Essential Library of Congress Subject Headings

Vanda Broughton

T0204218

Neal-Schuman Publishers, Inc.
New York

Published by Neal-Schuman Publishers, Inc.
100 William St., Suite 2004
New York, NY 10038
http://www.neal-schuman.com

First published in the United Kingdom by Facet Publishing, 2012.
This simultaneous U.S. edition published by Neal-Schuman Publishers, Inc., 2012.

Printed and made in the United Kingdom.

The paper used in this publication meets the minimum requirements of American National Standard for Information Sciences—Permanence of Paper for Printed Library Materials, ANSI Z39.48-1992.

ISBN 978-1-55570-640-1

Contents

Preface

The Library of Congress Subject Heading list (LCSH) is now used very widely in the English speaking world as a means of subject searching in library catalogues. In the UK this is a relatively recent phenomenon, and there is no substantial history of library school education in the use of LCSH or, indeed, of subject indexing or subject heading languages in general. *Essential LCSH* caters primarily for those unfamiliar with LCSH, and addresses the basics of locating, selecting and applying subject headings. It also aims to identify some of the common problems and misunderstandings experienced by beginners, and to suggest some useful strategies for coping with them. To this end, there are provided various practical exercises designed to test understanding and provide practice.

Because LCSH is not particularly systematic in its structure, it has been difficult to determine the best structure for the book. The early chapters provide some basic background, and describe the general conventions and policies at work in LCSH; after a section on content analysis, the following chapters deal with the way in which subject content can be expressed through the choice of headings, and the construction of structured headings. Otherwise, I have tried to concentrate on how various aspects of subject content can be represented, dealing with commonly occurring themes such as place, period, form, persons, name headings for people, organizations and places, and finishing with the specific subjects of literature and music, which have some of their own particular rules and practices. Two final chapters deal with electronic LCSH and LCSH online.

As with the previous titles in this series (*Essential Classification* and *Essential Thesaurus Construction*), the content is based very much on the content of the cataloguing and classification module of the MA in Library and Information Studies at University College London. As this particular title has a narrower focus than the other titles, it includes an extra helping of material designed to deal with some of the more obscure corners of LCSH. Nevertheless, it is still intended for the student and the novice cataloguer, and hence it is essentially an introductory work and not a comprehensive text. For a truly authoritative work on LCSH I recommend Lois Chan's *Library of Congress Subject Headings: principles and application*.

Because of the relatively recent introduction of LCSH in many UK libraries, it may be that some more experienced practitioners consult this work. I hope that you find it useful, and that you will forgive the didactic tone where this is all too apparent.

In this book LCSH is always referred to in the singular; this results in some inelegant sentences, but it serves the interest of consistency. Some typographical conventions are also used throughout. Examples of LCSH are in bold wherever they occur in the text. In other books in this series, bold type has been used to indicate terms in the glossary, but that practice has not been followed here in order to avoid confusion. No attempt is made to replicate exactly the appearance of LCSH except in those figures designed so to do. For the most part, the examples of headings use the same font as the main text of the book, but the use of bold, italics, punctuation and indentation is preserved, so that the examples look similar to LCSH itself. Extracts from the online version of Library of Congress *Classification Web* use the conventions of that format, including the Times New Roman font. Examples of bibliographic records are in Courier New font to differentiate them from the text proper.

Headings used as examples are not necessarily reproduced *in toto*. Most headings have numerous cross-references and textual notes, and to include all of these every time a heading is referred to would make the book uncomfortably long, as well as tending to obscure the particular point under discussion. Similarly, where lists of headings or subdivisions are shown, these usually consist of a selection from the complete list.

I hope that all the headings used are current, but LCSH is being revised and updated all the time and it cannot be guaranteed that every heading used in the book is still valid. All the examples of books and other resources are real. The great majority of them are taken from the Library of Congress catalogues, so that the choice of headings for a particular item can be compared with that of the Library of Congress itself. It goes without saying that all the headings are real, although some do strain the reader's credibility.

Thanks are due to my former colleague, Dr John Bowman, for reading the text, for making many useful suggestions, and for correcting my errors. Any that remain are entirely my responsibility. Over a number of years we shared an interest in LCSH, and regularly looked forward to the delights of the *Cataloging Service Bulletin* with its selection of 'Headings of current interest'. Thanks as well to the students of the Department of Information Studies, past and present, whose efforts to master LCSH have provided me with a good sense of where the difficulties lie, and where clarification is most needed. They too derive much enjoyment from the richness and variety of the headings, and usually manage to learn how to apply them successfully. A number of friends and associates have also made suggestions of particularly unusual or unexpected headings, for which I am truly grateful.

Vanda Broughton
University College London

1 Introduction

Today searching for information using words and phrases from natural language has become the norm. Everybody knows how to use a search engine, and most people will start a search by entering the name of whatever it is they wish to find out about. Although directory style methods of organizing information on websites are also common, many searchers find it simplest and easiest just to put some appropriate words into a search box. The existence of so much information in electronic format reinforces this approach, since it is easy to process huge quantities of text very rapidly, mechanically matching strings of characters to locate and retrieve the sought terms.

This increasing preference for language-based retrieval is mirrored in managed information resources, databases, indexes and bibliographies, and library catalogues. While the classification scheme was the dominant means of organization and retrieval in libraries for two-thirds of the twentieth century, with the arrival of the first automated systems in the 1950s and 1960s, there was an accompanying move towards language as the basis of indexing, and the emergence of tools such as keyword lists and thesauri. These have continued to be the norm for electronic collections or for collections where physical access and browsing are not important. In the library context, where automated retrieval by means of an online catalogue is combined with a substantial physical collection of documents, the subject heading list has usually been considered a more appropriate system.

This is particularly noticeable in the UK, where the use of subject headings in library catalogues has become widespread over the last 20 years. A number of factors have doubtless contributed to this situation: greater awareness of, and access to, subject headings through the medium of web-based catalogues; the advantages of bibliographic information sharing made possible by this phenomenon; the consequent need for standardization, particularly of the bibliographic tools used; and the ease of retrieval using words, as noted above. Why the subject heading list, rather than the thesaurus, should be preferred is not altogether clear, but it is now very well entrenched in most academic libraries of the developed world, the UK being one of the few countries not to have its own national system of subject headings.

As a consequence, the Library of Congress Subject Headings (LCSH) has been adopted by British libraries, in common with other English speaking nations, and several non-English speaking ones which use them in translation. Considerable impetus was provided by the British Library's decision in 1995 to abandon its Compass (previously PRECIS) subject indexing system in favour of LCSH, not only for the Library's own catalogues, but also on MARC records, and in the *British National Bibliography*. Since that time, LCSH has spread rapidly through the UK academic library community, although it has yet to be adopted in public library catalogues.

In the first instance, the Library of Congress developed LCSH as the principal means of subject access to its own collections, without any great expectation that anyone else would use them, although they were quickly taken up by a number of American libraries. For many decades this continued to be the situation, until libraries began to adopt them on a much greater scale, and on a worldwide basis. This meant that there was more incentive to make them less 'Americo-centric', and this need, together with the establishment of co-operative cataloguing projects, has led to a more considerable level of input from outside the Library of Congress. Nowadays it is possible to suggest new headings or modifications of existing ones via the Library of Congress website. When the British Library reintroduced LCSH in 1995, the first new heading proposed by them was **Luminescent probes,** and the first exclusively British heading was **Ring ouzel,** a bird of the thrush family unknown in North America.

LCSH, which was first conceived over a hundred years ago, has thus been in a state of continuous development and evolution during the twentieth, and into the twenty-first, century. LCSH is used today not only in library catalogues but in many bibliographic resources, abstracting and indexing services, and other databases. The current edition has more than 280,000 headings, from **A10 (Jet attack plane)** to **Zyxin,** and has been translated into many languages, including Turkish, Czech, Greek, Flemish, Hungarian and Portuguese, and is used in countries as far afield as Brazil, Belgium, Lithuania and Malaysia.

What is LCSH?

LCSH is an alphabetical list of the subject headings that are used in the catalogues of the Library of Congress, together with thesaurus-type cross-references that enable cataloguers to navigate the list and to find other appropriate headings. A typical section of LCSH looks something like this:

Moose (May Subd Geog)
  UF Alces alces
    Alces americana
    Elk, European
    European elk
  BT **Alces**
  RT **Cookery (Moose)**
  NT **Moose calves**

Moose calves (May Subd Geog)
  UF Moose--Infancy
    Calves, Moose
  BT **Animals--Infancy**
    Moose

Moose County (Imaginary place) (Not Subd Geog)
  BT Imaginary places

Moose (Dog) (Not Subd Geog)
  BT **Dogs**

Moose, Elliot (Fictitious character)
  USE **Elliot Moose (Fictitious character)**

Moose elm
  USE **Slippery elm**

When we consider the practical application of LCSH, we will look in more detail at the layout, and at what the different cross-references and typographical variations mean, so you don't need to worry about these at this stage.

The purpose of the subject headings is to allow users to find material on a particular subject. The classification scheme used at the Library of Congress is a very broad classification and although it aims to provide a unique call number for every book, this is achieved by using author names and dates of publication as additions to the classmark, rather than by very detailed subject classes. As a result, the classification functions primarily as a shelf location device, rather than as a tool for subject searching and retrieval. LCSH was developed for that role, and you will sometimes come across the phrase 'the burden of retrieval', which is borne by the subject headings; that is to say, the work of finding documents is carried out by the subject headings.

LCSH is an example of a controlled indexing language, which means there are strict rules for the way in which headings can be used. It is also a standard, which implies that all its users should conform to those rules so that LCSH is consistently applied in all the libraries that use it. This ensures that searches can be carried out on more than one catalogue (or in merged catalogues) and achieve comparable results for the same query. For this to happen, individual libraries should not change the headings or interpret them to meet local needs, although undoubtedly this does happen quite often.

The format of LCSH

The print version of LCSH comes in five volumes containing the headings themselves (sometimes called the red books), which is now in its 33rd edition (2011). The collection of rules for application of LCSH, the *Subject Headings Manual*, is published separately in a loose-leaf format. LCSH is also available on the web as part of *Classification Web* (http://classificationweb.net), although this product does not contain the *Subject Headings Manual*, which is available electronically as part of another Library of Congress electronic resource, *Cataloger's Desktop*.

Beginners often find the printed volumes easier to use than the online version, since it gives them a broader view and a better sense of the context of headings. When you are more familiar with the scheme, the online LCSH is undoubtedly quicker and easier to search, and it uses hypertext to link directly to the classification, which is immensely helpful if you are using both. The examples used in this book are taken from the online version of LCSH, and from the online catalogue of the Library of Congress.

The Policy and Standards Division at the Library of Congress maintains LCSH and produces the published version. Updates of the print version appear on an annual basis and *Classification Web* can be continuously updated. Weekly lists of new and changed headings are posted on the Acquisitions and Cataloging website, and updates to the *Subject Headings Manual* are available as a free download from the Cataloging Distribution Services website at www.loc.gov/cds/PDFdownloads/scm/index.html. Headings of current interest and amendments to headings are also published at regular intervals in the *Cataloging Service Bulletin* which is available as a free download at www.loc.gov/cds/PDFdownloads/csb/index.html.

The Library of Congress provides an excellent range of free online resources for cataloguers and classifiers, which can easily be explored starting from the 'Resources for librarians' link on the Library's home page.

2 History and principles of LCSH

Early subject headings

In the nineteenth century such library classification schemes as existed were very rudimentary, often consisting only of a few broad subject divisions with the books then arranged by size or author's name, or some other principle unrelated to the subject. Locating a book on a specific topic could be a very hit and miss affair, as the lack of detail in the classification meant that related material was usually scattered throughout the relevant class. The more usual method of subject searching was through alphabetically arranged subject catalogues. These might take the form of large 'guard books' or ledgers into which the catalogue entries were written or pasted, and which were commonly reproduced as printed books. The alternative form of card catalogue came into common use in British and American libraries from the 1870s onwards.

The earliest subject entries were usually simply names of topics, such as 'Geology' or 'Cricket'. In many cases the subject keywords or 'catchwords' were taken directly from the title of the book or article. Where necessary the subject headings might be combinations of two or more words, for example, 'Military history' or 'Education of women', and in some early subject catalogues and indexes headings can be found with subdivisions, rather in the manner of book indexes.

Whatever the format, most of these early headings were created on an impromptu basis, and there were no general rules applied to ensure that the format of headings was logical or consistent. It often appears that not much common sense was exercised in their selection, nor thought for what a reader might reasonably look up.

Cutter's Rules

The idea of systematic subject headings is usually credited to Charles Ammi Cutter, an American librarian, who, in 1876, the same year that Dewey created his Decimal Classification, published a slim volume called *Rules for a Dictionary Catalog.* This was one of the earliest comprehensive statements of theoretical principles for making entries in a catalogue, although several libraries had produced some sets of cataloguing rules during the mid-nineteenth century. Most of Cutter's *Rules* were concerned with how to enter the details of the author and title of a work, and what are known as the descriptive elements (the physical dimensions of a book and the number of pages, for example), but he also provided some guidelines on how to make *subject* entries in a catalogue.

Cutter said that the purpose of subject entry was twofold: to enable a person to find a book of which the subject is known; and to show what the library has on a given subject and in a given kind of literature. Within the context of today's online catalogues and digital resources, you can expand this to read 'documents, resources, information...' instead of 'a book', and 'is available' instead of 'the library has'. But the primary purpose of subject headings remains the same: to support information seeking by subject.

Cutter's *Rules* provided guidelines for the form of compound (multiword) terms and phrases when used in headings, and they also stated some general principles about the choice of language and how to deal with the problems of synonyms and other difficulties of natural language. They continue to be influential as can be seen in the IFLA publication *Principles Underlying Subject Headings*, which confirms almost all of Cutter's theory. We shall look more closely at these ideas in the next chapter.

Cutter was an influential figure at the Library of Congress (his Expansive Classification formed the basis of the Library's own classification scheme), and his *Rules* directly affected the management of the catalogues there. At around the same time that his rules were being implemented at Congress, the American Library Association (ALA) began to compile an authoritative list of subject headings that libraries could use in preference to making up their own, and Cutter's *Rules* were also used as the basis of this list. In 1895 an edition of Cutter's *Rules* was published with these headings as an appendix. The ALA list was taken up by the Library of Congress, which used it as a starting point for its own system of headings, the Library of Congress Subject Headings. Work on the subject authority list began at Congress in July 1898, and the first published list of headings appeared in 1914, under the title *Subject Headings used in the Dictionary Catalogs of the Library of Congress.*

Cutter's *Rules* brought order and consistency to the business of making subject headings, and introduced the first elements of what we now call vocabulary control, the business of streamlining the use of language with a view to improving the effectiveness of retrieval.

Subject cataloguing and the dictionary catalogue

In order to appreciate Cutter's purpose, you should understand the notion of the dictionary catalogue that he proposed. Nowadays, almost all libraries have a single automated catalogue in the form of a database; this holds all the information about individual items in the collection in a single record for each one. This record usually includes the author, title, publication and descriptive elements, as well as any subject headings, keywords, or classification codes, and also extends to administrative data such as loan status and physical location. Naturally, the information has only to be entered once, and anyone using the catalogue can access any element or combination of elements, in a single search.

In Cutter's time this was obviously far from the case. The central problem of physical catalogues is that they are one-dimensional or linear in nature, and therefore only one aspect of the record could be used as the basis of ordering the catalogue. If, for example, the authors' names were used in alphabetical sequence, the classmarks were scattered and could not be searched for. If readers were to be able to search for authors, titles and subjects, separate sequences had to be created, and multiple copies of the records made to be filed in the different sequences. Life could be simplified for the reader if the separate sequences could be merged, and this was what happened in the dictionary catalogue. A single alphabetical sequence incorporating authors' names, titles of books, and alphabetical subject headings became the norm in American libraries. For Cutter, then, any statement of cataloguing rules necessitated rules for subject entries.

In British libraries the dictionary catalogue was not so common, and it was more usual to find one catalogue for authors and titles, and a separate catalogue for subjects. The latter was frequently in the form of a classified catalogue (one arranged by classmark, which mirrored the order of books on the shelves), supplemented by an alphabetical index to the classification; the alphabetical index would tell the readers the appropriate classmarks for a particular subject, but they would then need to consult the classified catalogue itself to find out which actual books were held. However, many libraries published catalogues arranged by names of subjects, for example, the British Museum Subject Index; others adopted an alphabetico-classed approach, with names of broad classes arranged alphabetically and the titles within these sections ordered by their classmarks.

Even when classification schemes became more detailed and sophisticated, and as a consequence the arrangements of books in libraries were more logical and helpful, using the catalogue as a means of searching for subjects remained a popular way of locating material. The two methods can be contrasted as browsing (scanning a systematic arrangement where similar resources are placed in proximity, and there is a logical sequence of topics) and retrieval (where a specific topic is searched for independently of its context). In contemporary terms, this is equivalent to the difference between using a directory style approach, such as that of Yahoo! or the Open Directory Project, and entering the name of a topic directly into a search engine.

LCSH in the catalogue

In today's online catalogues LCSH is used as a source of subject metadata. It provides us with a source of terms that can be attached to a document to let us know what it is about. In a digital situation metadata may be inserted into the html or other source code in which the digital object is written, and is invisible to the end-user, but in conventional libraries the metadata comes in the form of a catalogue record, and can be easily seen. This is separate from the item itself, but is a representation of the item in the sense of recording its key aspects, including its subject content. In older literature, this formal representation of a document is sometimes referred to as a document surrogate.

Users will therefore normally come across LCSH when searching a catalogue, either as a component part of the records themselves, or in the subject index to the catalogue. (There is more about the Library of Congress online catalogue and how to use it in Chapter 18.)

In Figure 2.1 you can see the subject headings for a particular book entered in the subject field of the catalogue record. This is the part of the record searched in a subject search. The individual subject headings are also held within the subject index, which can be browsed to see which books have been allocated any given heading. In the example of Library of Congress's subject index in Figure 2.2 you can see how many items have used each heading; clicking on a heading will bring up the list of titles.

The subject headings can therefore be used to retrieve items (in a subject search) and to browse (using the subject index), but both of these operations can only be performed by means of the catalogue. In a conventional library

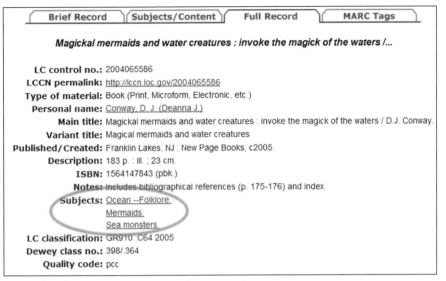

Figure 2.1 Subject headings on a catalogue record

#	Hits	Headings (Select to View Titles)	Type of Heading
[1]	28	Mermaids	LC subject headings
[2]	3	Mermaids	LC subject headings for children
[3]	1	Mermaids 1750-1800.	Thesaurus for graphic materials: TGM I, sub. terms
[4]	1	Mermaids 1930-1940.	Thesaurus for graphic materials: TGM I, sub. terms
[5]	2	Mermaids Drama.	LC subject headings
[6]	1	Mermaids Drama.	not applicable
[7]	8	Mermaids Fiction.	LC subject headings
[8]	181	Mermaids Fiction.	LC subject headings for children
[9]	1	Mermaids Florida Weeki Wachee History.	LC subject headings
[10]	4	Mermaids Folklore.	LC subject headings
[11]	5	Mermaids Folklore.	LC subject headings for children
[12]	6	Mermaids in art	LC subject headings
[13]	2	Mermaids in art Catalogs.	LC subject headings
[14]	1	Mermaids in art Exhibitions.	LC subject headings
[15]	8	Mermaids in literature	LC subject headings
[16]	1	Mermaids Ireland.	LC subject headings

Figure 2.2 Subject headings in the catalogue's subject index

where the books need arranging on the shelves, LCSH must always be used in conjunction with a classification scheme. This classification doesn't have to be the Library of Congress Classification, and LCSH can be (and is) used with the Dewey Decimal Classification, the Universal Decimal Classification, the Bliss Bibliographic Classification and many specialist and in-house schemes.

Major characteristics of LCSH

In the introduction to the fourth edition of LCSH in 1943, David Haykin stated that there were no guiding principles or theoretical basis to the subject headings and this is largely true; they were just developed as needed. But it is also true to say that Cutter's *Rules for a Dictionary Catalog*, and the American Library Association subject headings that were published as an appendix to the *Rules* in 1895, were influential on the style and direction of LCSH. It does suffer from the fact that it was not originally based on any clear structural principles, but it is now too large for the problem to be addressed in a systematic way. Nevertheless, it is an immensely useful working tool, as well as a real treasure house of the weird and wonderful in document description. It is hardly possible to open any page of LCSH without finding something to surprise and delight.

The Library of Congress and literary warrant

If there are no philosophical principles underpinning LCSH, there is a very strong influence on its content and coverage, and that is the Library of Congress itself. LCSH was developed for the subject cataloguing of books at Congress and remained exclusively so for a long time. New headings were added as needed for cataloguing items in the collections there, rather than to fill in gaps in a theoretical structure. This notion of a cataloguing tool reflecting the material it is required to cope with is called the principle of literary warrant; it is an important feature of any subject organization system that its content should be based on actual documents, and not on some abstract philosophical idea of what constitutes knowledge. In the early history of LCSH this was a rather exaggerated feature, since only documentation held by Congress formed the literary warrant, rather than documentation generally. This inevitably means that the content of LCSH mirrors the content of the Library of Congress, and more importantly, it reflects any weaknesses in that collection.

This might seem not to be too enormous a problem in a great national library (the largest in the world), and indeed there are no serious shortcomings in terms of the content of LCSH. Some subjects, however, are not collected by the Library of Congress (medicine and agriculture, for example, are the responsibility of other US national libraries), and the headings for those subjects are correspondingly fewer and less detailed than in 'strong' Library of Congress subjects such as history and politics.

Bias in LCSH

Critics of LCSH sometimes condemn its American bias, but that seems to me largely unimportant. There is certainly a proliferation of all things American: place names; names of individuals; details of events in US history; and an avalanche of US family history headings (which, one imagines, no one outside the family concerned will ever want or need). This could hardly be otherwise, and in any case, LCSH is not rationed. These headings don't exclude other, more generally useful ones, and you can simply ignore the ones you don't need.

The existence of cultural bias, and political incorrectness, seems a more serious criticism, and LCSH has suffered a number of attacks on this front over the years. It is quite easy to find headings that infringe all sorts of unwritten laws, and many current written ones. There is considerable gender bias; there have been headings for **Women as judges, Women as composers, Women as astronauts,** perhaps inevitably **Women as automobile drivers** and even **Women as librarians,** without any mention of men in the same roles. The criminal fraternity is packed with minorities too; apart from **Women criminals,** there are **Alien criminals, Chinese American criminals, Jewish criminals, Catholic criminals, Deaf criminals,** even **Aged as criminals.** Needless to say, no white, male Anglo-Saxons feature as criminals, although this may be the default definition for criminals.

Of course, no one at the Library of Congress, now or in the past, decided to create these headings out of malevolence or a sense of mischief. We know that LCSH is not built on a philosophical model, and that headings only come into being on the basis of need. These particular headings exist to accommodate a literature produced before such attitudes became unacceptable, and, because the literature will continue to exist, so will the offending subject headings. It is a problem of the material rather than the system used to organize it.

Nevertheless, the Library of Congress has taken notice of its critics, and in recent years has changed many of the headings to more acceptable forms. Most of the **Women as authors** type headings have been replaced by **Women authors,** or similar, and a few **Men...** headings have come in, although these are usually attached to unusual male occupations such as **Men caregivers** or **Men elementary school teachers.**

You can easily test the literary warrant of LCSH by matching new headings from the *Cataloging Service Bulletin* against the Library of Congress catalogue. The appearance of a new heading is usually accompanied by a new item requiring that heading. Indeed, looking at the catalogue will normally account for all the oddities of LCSH. A recently added curious heading is **Dog scootering**; if you run a subject search on The Library of Congress for this heading, you will find the document that brought it into being, and be able to discover what dog scootering is. Other headings that have arisen in this way include **Homing pigeons in the Bible**, **Ear plugs (Whales)**, **Also (The English word)**, **Middle-finger gesture** and the delightful **Ungulates in art** (a book about painting deer and other hooved animals).

3 Subject heading lists and the problems of language

In this chapter we will look at the alternative ways in which information can be organized, and the role that language plays in ordering and retrieval. Many of the challenges associated with indexing and searching, the design of indexing tools, and the consequent effectiveness of retrieval arise in large part from the richness and diversity of language. This is true of all languages, but is particularly the case in English, which has a huge stock of words and many linguistic influences.

Systematic and alphabetic approaches to information

There are two fundamental approaches to the organization and retrieval of information for its subject content. First, the information may be arranged in a systematic way using some sort of scheme or map of knowledge that provides an overview of a subject area and shows the structure and relationships between topics. This is a very useful approach for users who are not very clear about what might be available, or not very precise in their search requirements. It allows users to scan material, to find items on the same topic together, and related topics nearby, and to discover more specific items within broad subject groups. This browsing behaviour is supported by schemes of classification or categorization for the physical arrangement of resources, such as those used in libraries and bookshops. Similar approaches are often found in digital libraries and subject gateways and portals, where a directory style arrangement offers users some basis for the initial search and encourages them to focus and refine search by drilling down into the various categories and sub-categories. The bringing together of topics is known technically as collocation.

Such systematic structures are essentially conceptual in nature; they work on the basis of abstract classes, categories, or ideas, and, in order to keep the systematic structure in place, codes (such as classmarks or URIs) may be used to represent the concept. Tools that assist this kind of search include conventional library classification schemes (such as the

Dewey Decimal Classification and the Library of Congress Classification scheme), and user interest classifications common in many public libraries. For digital resources, taxonomies and concept maps work in a similar way.

The alternative is to disregard the problem of physical arrangement, and concentrate instead on providing each document with subject index terms, tags or metadata, so it can be discovered by searching a catalogue or database using subject related words or phrases. These index terms are added to the item's record in the catalogue or database, and the search operates on this data, rather than by scanning the resources themselves; more or less the same method is used in search engines where enormous indexes are built using keywords extracted from the material. This approach is more effective for users who are clear and precise about their information requirements, since they can go straight to the information they need without wading through all those items that aren't relevant.

The essence of this method is that it uses words themselves as the basis of search. Now, when virtually all searching is carried out using automated systems, this type of search has become dominant, largely because of the extensive use of search engines. It has, however, provided an alternative to browsing for a very long time, going back to the subject entries in catalogues and indexes in nineteenth century libraries, before the beginnings of LCSH. As with the systematic method, there are several kinds of subject indexing tool, including keyword lists, thesauri and the subject heading list.

In many situations the two systems are used complementarily, and an interface that supports both browsing and retrieval is perhaps the most useful for the end-user. For example, a user who wants to find out about British wildlife in a general way might browse a systematic arrangement to identify the different categories of plants and animals, and the various aspects of wildlife which are studied or which are of current interest. Someone wanting just to find out about the ecology of slime moulds can retrieve this more easily by searching with keywords. In a conventional library, the classification scheme provides the browsing mechanism, and the subject headings perform the retrieval function.

The alphabetical, or word-based, approach to organizing information has been very much in the ascendant recently with the great improvement in search mechanisms. Nowadays it is much more likely that libraries will use relatively broad systems of classification for physical organization of collections, and rely on the online catalogue to make specific searches using keyword and subject queries.

We don't need to concern ourselves here with the problems of classification schemes, but it is necessary to look at the advantages and disadvantages of word-based systems, at why they sometimes are inefficient, and how these inherent difficulties can be managed.

Summary

- Information can be organized either in systematic order, or in alphabetical order.
- Systematic orders place similar topics near to each other and indicate relationships between topics.
- They provide an overview of the subject and assist browsing.
- Library and bookshop classifications are examples of systematic structure tools, as are taxonomies and concept maps.
- Alphabetically ordered tools are presented as lists of keywords, descriptors, metadata tags, or verbal headings, which are added to the item or its record.
- They support word-based search, and the retrieval of specific information.
- Thesauri and subject heading lists are examples of alphabetical tools.
- Most collections (either physical or digital) will use a combination of the two approaches.
- Alphabetic systems tend to dominate, and there is less concern today for detailed, or close, classification.

Advantages of alphabetic systems

The obvious advantages of using words as a basis for retrieval are the intuitive nature of searching in this way, and the immediate accessibility of it. There is no need to learn a system or to be familiar with the organizing principles of a collection. In an online environment anyone can formulate a search by using words from the subject, and there is usually no need to put these in any particular order. When searching an index or a printed list for information, alphabetical order is easily understood by everyone. Nevertheless, the very accessibility of language creates some problems for retrieval which need to be addressed.

Disadvantages of alphabetic systems

The difficulties of word-based systems are linked to two major characteristics: problems inherent in the nature of language, and problems associated with alphabetical order as an organizing principle. Both of these are addressed by standard design features of indexing vocabularies, and in following chapters we will look at how these features are implemented in practice.

Language related disadvantages
Natural language indexing and searching

Any sort of indexing, classifying, or subject description of documents is, on the whole, a very time-consuming and intellectually demanding process. This is one of the reasons why copying or downloading catalogue records from other libraries is so prevalent nowadays; it simply saves a great a deal of money. We might therefore ask whether the use of complicated systems of cataloguing and indexing is really necessary. Why not use the language of our everyday speech, since surely this would make the assignment of the keywords much quicker and easier? The titles of documents, or the text itself, could provide us with the terms needed for indexing, and in any case, whatever we as cataloguers do, there is no guarantee that end-users will choose the same terms, and they will certainly not be familiar with the cataloguing system.

On the face of it, it would appear to be easy to use such a natural language approach to index documents for the initial indexing and also for the retrieval process, particularly where machines can help with the process. There are some real advantages in the use of natural language: it is quick and easy for the cataloguer, and intuitive for the user. Nobody has to learn cataloguing rules, or how the system works, and indexing can be carried out by untrained staff; in some cases authors can provide their own keywords. One school of thought maintains that language derived from the literature itself is more accurate, representative of the subject and up to date than that of classifications and other subject tools. New terms and ideas are added to the language as they appear in the documentation, and as terms become obsolete they naturally disappear from use; such language needs no costly maintenance regime, and it is free to the user. Indexing of this kind was very popular when automated systems first started in the 1950s and 1960s, and it is the basis of user driven Web 2.0 applications, such as social tagging, or folksonomy.

However, experience of searching the world wide web will show how difficult it is to achieve sensible results from this kind of free form searching. Masses of irrelevant material is retrieved because it is impossible to differentiate between alternative meanings of words, hard to predict how words will have been used in different contexts, and difficult to separate people and things with the same name. And what do you do about all the relevant data which you can't find because words other than your particular search terms have been used in the title or metadata? The disadvantages of natural language are very considerable, and we will look at some of them in detail below: differences in how people understand the meaning of words, variations in the use of a word in different contexts, problems of synonymy and homonymy, and different orthographic (spelling) systems. Added to this is the problem of how we deal with indexing and retrieval across different natural languages, although this is largely beyond the scope of this book. All of these difficult aspects of words, their vagueness and imprecision, affect indexing, and more particularly they affect searching.

Summary

- Alphabetic systems are more natural and intuitive than systematic ones.
- Alphabetical order is widely understood, and unambiguous.
- Natural language indexing, using the language of the document, or terms created *ad hoc* by the indexer, has some advantages.
- The vocabulary will be current and naturally updated, and obsolescent terms will drop away through lack of use.
- Natural language indexing is cheap to use, and has no maintenance costs.
- Nevertheless, there are difficulties inherent in natural language that make it less effective in retrieval.

What words mean

At the most basic level, the problem of the meanings of words is a considerable one. It can be impossible to know if two different people understand a word to mean exactly the same thing, since both will attach their own associations and nuances to a word. In different nations and cultures this phenomenon can be formalized, the most striking example being that of the mismatch between British and American English.

American usage is more familiar now that US television programmes are common on the British media, and many of the differences only occur in slang words, but large numbers of English words have multiple meanings, some peculiar to the USA or UK, some shared by both, and many having combinations of these. Figure 3.1 shows some familiar examples.

Because of this phenomenon, searching in an international database can return some unexpected results. Although the examples below are fairly

Concept	American	British
bedcover	comforter	duvet
car storage area	trunk	boot
engine cover	hood	bonnet
fruit preserve	jelly	jam
fuel	gas	petrol
porcine animal	hog	pig
trouser straps	suspenders	braces

Figure 3.1 Differences in terminology between British and American English

trivial, real difficulties could be experienced if trying to find, for example, information about 'private schools' and 'public schools', which are quite different concepts in the USA and UK. A British searcher will also have some problems searching an American database if he doesn't know the appropriate terms for his subject in American English.

The problem is further compounded by the continuous evolution of language: the meanings of words change over time, and in different environments they may change in different ways. Differences in understanding of this kind are also common in different societies and cultures.

Synonyms and homonyms
Synonyms
Systematic structures used for knowledge organization work on the basis of concepts, often with a code used to represent the concept. In a classification system this is the classmark, and the way in which users will locate an item on the shelves. For example, the concept of 'pirates' is represented in the Library of Congress Classification by the code G535. Anybody searching for books with the classmark G535 will find lots of items with pirates as the subject. But the full heading for G535 also specifically includes 'buccaneers' and, by implication, 'corsairs', 'privateers', 'picaroons' and any other labels for pirates that may occur. These books classified at G535 in the Library of Congress use lots of different terms in their titles, and some do not mention pirates at all:

Freebooters of the Red Sea
Sea wolves of seven shores
Buccaneers of the Pacific
Life under the Jolly Roger
French corsairs

The occurrence of many terms for one concept is known as synonymy, although you may more often find it defined as words with the same or very similar meaning.

When searching using words, this creates a problem because we don't know which of these synonyms the indexer may choose to apply to a document, nor indeed which word the searcher may choose to look for. The chance of the indexer and the searcher choosing the same word on every occasion is remote and the consequence is that much relevant material would fail to be found by the end-user.

Words that have more or less the same meaning create one of the thorniest problems in indexing and searching. English, because it has been subject to a great number of linguistic influences, is particularly rich in synonyms. A familiar example is the use of Anglo-Saxon words for animals, such as cow, sheep and pig, and their Norman French words for the cooked equivalents, beef (*boeuf*), mutton (*mouton*) and pork (*porc*). Many words have also been imported into English through the influence of Germanic, Celtic and Norse languages and through Latin, all contributing to a large and diverse word stock. American English, too, has developed against a background of enormous ethnic diversity, which accounts for the very many words peculiar to American English.

When a concept has a variety of labels attached to it, the cataloguer or indexer has difficulty in knowing which one to choose in describing a document, and the searcher has a corresponding problem in knowing which one to select for searching. The chance that they will both opt for the same term seems remote.

Homonyms

Homonyms present us with the reverse problem; words that look the same but have different meanings, or, to contrast it with our definition of synonyms, words that are equivalent to several concepts. A classic example is provided by these titles:

```
A history of reading / by Steven Roger Fischer. - London:
Reaktion, 2003
A history of Reading / Stuart Hylton. - Chichester:
Phillimore, 2007
```

Here, only the capital R tells us which is a history of an activity, and which the history of a place, and in a system of citation, for example, in which initial letters of words are all capitalized, it would be impossible to distinguish them. An example like this is more accurately a homograph, since it is confusing only when written down, but there are thousands of instances of true homonyms, that look, and sound, alike (bank, break, dog, fine, mole, row, ring, stalk, wood and so on). Another name for this phenomenon is polysemy, and such words are referred to as polysemous: having many meanings.

Homophones (words that sound alike but are spelled differently, such as 'allowed' and 'aloud'), are not problematic from a cataloguing point of view, since they are clearly different in their written form. Homophones are useful ingredients of jokes, particularly puns and 'knock-knock' jokes, which may explain why very many of the examples of so-called homonym lists on the world wide web turn out to be lists of homophones. A curious quirk occurs with the English language when variations between American and British spelling create homonyms in one and not the other (such as the troublesome homonyms 'tire' and 'tire' in the USA, but straightforward homophones 'tire' and 'tyre' in the UK).

Homonymy is not a nuisance on the same scale as synonymy, but it still hampers retrieval. Whereas the synonym causes us to miss relevant documents in searching, the homonym causes us to retrieve irrelevant ones.

Meaningful words

In addition to the problem of having too many words, or the wrong words, classifiers also have to think about whether the words they use are *useful* terms: they need to be terms that the searchers will look for when trying to find material on a topic.

One of the earliest books on indexing, *How to Make an Index* by H. B. Wheatley, gives some excellent examples of the bad indexer at work. These examples from an index to the periodical *The Freemason* illustrate well the rotten indexer's art:

```
An oration delivered
Another Masonic manuscript
Interesting extract from an old Masonian letter
Our portrait gallery
Recent festival
```

Put into alphabetical order in an index, these headings will not help the searcher at all, since someone looking for, say, Masonic manuscripts, is likely to look under 'Masonic' or 'manuscripts'.

Words like 'an', 'another', 'our', 'according' and 'up' are not words that the searcher will look for – they are not sought terms. Although they will appear in the text of documents, they don't tell us much about the content of documents, so indexers don't normally use articles, conjunctions or prepositions because they are not significant words. Adjectives and adverbs are not much favoured either, unless they form part of a phrase (such as 'rapid transit systems' or 'green politics'). Instead we use nouns and noun forms of verbs ('management', 'co-operation'), because these are the words that searchers will look for.

Structural disadvantages of word-based systems

The second problem of alphabetically based systems is that they scatter related concepts. In our example of pirates, the Library of Congress Classification places them next to 'filibusters', and close to 'sea-faring', 'adventures', 'shipwrecks' and 'buried treasure', all suitably piratical topics. If, however, we look at 'pirates' in the alphabetical index we find:

Piranhas
Pirate radio broadcasting
Pirates
Piray River
Pirbuterol
Pirc defense (Chess)
Pirenzepine

Buried treasure is miles away, with burglars, buried cities, and buried telephone lines, while the buccaneers are keeping company with *bubo lactaeus* (the giant eagle owl) and bubonic plague. Clearly, browsing isn't possible in the alphabetically organized world, and there is no obvious way to find out what other relevant topics there might be. If an alphabetical system is to function properly it must have a system of cross-referencing, so that related terms can be linked, and cataloguers can navigate the headings, and find more general or more specific entries.

This is one of the problems Cutter addressed early on, although in his rules the cross-references were only made downwards, to more specific headings.

It seems then that if we leave the cataloguer or indexer to use natural language, there are far too many words to choose from, many of which have the same meaning, or share the same form, or are not words that anyone would look for. Using natural language makes efficient finding really very difficult. When trying to describe the subjects of documents, on the whole it is better if we impose some rules and restrictions on the process, and limit the number of choices open to the cataloguer. It is more effective to use instead what we call a 'controlled language' or 'controlled indexing language'.

Summary

- Variations in meanings of words in different places or contexts make searching less accurate, and retrieve irrelevant material.
- Synonyms (more than one word for the same concept) also complicate searching, because it can be impossible to know which words have been chosen to describe the subject of a document.
- Homonyms (more than one concept for the same word) create difficulties because it is hard to distinguish between the different meanings of the homonym.
- Some parts of speech (articles, pronouns, conjunctions) are not useful in describing a subject, so do not make good index terms.
- Others (adjectives, adverbs, verbs) are not naturally chosen by searchers.
- Putting concepts in alphabetical order obscures the relationships between them and scatters related ideas.
- Cross-referencing is required to deal with this problem.

Controlled indexing languages

A controlled indexing language is a system for indexing or subject cataloguing documents that addresses and attempts to minimize the problems of natural language indexing. The mechanisms for doing this are referred to as vocabulary control. Rather than using the whole range of words in English or any other natural language, the controlled indexing language restricts the number of terms that the indexer can choose from; it does this by the following means:

- It cuts out synonyms and gives the indexer a single term for each concept (the preferred term).
- It excludes useless words that no one will look for.
- It helps to make sure that everybody uses the same words for the same ideas.
- By improving consistency in this way, it makes retrieval more efficient.

Experiments in information retrieval have shown that imposing some constraints on the use of language improves indexer consistency in selecting index terms, and consequently enhances the performance of the indexing system.

In addition to these general objectives, there are usually more detailed rules about how different kinds of terms are identified and managed, and which forms of terms will be preferred. There will also be a system of cross-referencing, allowing the indexer to browse upwards and downwards through the subject hierarchy, and identifying other kinds of relationships between index terms.

A subject heading list is a prime example of a controlled indexing language, and LCSH is probably the most widely used individual controlled vocabulary in the world. In Chapter 5 we will look at the specific ways in which LCSH implements vocabulary control, and addresses the problems of navigating the system.

Standards for document description

One final advantage of using a controlled indexing language is that it improves consistency on a grand scale. Limiting the use of synonyms and giving rules for describing documents undoubtedly makes searching and finding much better within the library or document centre, but there is a much broader dimension to this. In these days of web-enabled OPACs and of shared cataloguing there are real management and financial benefits in using standardized systems, rather than operating home-made or in-house regimes.

So far we have only considered the 'vocabulary' part of the indexing language, but indexing languages, like natural languages, also have rules for joining the words together, what is called syntax. The chapters on structured subject headings will examine the way in which various parts of the vocabulary can be joined together to make more complex statements of subject content.

Summary
- The use of natural language in classification and indexing creates some problems for classifiers and searchers.
- Controlled indexing languages limit the number of indexing terms and regulate the form and type of words used.
- This management of the indexing terminology is known as vocabulary control.
- The process improves consistency of indexing and makes search more effective.

- Controlled indexing languages also use systems of cross-referencing so that indexers can locate related topics.
- As well as improving indexing at the local level, the use of standard indexing languages allows for the sharing of records between different organizations and the exchange of information in different languages.

4 The format and display of LCSH

In this chapter we shall examine the way in which the subject headings are visually presented. LCSH uses a number of conventions of format, which are not necessarily intuitive for the novice user, and the system of cross-referencing is peculiar to vocabularies of this kind. The printed list of LCSH and the online version vary very slightly, so we shall concentrate on the print format, which has elements that are potentially more likely to cause confusion. There is some slight duplication of material in this and the following chapters, as it is sometimes hard to determine the difference between conventions of formatting, and the form of the heading.

Filing and alphabetization

It is worth starting out by explaining the rules for filing, since these are arbitrary in most alphabetical listings, and you need to be clear how spaces, symbols and punctuation are treated if you are ever to find your headings. This might seem very trivial, but there are hundreds of thousands of headings and there may be dozens, or even hundreds, beginning with the same word.

The most important distinction in filing systems is whether entries file word-by-word or letter-by-letter. In word-by-word filing, sometimes called 'nothing before something', spaces file before letters, and it is the first whole word that is the most important part. In contrast, letter-by-letter filing treats all the words in the heading as a single string of characters, ignoring the spaces for filing purposes:

Word-by-word filing	Letter-by-letter filing
Fat cells	**Fatal familial insomnia**
Fat dormouse	**Fatalism**
Fat embolism	**Fat cells**
Fat persons	**Fat dormouse**
Fat substitutes	**Fat embolism**

Fatal familial insomnia	Fathead minnow
Fatalism	Father and child
Fathead minnow	Father Christmas
Father and child	Fatherhood
Father Christmas	Fathers
Father Tim	Father Tim
Fatherhood	Fat persons
Fathers	Fat substitutes

You can see that this makes quite a lot of difference to the relative position of the headings, and might affect whether you are able to locate them. LCSH uses word-by-word filing, which is, I think, more intuitive for the majority of people.

You should also note that all the words in a heading count for filing purposes, even apparently insignificant words:

Dancing and society
Dancing for the aged
Dancing improvisation
Dancing in art
Dancing injuries
Dancing mice
Dancing on postage stamps
Dancing schools
Dancing with dogs

Non-alphabetic characters

There are few examples of characters other than the letters of the Roman alphabet anywhere in the headings, and when they do occur they are treated in a very straightforward manner. Numbers file before letters, as you might expect:

Rua 26 de Agosto
Rua Afonso Pena
Rua da Corredoura

Motorola 88200 (Microprocessor)
Motorola computers

Group 14 elements
Group accounts
Group algebras

However, the decimal filing of numbers is perhaps less to be expected, and something to watch out for:

1 Wall Street
10 Downing Street
141R (Steam locomotive)
1080 Degree Snowboarding (Game)
221B Baker Street
87th Precinct (Imaginary place)
9 d'Octubre Bridge

These numerals are the exception rather than the rule, for, in line with the general conventions of vocabulary control, LCSH likes to turn numbers into words wherever possible:

Fifth Avenue (New York, N. Y.)
Four-color problem
Nineteen sixties
One-letter words
Seven hundred (The number)
Three bears (Tale)
Twelfth century

It is a mystery why some numbers which could be easily spelled out are not, but that is not untypical of LCSH.

Other than numbers, LCSH largely avoids the use of characters which are not Roman letters. Terms in headings deriving from languages in other scripts are anyway Romanized using standard tables for transliteration. Where Greek letters occur as a part of an English word or phrase, they are written out, thus:

Alpha rays
Chi Rho symbol
Pi calculus
Sigma particles

One very rare departure from this practice is the use of the letter 'Þ' (found in Old English, Old Norse and Icelandic). Despite the fact that this could easily be converted to 'th', it is retained in four headings, and these file right at the end of the alphabetical sequence:

Þingvallavatn (Iceland)
Þingvellir þjóðgarður (Iceland)
Þórisdalur (Iceland: Valley)
Þórsmörk (Iceland)

It is worth noting that in the indexes to the catalogue of the Library of Congress the 'Þ' is filed as if it were 'th'.

Punctuation

For filing purposes most punctuation is ignored. In the following selections we can see how both commas and apostrophes are discounted, as are brackets or parentheses:

Horses	Boxers
Horses, Fossil	Boxers, African American
Horse's Head Nebula	Boxers (Dogs)
Horses, Hobby	Boxers, Irish American
Horses in art	Boxers, Italian American
Horses in heraldry	Boxers (Sports)
Horses in literature	Boxers' spouses
Horses, Merry-go-round	Boxers (Underwear)
Horses on postage stamps	
Horses, Rocking	

The full stop, or period, is occasionally used in headings for works of literature and the like. The Bible is a good, if complicated, example. Again, the punctuation mark is ignored for filing purposes:

Bible
Bible films
Bible games and puzzles
Bible. Greek
Bible in literature
Bible in music
Bible. Latin
Bible. N. T.
Bible plays
Bible. Polyglot

The only major exception to this general principle is the hyphen. At first glance, hyphens look as if they don't matter for filing, but in fact they have the same value as a space. The hyphenated word is effectively treated as if it were two separate words:

Egg family
Egg-free diet
Egg gathering
Egg hunts, Easter
Egg-laying snakes, Harmless
Egg mushroom
Egg-plant tortoise beetle
Egg yolk
Eggbeaters
Eggcups

Typography

There is not much variation in the typography used in LCSH. The same font is used throughout, and only very rarely are italics used to give information about a heading.

But it is helpful to know that preferred headings are always in bold type, and that non-preferred headings (those that are not to be used) are in normal type. There is no real confusion because the non-preferred headings will always refer the user to the proper form, but the bold type helps to confirm which are valid headings and which are not:

Carpet and rug industry
    USE **Rug and carpet industry**
Carpet auctions
    BT   **Auctions**
Carpet backing
    BT   **Carpets**
Carpet beetle, Furniture
    USE **Anthrenus vorax**
Carpet beetles
    UF   Buffalo bugs
        Buffalo carpet beetles
        Carpet bugs
    NT   **Black carpet beetle**
Carpet bugs
    USE **Carpet beetles**

Summary

- LCSH uses a range of conventions in presenting the headings.
- Filing order is word-by-word.
- All words (even insignificant ones) count for filing purposes.
- Numbers file before letters.
- Numbers file decimally.
- Non-Roman letters file at the end of the alphabetical sequence.
- Most punctuation marks (commas, apostrophes, brackets, full stops) are ignored for filing.
- The hyphen counts as a space.
- Valid headings (or preferred headings) are in bold type.

Notes and references under headings

All of the above is to do solely with the sequence of headings, but they do not in reality appear as a simple list. Most headings have cross-references and notes of various kinds attached to them, so that the entry for a heading is, in most cases, more than just the heading itself, and sometimes the entries are fairly long and complicated. Figure 4.1 is a typical entry for a heading and you can see that there are a number of different notes and codes and subdivisions. We will look at each of these separately.

Scope notes

One of the first elements of the complete heading entry may be a note or explanation of the heading where this is open to debate:

Sex discrimination
> Here are entered works dealing solely with discriminatory behavior directed toward both of the sexes. Works on sexism as an attitude as well as works on both attitude and overt discriminatory behavior are entered under Sexism.

Scooby-Doo television programs
> Here are entered works on Scooby-Doo television programs discussed collectively. Works on individual Scooby-Doo television programs or series are entered under the specific title.

These are usually referred to as scope notes, since they indicate how the heading is to be used, what the 'scope' of its application is, and how, alternatively,

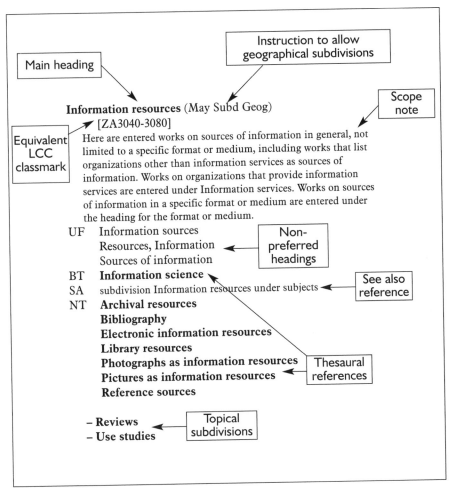

Figure 4.1 Typical entry for main heading

works which fall outside the scope are to be handled. Notes of this kind are not very common in LCSH, and usually they are brief and to the point.

Cross-references to the Library of Congress classification

Although there is no structural relationship between the headings and the classification, there are nevertheless various points of correspondence where a heading is equivalent to a classmark. When this happens the appropriate class is listed immediately under the heading:

Scooby-Doo television programs
    [PN1992.8.S36]

Parsnip
 [QK495.U48 (Botany)]
 [SB211.P3 (Culture)]

Dog walking
 [SF427.46]

Spies
 [UB270 (Military)]
 [VB250 (Naval)]

In the electronic LCSH these references are active hypertext links to the online classification. The fact that LC is a broad classification is demonstrated by the low number of links of this kind; perhaps only one in ten headings has a corresponding classmark, since they are so much more specific and numerous than the classes in the LC classification.

Geographic subdivision instructions

We shall look at the how geographic subdivisions are dealt with in Chapter 10, but for the moment you should simply note that the majority of headings can have these subdivisions added, and this is indicated by the legend (May Subd Geog) immediately following the heading:

Booby traps (May Subd Geog)
Electromagnets (May Subd Geog)
Plasma astrophysics (May Subd Geog)
Pole dancing (May Subd Geog)

If geographic subdivision is not allowed, this instruction is simply omitted, although occasionally subdivision is expressly forbidden. It is not entirely clear why some headings are singled out like this; they tend to be headings for people or characters, although this is not always so:

Book burning in literature (Not Subd Geog)
Cinderella (Legendary character) (Not Subd Geog)
Moonquakes (Not Subd Geog)
Potatoes in art (Not Subd Geog)
Woofter family (Not Subd Geog)

Summary

• Scope notes indicate how a heading is to be understood and applied.

- Where appropriate, links to Library of Congress Classification codes are provided.
- In the online LCSH these are live hypertext links.
- (May Subd Geog) indicates where geographic subdivisions can be added to a main heading.

Thesaural references

The next element in the heading, after the scope notes, the references to LC classmarks, and the geographic subdivision instructions, is that of cross-references to other headings.

The role of the thesaural references in locating a fuller range of headings is explored in Chapter 7, so here we shall confine ourselves to a very brief examination. There are five of these thesaural codes or tags (USE, UF, BT, NT and RT) and they divide into two groups: those that indicate which are the preferred headings (USE and UF) and those that refer to alternative headings (BT, NT and RT).

USE and UF tags

In the section on vocabulary control in Chapter 3 we considered briefly the idea of preferring one form among headings that mean the same, or roughly the same, and how this improves retrieval. (This is explored in more depth in Chapter 5.) USE and UF tags are employed to make the link between preferred and non-preferred headings, and to ensure that the correct form is used. Each UF tag will have a corresponding USE tag referring in the other direction. For example:

Football and war
> UF War and football

War and football
> USE **Football and war**

Sometimes a heading will represent more than one non-preferred heading. In that case they are listed in alphabetical order:

Soccer
> UF Association football
> > English football
> > European football
> > Football (Soccer)

BT, NT and RT tags

These are the standard thesaurus tags that indicate more general or broader terms (BT), more specific or narrower terms (NT), and terms related in other ways (RT). They serve the purpose of identifying potential alternative headings, and for getting a sense of what headings are available in particular subject areas:

> **Shepherds** (May Subd Geog)
> | | |
> | --- | ------------------ |
> | UF | Sheepherders |
> | BT | **Herders** |
> | RT | **Sheep** |
> | | **Sheep ranchers** |
> | NT | **Women shepherds** |

As with the USE and UF references, there are reciprocal references making the links in the reverse direction.

Note that where there is more than one example of the same kind of tag, the tag itself is not repeated.

See also references

Occasionally among the thesaural tags you will need a note marked SA. This stands for 'See also' and in most cases the reference is necessary because the topic occurs both as a main heading and as a standard subdivision. These are not very common, and references between main headings are always managed through the thesaurus tags.

Summary

- Thesaurus-type codes, or tags, are used to cross-reference the headings.
- USE and UF indicate which are preferred (authorized) and non-preferred headings and link between the two.
- BT, NT, and RT references point to other headings which are more general, more specific, or related in some other way.
- The cross-references provide a useful means of locating alternative headings.
- SA references are used mainly to indicate where headings occur both as main headings and subdivisions.

Topical subdivisions

The final element in the entry is likely to be a list of what are called 'topical subdivisions'. We shall look in some detail at the use of subdivisions in subsequent chapters, but they need to be briefly mentioned here because of the risk of confusion with the cross-references.

Topical subdivisions are subdivisions of the main heading, which are used to make a structured heading. For the sake of economy, in the printed LCSH, the subdivision part only is given, preceded by a dash. This dash alerts you to the fact that the word or phrase is not a heading in its own right, but must be added to the main heading:

Yoga
      UF   **Yoga--Hinduism**
      BT   **Philosophy, Indic**
      NT   **Chakras**
             Christianity and yoga
             Hatha yoga
             Music for yoga
             Siddha yoga
             Yin yoga
             Yogis

    --Bon (Tibetan religion)
    --Jainism

For use as headings these have to be written out in full:

Yoga--Bon (Tibetan religion)
Yoga--Jainism

Sometimes the topical subdivisions have further levels of subdivision, indicated by additional dashes:

Uranus (Planet)
         [QB387(Theoretical astronomy)]
         [QB681-683 (Descriptive astronomy)]
      BT   **Outer planets**
    --Color
    --Satellites
    -- --Ephemerides

These headings should be written fully as:

Uranus (Planet)
Uranus (Planet)--Color

> **Uranus (Planet)--Satellites**
> **Uranus (Planet)--Satellites--Ephemerides**

In my experience, a common problem when starting out with LCSH is failing to distinguish between the cross-references to other headings, and the topical subdivisions. Some students read the cross-references as subdivisions, and others take the subdivisions to be headings in their own right. The first of these errors is the more usual, so be careful to ensure that what you see is what you think you see.

In *Classification Web* this isn't problematic since the main headings with topical subdivisions are listed in their full form:

Uranus (Planet)
> [QB387 (Theoretical astronomy)]
> [QB681-683 (Descriptive astronomy)]
> BT   Outer planets

Uranus (Planet)--Color
> BT   Color

Uranus (Planet)--Satellites
> [QB406]
> UF   Satellites--Uranus [Former Heading]
>   Uranian satellites
> BT   Satellites
> NT   Ariel (Satellite)
>   Miranda (Satellite)

Uranus (Planet)--Satellites--Ephemerides
> [QB681]
> BT Ephemerides

Summary

- Topical subdivisions of a heading are shown preceded by a dash.
- These should not be used on their own, but only in conjunction with the main heading.
- Where there are further levels of topical subdivision, all the levels must be represented in the final heading.
- *Classification Web* expands the headings to include topical subdivisions, so that the correct format is given.

- Be very careful not to confuse cross-references to other headings with the topical subdivisions.

5 The choice and form of headings

Where do LCSH headings come from?

New cataloguers sometimes wonder who decides which headings are to be created. The answer is that headings are created in response to the books that are to be catalogued. There is no underlying theoretical framework to the headings, and they are just invented as needed. This has been the practice from the beginning of LCSH, and it explains many of the odd and unusual entries, such as **Also (The English word)** or **One-leg resting position**. If you feel doubtful about this you can always trace the book for which the heading was made through the Library of Congress catalogue (http://catalog.loc.gov/). Simply click on the heading in the subject index to bring up all the records to which it has been assigned. So, to explain a heading such as **Dog day care**, carry out a subject browse and click on the link to bring up the single title responsible for this heading (Figure 5.1).

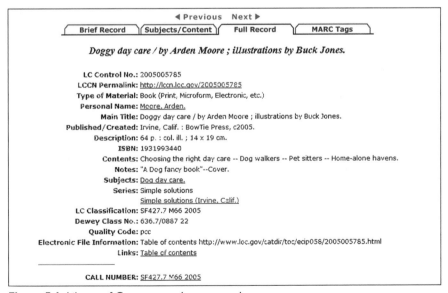

Figure 5.1 Library of Congress catalogue record

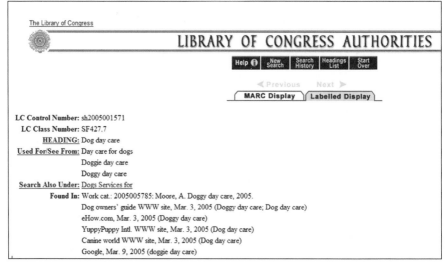

Figure 5.2 Library of Congress authority record

A single occurrence of a topic would not in itself be enough to warrant a new heading, and if you consult the subject authorities (http://authorities.loc.gov/) you will see that it must be found in several different sources before it is added to the list (Figure 5.2).

Of course, the headings are not added on an *ad hoc* basis, and new headings are approved by a central editorial body. In recent years institutions outside the Library of Congress have been able to suggest new headings. The British Library's re-introduction of LCSH to the records in the British National Bibliography in 1995 resulted in closer co-operation between the two libraries, and the opportunity for BL to propose additions to the headings list. The first heading contributed by BL was **Luminescent probes** and the first uniquely British heading was **Ring ouzel,** a bird of the thrush family native to Europe. This general principle is known as literary warrant, since a topic must be endorsed by its appearance in published literature in order to feature in the LCSH.

Summary

- LCSH is not built on a theoretical structure.
- Most headings are created as needed for books that have to be catalogued.
- This principle of validating headings is known as literary warrant.
- Editorial control is exercised over the process, and topics need more than one occurrence in the literature to justify the creation of a heading.

- The source of new headings can be seen in authority records for each heading.
- Libraries using LCSH are now able to suggest new headings.

Cutter's Rules and the choice of preferred terms

Although there is not very much in the way of theoretical principle under-lying the subject headings, there are policies that address the selection, or not, of different kinds of vocabulary, such as the use of either scientific or popular names for animals and plants. Over time, standard patterns of head-ing structure have also emerged, and there are a number of conventions affecting the way that the headings are formed. Many of these practices date back to the ideas of Cutter, and some of them reflect the conditions of phys-ical catalogues, the way in which compound headings should be handled there, and the part played by linear order in retrieval.

Cutter laid great stress on the end-user, whose convenience he said should always take precedence over that of the cataloguer. In other words, the cataloguer (or perhaps the designer of cataloguing systems) should take trouble in the creation of the catalogue record, and its various constituent parts, to ensure that using it was as easy and natural as possible for the reader.

Cutter said that consideration in the creation of headings must be given to the expectations of the users. In a general library Cutter's imag-ined reader was the average person, the 'man on the Clapham omnibus', rather than the scholar or the specialist. This emphasis on the common reader is retained today, with most headings preferring vernacular or everyday language over technical terms. Cutter also considered the form of the heading, which parts of speech (nouns, verbs, adjectives and so on) were acceptable, and whether headings should be inverted ('Art, Modern' as opposed to 'Modern art'). Many of his decisions were constrained by the physical catalogue, and its linear order, and are not really necessary now that catalogues are almost exclusively automated. Nevertheless, a number of these conventions persist in the contemporary LCSH.

The soundness of Cutter's theory, and of the policies developed by the Library of Congress, is evidenced by the study of subject heading lists con-ducted by the IFLA Classification and indexing committee, *Principles Underlying Subject Heading Languages (SHLs)*. This shows that virtually all of the general principles implemented in LCSH, which we will look at in the next section, are endorsed by other systems and constitute a body of good practice in subject cataloguing.

Summary

- Despite the lack of underlying theory, various policies affect the selection and form of headings.
- Some of these date back to Cutter's ideas of good practice in subject cataloguing.
- Preference is shown for everyday language and the needs of the average user.
- Some conventions result from the nature of physical catalogues and the way in which linear order affects them.
- Cutter's thinking is largely confirmed by modern practice in the design and application of subject heading languages.

Vocabulary control in LCSH: selection of terms

As we saw in Chapter 3, some restrictions need to be exercised in the use of language, if consistency in indexing is to be achieved and the efficiency of retrieval improved. Some styles of language need to be given priority over others, and policies need to be in place to ensure that this is done in a consistent way, and not *ad hoc*. Making sure that indexing practice is predictable is important too for end-users, who should have some expectation of how a topic will be expressed if they are to conduct successful searches.

These policies collectively constitute a form of vocabulary control, and the subject terms chosen as a result of their application are the authorized headings, or preferred terms, in the LCSH vocabulary.

Uniform headings

The principle of the uniform heading states that there should be only one heading to represent a particular topic. The idea of a uniform heading is an abstract one, but it has an important practical purpose: that the user should not have to search under several different headings to find information on a topic, but that all that information is brought together under a single heading. If you have come across uniform titles in cataloguing you will see that, while the uniform heading is something different, it has essentially the same purpose of keeping everything related together.

It is the main means of controlling synonyms, and ensuring that preferred terms are selected, and non-preferred terms discarded. If you look at any example of a heading that has USE or UF references attached you will see how it works:

Intellectual freedom
> UF   Access to ideas
> Freedom of thought
> Freedom to read

Dogs
> UF   Canis domesticus
> Canis familiarus
> Canis familiarus domesticus
> Canis lupus familiaris
> Dog
> Domestic dog

Intellectual freedom is chosen in preference to 'Access to ideas' or 'Freedom of thought', and becomes the authorized heading (the preferred term) for this concept. 'Access to ideas' is still entered in the list, but the entry there will read:

> Access to ideas
> USE **Intellectual freedom**

This ensures that **Intellectual freedom** is used consistently as the heading for this topic, so that everything about it is brought together under the same search term. The same principle applies to the heading for **Dogs**, which shows the application of some additional criteria in the choice of the preferred term, and which we shall return to later.

There are other ways in which headings for a topic can take different forms: an important one is the occurrence of different spellings of a word; a second is variation in the word order in the heading.

Variations in spelling

It may be that the chosen heading can be spelled in more than one way, in which case the preferred version must be determined to maintain the uniform heading principle. For example:

> Civilisation   or   Civilization
> Mediaeval   or   Medieval
> Behaviour   or   Behavior

In the case of LCSH, *Webster's Third International Dictionary* is used as an authority. It is useful to have an external reference source of this kind, since often there is not much to choose between different forms, and it provides a quick and easy resolution of any dispute. British users of LCSH should watch out for the American spelling, which is not always predictable; having seen **Encyclopedias**, for instance, you may be expecting 'Archeology', but the form is **Archaeology.**

Similar problems occur with different forms of names, this being a particular problem when names are transliterated from non-Roman scripts. For instance, we may have to make a choice between:

> Tchaikovsky
> or   Tchaikovski
> or   Chaikovsky
> or   Tschaikowski

The Library of Congress uses standard tables for transliteration so there is some degree of uniformity in the way this is done. The results of their deliberations can be found in the name authorities on the Library of Congress website (http://authorities.loc.gov/). Similar problems are found in the spelling of place names (of which more in Chapter 14), and are resolved in the same way. An important example is the change in the spelling of 'Peking' to 'Beijing', which happened when the Library changed the system of Romanization of Chinese from the Wade-Giles system to Pinyin during the 1990s.

Inverted headings

You will find both inverted headings (**Prisoners, Foreign**) and natural word order headings (**Prisoners' songs**) in LCSH, and it is often difficult to discern any reason why one is preferred in any given case. What is clear is that under the uniform heading principle only one form can be used for a particular topic. So, for example, we have:

> **Church history**
> **Local history**
> **Social history**

and:

> **History, Ancient**
> **History, Modern**

but not:

Modern history

or: Ancient history

or: History, Local

Summary

- Vocabulary control is used to manage the selection of headings.
- This improves consistency in cataloguing and makes searching more effective.
- An important principle is that a topic should be represented by only one heading (uniform heading principle).
- This means that one preferred version is chosen from any potential synonyms or synonymous phrases.
- Variation in spelling and in the transliteration of foreign words is managed by the use of reference tools.
- A choice is made between inverted and non-inverted forms.

Principles of synonym control

The spelling situation and the inverted or non-inverted entries are both examples of variant forms of essentially the same heading. True synonymy, where different terms represent the same or similar topics, is more complicated and we need some rules for making consistent choices. Cutter's idea that the 'average' reader, or non-specialist, should be kept in mind, explains some of the policy decisions that affect LCSH. It is a system of headings for general use, in libraries that may contain any or all subjects, and this universality is important in making it widely usable.

Some broad and fairly vague policies apply, such as a preference for language that is unambiguous, familiar to users, and unbiased. Many critics of LCSH would say that it has been singularly unsuccessful in the last objective, but nevertheless its purpose is to provide, as far as possible, a neutral vocabulary. There are other, more specific choices to be made between various forms of terminology.

Scientific and technical terms

This is a perfect example of where the average user is given priority. Wherever possible, everyday language is preferred to its technical equivalent, and vernacular forms to scientific ones. So we see:

Horses

UF   Equus caballus

Hippology

Mumps

UF   Epidemic parotitis

Aspirin

UF   Acetylsalicylic acid

English bluebell

UF   Endymion nonscripta

You can see that in a scientific library it could be better to use the alternatives, since a botanist no doubt thinks of endymion rather than bluebell, but for general libraries the common form is more likely to be sought. This is not to say that technical terms are not used, since in many cases there is no more familiar equivalent. A great number of scientific terms, for example, will not be in common usage, nor are many technical terms in other disciplines:

Bretylium tosylate

Fissurellidae

Supervenience (Philosophy)

Nonatherosclerotic myocardial ischemia

Cartularies

Obsolete terms

LCSH has a policy of eradicating out-of-date terminology (including dated spelling), and it seems only sensible that the current way of referring to a topic should be preferred. One practical result of this policy is that only the current name of a place is used in headings, hence:

Cambodia	rather than	Khmer Republic
Canaveral, Cape (Fla.)	rather than	Kennedy, Cape (Fla.)

This extends to historic names of things, as well as more recent changes in terminology:

German shepherd dog	rather than	Alsatian dog
Mercury	rather than	Quicksilver
Radio	rather than	Wireless
Sulfur	rather than	Brimstone

However, it can be difficult to decide when a term is old-fashioned, or if its meaning has changed, other than with the benefit of hindsight. Some of these preferences can be culturally linked, as in the case of **Bathing suits**, which looks quaint to British readers, as does **Betrothal** in preference to 'engagement'. It is also hard to know how to accommodate books about obsolete topics if the headings are removed, and this probably accounts for the retention of some rather antiquated looking headings, such as **Coster-mongers** or **Mesmerism**.

Foreign terms

LCSH, like most controlled vocabularies, prefers to avoid the use of foreign words. This is perfectly reasonable where an English language equivalent can be found. The exceptions are where the word is now commonly used and understood in English, for example, **Aperitifs**, **Cinéma vérité**, **Sputnik satellites** or **Chiaroscuro**. Words like this are usually referred to as loan words.

In practice, there are very few words indeed that do not have an English counterpart, and don't fall into the category of loan words, since such terms would hardly ever be needed. The usual example given is **Reallast**, a German legal term referring to a kind of land tenure, which is peculiar to Germany. Other examples of legal terminology of foreign origin can be discovered (**Jus primae noctis**, **Scutage**, **Fiefs**, **Gavelkind**), although it is difficult to say with confidence whether these are really foreign words, or part of the standard technical vocabulary of English law derived from Latin, Norman French and Middle English.

A comparable situation exists with the use of Latin names of plants and animals. Again, vernacular names are preferred, but in many cases there is only a Latin version, and who is to say whether or not these are part of the normal technical vocabulary of the biological sciences. The situation is not helped by the fact that LCSH is not entirely consistent in its application of this policy. We have seen above some examples of where English is preferred to Latin (as expected), but there are also instances of the reverse:

Thais clavigera	UF	Dog whelk
Leptodactylus melanonotus	UF	Fringe-toed foamfrog
Pelorneum ruficeps	UF	Spotted babbler
Nipaecoccus viridis	UF	Fluffy mealybug

Unique headings

Whereas the principle of the uniform heading is intended to cope with synonyms, the unique heading principle deals with homonyms. So while the uniform heading ensures that there will be only one heading for each topic or concept, the unique heading principle deals with the inverse situation, to ensure that there will be only one topic or concept for each heading.

Homonyms (or more strictly, homomorphs) are differentiated by the use of contextual terms placed in brackets, which are known as qualifiers. The qualifier forms part of the heading and should be included in it.

The qualifier clarifies which meaning of the word is intended:

Rings (Algebra)	**Polarity (Biology)**
Rings (Gymnastics)	**Polarity (Linguistics)**
Boxers (Dogs)	**Polarity (Philosophy)**
Boxers (Sports)	**Polarity (Psychology)**

Some potential conflicts are avoided by using alternative forms of the heading:

Squash (Game)
Squash (Vegetable)   USE   Squashes

This process is called disambiguation. A very common use of qualifiers is to disambiguate name headings, particularly for places with the same name, and less frequently for persons (these are more commonly distinguished by providing dates of birth and death):

Memphis (Extinct city)
Memphis (Tenn.)

Disambiguation is not the only function of qualifiers, and other examples are dealt with later in this chapter.

Summary

- Synonyms are managed by a number of editorial policies.
- Vernacular, or everyday, language is generally preferred.
- Scientific and technical terms are not used where a common term is available.
- Obsolete terms are avoided.
- Foreign terms are not used except where they are commonly used in English, or where there is no English equivalent.

- These rules are not applied absolutely rigorously, and many exceptions can be found.
- Words that look the same (homonyms, or homographs) are qualified by additional terms in brackets which establish the context or meaning.

Vocabulary control in LCSH: form of terms

As well as deciding which synonyms or variant terms are to be preferred to others, some choices have to be made about the format of headings. There are various statements of good practice, such as the national and international standards for thesauri and other controlled vocabularies, and although LCSH was developed long before these were published, it does observe the majority of the conventions recommended there. It also has its own traditions about the style of headings, and certain patterns of form can be observed; the regular user will soon come to recognize these, and the conventions applied in constructing them.

We will examine a variety of different kinds of form, including a more detailed look at inverted headings and qualifiers, and the way in which punctuation is used.

Single word headings

There are probably far fewer of these than you might expect, despite efforts in recent years to simplify the headings and make them less complex in structure. Most single word headings are the names of disciplines, activities, classes of persons, objects, phenomena, and organisms:

Actors
Anthropology
Burglars
Chemotherapy
Cloudiness
Dinosaurs
Dreams
Knitting
Mosquitoes
Teapots
Tulips

Nouns and other parts of speech

You will notice that all of these terms are nouns. It is accepted good practice in subject indexing to use nouns or nominal forms, because it reduces the number of possible forms, and because searchers are much more likely to use nouns as search terms. Verbs occur frequently as headings for activities and processes of all sorts, but they are always presented in the noun form:

Classification	rather than	Classifying
Dance	rather than	Dancing
Digestion	rather than	Digesting

Other forms of verbs, such as infinitives and participles, should be avoided, and are in LCSH. In English the present participle of a verb is often identical to the noun form known as a gerund, so there are plenty of examples of headings that may initially look like verbs, such as **Bricklaying, Fishing, Learning, Painting, Singing, Swimming** or **Wrecking**.

Adjectives and adverbs are similarly taboo, except where they occur as part of phrases. There are lots of examples of these (see below). Adjectives and adverbs, like verbs, should be converted to noun equivalents:

Cloudiness	rather than	Cloudy
Elasticity	rather than	Elastic
Benevolence	rather than	Benevolent

Most of the published standards also exclude the use of the more minor parts of speech, such as pronouns, conjunctions and prepositions, and they provide guidelines for when definite and indefinite articles are permissible.

Because LCSH includes some very complex headings, these other word forms occur fairly frequently. But they don't stand on their own, except in the rare situations where the word itself is the subject, and then they are qualified to that effect; a good example is **But (The English word)**. Some (unsuccessful) trial searches for words like 'for', 'how', 'under', 'what', 'who' and 'why' will demonstrate how exceptional this heading is.

Singular and plural forms

Names of physical objects or entities (which include types of persons) are known as concrete nouns and these are usually represented as plurals.

Names of abstract concepts are naturally used in the singular form. Another way of determining whether terms are to be singular or plural is to decide whether they are 'count nouns' or 'non-count nouns' (whether the object can normally be counted). This means that some concrete phenomena, such as substances, appear in the singular. This gives rise to such headings as **Cheese, Uranium** and **Wool**. It could be argued that cheeses exist as physical objects, or that cheeses ought to be plural because there is more than one kind of cheese, but if that view is taken it becomes very difficult to find any examples of singular substances (the 'snows of yesteryear' and the 'season of mists' immediately spring to mind, and any Google search will retrieve numerous examples of fogs, bubble gums, custards and so on). LCSH takes a more pragmatic line and substances and materials normally take the singular.

Regular exceptions to the pluralization of count nouns include parts of the body and musical instruments (**Brain, Ear, Didjeridu, Bass trombone**), as well as named species and varieties of plants and animals (**English bluebell, Turnip aphid, Norwegian forest cat**), although more general categories of these last two can be pluralized, as with **Hairless dogs** or **Dangerous plants**.

Summary

- LCSH uses various conventions in forming headings, and there is a consistent style.
- This conforms with much of established good indexing practice as expressed in national and international standards.
- Some headings take the form of single words.
- These are expressed as nouns, or as the noun equivalent of verbs.
- Other verb forms, adjectives and adverbs, prepositions and conjunctions are never used as single word headings.
- Concrete nouns (or count-nouns) are made plural, while abstract nouns are in the singular form.
- Exceptions to this rule include parts of the body, musical instruments, and species of plants and animals.

Multi-word headings

In practice, the number of concepts that are represented by a single word is fairly limited, and the great majority of objects, persons, phenomena, and so on, require multi-word headings:

Ball lightning
Coffee tables
Folk singers
International relations
Machine knitting
Quantum chemistry
Project managers
Shrub roses
Toasting forks

The concepts here are not necessarily complex, and very often they are varieties or sub-classes of a more general class of things. It is sometimes just a matter of linguistic accident whether a term is single or multi-word, for example **Bullfrog** or **Spotted frog**, **Medical physics** or **Astrophysics**. Note that only the first word in these headings has a capital letter.

Expressions of this sort are sometimes referred to as noun phrases, where a noun is qualified by an adjective or another noun. If you follow this up in reference sources, you will find that sources from linguistics use terminology slightly differently from those in indexing or library science. In indexing jargon, the noun is sometimes referred to as the focus, and the qualifying adjective or noun as the modifier, or difference:

Aquatic sports
Brown bear
Dwarf trees
Human growth
Jewish authors
Mercenary troops
Molecular biology
Private libraries

In these examples using adjectives as modifiers, the adjective creates a subclass of the focus.

Inverted headings

Sometimes headings of this kind are inverted, bringing the noun into the lead position. Most of the adjectives here refer to period, or to nationality or culture. Note that in these headings the adjectival element, which would otherwise have been in the lead position, has an initial capital letter:

Architecture, Domestic
Boats, Ancient
Chemistry, Forensic
Cookery, Albanian
History, Modern
Journalism, Scientific
Manuscripts, Medieval

This practice originates in the days of the card catalogue, and the purpose is to bring together all the varieties and subdivisions of a subject. This creates a more logical and structured sequence when searching a linear file and it achieves the same objective in the subject index to a catalogue. From a retrieval point of view it doesn't matter very much where an individual word comes in the phrase, as the software in an automated catalogue normally allows the searcher to retrieve records using keywords.

Although, as we established above, an individual heading can exist only in either the inverted or the natural word order form, there are thousands of examples of both forms, and it is hard to predict which will be preferred. Recently many inverted headings have been revised to use natural word order, for example:

Australian literature
Domestic engineering
Industrial accidents
Melodic analysis
Nonfiction novel
Quadratic fields

There is no consistent policy in the use of natural language and inverted forms, although there appears to be a gradual move away from inverted forms, and there is not much evidence of new headings in the inverted form.

Summary

- The great majority of LCSH are multi-word headings.
- Most of these are noun phrases, that is, nouns qualified by another noun or an adjective.
- In some cases the order of words is turned round to create an inverted heading.

- This practice began in printed and card catalogues to bring significant words into the lead position.
- There is now a move away from inverted headings toward natural language order.

Qualifiers

Some headings contain terms in brackets, or parentheses, known as qualifiers. We have seen already how they are used to distinguish, or disambiguate, homomorphs, but they may also serve to clarify the meaning or context of a heading, even when it does not necessarily have more than one potential interpretation. Hence:

Gram (Unit)
Hecate (Greek deity)
Instrumentalism (Philosophy)
Parsing (Computer grammar)
Paseq (The Hebrew accent)
Symmetry (Physics)

Occasionally a qualifier may appear in the middle of a heading, as in the case of **Naps (Sleep) in the workplace**.

Headings for fictitious and legendary characters (and for legendary and imaginary places) are also indicated as such by these parenthetical qualifiers:

Little Orphan Annie (Fictitious character)
Paddington Bear (Fictitious character)
Superman (Fictitious character)

Anansi (Legendary character)
Brer Rabbit (Legendary character)
Friar Tuck (Legendary character)
Scheherazade (Legendary character)

221B Baker Street (London, England: Imaginary place)
Camelot (Legendary place)

Recently, some of these imaginary places have been redefined as imaginary organizations, reflecting the frequent confusion between places and organizations in indexing practice:

Hogwarts School of Witchcraft and Wizardry (Imaginary organization)

A strange use of the parenthetical qualifier occurs in the various terms for **Cookery**, such as **Cookery (Cheese)**, **Cookery (Puddings)** and **Cookery (Emu)**, which you might reasonably expect to be in the form Cheese (Cookery). There is no explanation of this oddity, and no other comparable example; it is just another of LCSH's quirks.

Summary

- Words in brackets (qualifiers) are used to establish the meaning or context of headings.
- Sometimes they are just explanatory, but more often help to distinguish between headings with the same verbal form (disambiguation).
- Qualifiers are also used routinely with the names of legendary and fictitious characters, and with imaginary places and organizations.

More complex headings

Very many of the LCSH are not only multi-word terms, but also represent more complicated subjects than the relatively simple concepts listed above. The practice of pre-combining two or more simple concepts in a 'ready-made' heading is known as pre-coordination. The majority of LCSH display some degree of pre-coordination, and some headings exhibit very high levels. This is in marked contrast to many indexing vocabularies used in automated catalogues and databases, which consist of only simple terms in the form of, for example, keywords or tags.

Pre-coordinated headings in LCSH fall into a number of distinct categories.

'And' headings

Headings of the 'A and B' type are very common. These may express a general relationship between two disciplines, or between two more specific topics. Sometimes this relationship is one of comparison or opposition:

Art and business
Music and mythology
Science and law

Fascism and freemasonry
Internet and teenagers
National socialism and soccer

Good and evil
Freewill and determinism

You should understand these headings to be about the interaction or relationship of the two topics rather than their separate treatment in the document. In contrast, many other 'and' headings are intended for closely associated topics, which are often dealt with together. These may be similar concepts (quasi-synonyms) or an object and an associated activity:

Encyclopedias and dictionaries
Kangaroo deterrents and repellents
Mormon wit and humor
Wounds and injuries

Books and reading
Dinners and dining
Salt mines and mining
Type and type-founding

You can see that there is probably no useful distinction, from a retrieval point of view, to be made between salt mines and salt mining, and that a document on one is likely to deal with the other.

Prepositional phrases

Similar expressions of relationship between two concepts may be found in the many headings using prepositions and conjunctions of various kinds. Like the 'and' headings, they normally express some general relationship, but the inclusion of the preposition creates a more elegant statement of subject. In other situations the preposition actively clarifies the subject, which might be less than obvious if expressed as keywords. For instance, the meaning of a string like 'History--Mathematics--Education' could be understood in several different ways, whereas **History in mathematics education** is quite unambiguous.

A more precise relationship may be intended, as with the 'for' headings, many (although not all) of which indicate a target audience or readership:

Automobile parking for people with disabilities
Deer hunting for teenagers
Dust ingestion by animals
Enzymes in animal nutrition
Internet access for library users

Mothers of criminals
Parties for dogs
Poisoning in honeybees
Worms as pets

A very common type of prepositional heading is that which deals with the representation of a topic in the arts and media. Sometimes it seems that almost every main heading has associated headings . . . **in literature** . . . **in art** . . . **in motion pictures,** and occasionally. . . **in music** . . . **in advertising,** and . . . **on television:**

Buddhist nuns in art
Ceramics in rabbinical literature
Pregnant women in advertising
Smoking in popular music
Teachers on television
Tree of life in literature

A specialized (and somewhat unexpected) sub-category is the liberal provision for themes on postage stamps:

Cows on postage stamps
Dance on postage stamps
Parsees on postage stamps
Space flights on postage stamps

Compounds and combinations

Occasionally LCSH goes to extremes in the level of pre-coordination. Mostly this is because it employs combinations of qualifiers, 'and' headings and prepositional constructions, but other highly pre-coordinated headings may defy categorization. It is most likely that these headings have been created for particular documents, and if you look at the Library of Congress subject indexes, you will see that often these very complex headings have only one associated title:

Contempt (Attitude) in literature
Dinners and dining in the Bible
Gay man-heterosexual woman relationships in motion pictures
Gold mines and mining on postage stamps
Pinocchio (Fictitious character) in advertising

> Liability for emotional distress (Jewish law)
> Animals as represented on the stage
> Business enterprises owned by people with social disabilities
> Church work with the baby boom generation
> Non-timber forest products industry

Although it is useful to represent subject content very exactly, it may not necessarily match the way end-users will naturally search, so the value of pre-coordination and the use of linking words in making the subject plain have to be balanced against this disadvantage.

There appears to be a move on the part of Library of Congress to replace some of these very complex combinations with more structured headings. For example, **Front pages of Brazilian newspapers** has been superseded by **Brazilian newspapers--Sections, columns, etc--Front pages**, which is likely to reflect more closely the way in which searchers think. A fuller discussion of structured headings can be found in Chapters 8–12.

Summary

- Some LCSH take much more complicated verbal forms.
- These may be referred to as pre-coordinated headings because they combine more than one concept or idea in the heading.
- 'And' headings link related topics, or an object and associated activity.
- Other headings use prepositions to link topics.
- More complex headings may have combinations of noun phrases, 'ands', prepositions, and qualifiers.
- Recently there is a move away from pre-coordination towards structured headings.

Punctuation of headings

As mentioned above, there are some well established conventions in the use of punctuation in headings, and when you become familiar with them, wrongly punctuated headings look very odd.

Capitalization

This has been briefly touched on above, but is worth repeating, as it is an important element of LCSH style. LCSH uses an initial capital only for the first word in the heading, no matter how long and complicated the heading may be:

Advanced very high resolution radiometers
Drinking of alcoholic beverages in motion pictures
Lodgepole pine dwarf mistletoe
Waste disposal in the ocean

Words that would normally take a capital letter (personal names and the names of languages, for example) are capitalized as usual:

African American agricultural labourers
Anglo-Norman dialect
Kate Greenaway Medal
Light and darkness in the Bible

Otherwise, initial capitals are used only to indicate structural elements in the heading, such as qualifiers, inversions and subdivisions:

Atomic swerve (Philosophy)
Pink flamingos (Lawn ornaments)
Christian literature, Early
Marine reptiles, Fossil
Jumping--Records
Theaters--Fire and fire prevention

There is further discussion of the way in which structured headings are created in Chapters 8–12.

Hyphens and dashes

As we have seen above, dashes are used to indicate subdivisions of a main heading. The convention in LCSH is to use double dashes to denote the subdivision, and these can be seen in the online version, *Classification Web*, and in the Library of Congress catalogue, for example:

Popes--Infallibility
Oak--Diseases and pests
Watersheds--Angola

These double dashes are used to differentiate structured headings from headings containing hyphenated words, such as **X-ray astronomy** or **Human-computer interaction**. But on the whole, LCSH does not like hyphens, and they are used only where they are unavoidable if sense is to be maintained. In other examples where hyphens might reasonably be expected, LCSH omits them, although this practice is not invariable and, as with most aspects of LCSH, exceptions can be found:

Coordinate indexing
Multimedia cartography
Postoperative care
Preschool teachers

Poly-aquaculture
Post-translational modification

Periods or full stops

The period, or full stop, is used in headings for named created works, such as literary texts or musical compositions:

Shakespeare, William, 1564-1616. Hamlet
Wagner, Richard, 1813-1883. Parsifal

These are normally created by the cataloguer as needed, so there are not many pre-existing headings of this sort. The Bible is a notable exception, although the headings in the published LCSH are not exhaustive, and the Library of Congress catalogue should be consulted for more examples:

Bible. N.T. Epistles of Paul

There is further discussion of these kinds of headings in Chapters 15 and 16.

Other punctuation marks

Apart from the commas used in inverted headings, there are virtually no other marks or symbols in LCSH. Arabic numerals are occasionally found, but non-Roman letters used as symbols are spelt out, as in **Chi Rho symbol** or **Beta rays**.

Summary

- Headings are punctuated according to strict rules.
- The first word in each heading has an initial capital letter.
- Initial capitals are also used for the first word in a subdivision, or in a qualifier.
- Inverted headings capitalize the original lead word.

- Otherwise capitals are only used for proper nouns.
- Hyphens are avoided wherever possible.
- Double dashes are used to separate the elements of structured headings, to avoid confusion with hyphenated words.
- Full stops (periods) are used in headings for literary and musical works.
- Commas are used in inverted headings.
- No other punctuation marks or symbols are used.

6 Content analysis

The preceding chapters have been mainly concerned with how the subject headings are presented, and what form they take. The form of headings is decided by the Policy and Standards Division of the Library of Congress, and you as cataloguer don't have any control over this; individual headings must be used consistently by everyone, both at the local level to ensure efficient retrieval, and across institutions to support the exchange of information and interoperability of catalogues.

In selecting headings for individual documents, however, you have much more freedom to do as you think best for your own situation. In this and the following chapter we shall look at how to choose headings in order to represent documents accurately and in a manner useful to end-users.

Before you can do that it is necessary to decide what the item being catalogued is about. Whatever system of subject headings (or classification scheme or thesaurus) is being used to describe a document, you should try initially to make an independent assessment of what the subject of that document is. In practice, you will almost certainly be unable to represent this exactly using the artificial language of your system, but you should at least begin by deciding objectively what it is you want to express. This process may be called 'subject analysis', or 'document analysis', 'content analysis' or 'concept analysis'. The subject content of items is sometimes also referred to more grandly as 'intellectual content' or 'semantic content', but these are simply other ways of defining what a document is about.

The problem of 'aboutness'; indexer consistency and subjectivity

The process of determining 'aboutness' is an essential part of subject cataloguing, but it contrasts markedly with the task of descriptive cataloguing. In the majority of cases the cataloguer has only to inspect the title page to determine the author and the title, and other bibliographic details of a book, and having found the author and title there is generally no dispute as to what they are. In some cases the subject is similarly straightforward, but in others the situation is more complicated. Unfortunately there is nowhere to look in a book which will tell you plainly and unequivocally what its subject is; you must decide this for yourself.

Deciding on the subject of a book can be tricky because it is a very subjective activity. Two people may interpret the subject of a book quite differently, and research has shown that if the same indexer thinks about the same item on two different occasions, he or she doesn't reach exactly the same conclusion about its content. Even experienced cataloguers find it hard to describe what exactly they do when deciding on the subject of a book because it is largely an intuitive process. And much of the time the titles and subjects of books may be mystifying:

```
The diseases of electrical machinery / by George W.
Stubbings. - London, E. & F. N. Spon, ltd., 1945

Proceedings of the third International Workshop on Nude
Mice, Montana State University, Bozeman, Montana, September
6-9, 1979 / edited by Norman D. Reed. - New York: G.
Fischer, c1982

On the flexure of a large elastic plate containing an
unstressed circular hole, by Ernest E. Burniston. -
Raleigh, North Carolina State University, Applied
Mathematics Research Group, 1967

Cleaning up coal: a study of coal cleaning and the use of
cleaned coal / authors, Cynthia A. Hutton, Robert N. Gould;
research consultant, Sophie R. Weber; editor, Richard C.
Allen. - Cambridge, Mass.: Ballinger Pub. Co., c1982
```

Nevertheless, there are some techniques of content analysis that can be learnt, and which will help you to establish standards of good practice and produce effective subject indexing. In the following pages we shall consider:

- *where* to find indications of subject content
- *how* to construct a statement of subject content.

Where to look for content
The title

The novice cataloguer often assumes that the logical indicator of a book's subject is the title. Of course often the title *is* an accurate reflection of the content, and this is especially true of scientific publications, where the titles tend to be fairly literal and descriptive of the content. Take the following example from a set of conference proceedings:

```
Pineapple research in Brazil/ J. H. Reinhardt and J. da S.
Sousa in Proceedings of the Third International Pineapple
Symposium: Pattaya, Thailand, 12-20 November 1998/ editors
S. Subhadrabandhu, P. Chairidchai
```

The authors of this paper, when asked to describe the content, have assigned to it the descriptors, or subject keywords, 'pineapple', 'research' and 'Brazil', which correspond very closely indeed to the title. The following titles also demonstrate the descriptive quality of titles of scientific and technical papers:

```
Characterization and treatment of brine wastewaters from
the cucumber pickle industry / by Linda W. Little, James
C. Lamb III, Louise F. Horney. - Raleigh: Water Resources
Research Institute of the University of North Carolina,
1976
```

```
The anatomy of the forelimb in armadillos and anteaters
(Mammalia: Edentada) [microform] / Bruce Kenneth Taylor. -
Thesis (Ph. D.)-University of Chicago, 1976
```

You can fairly safely assume that the subjects of these documents are those stated in the titles. This is not always the case. *Don't put socks on the hippopotamus* doesn't sound very much like a handbook of hippopotamus management, which is more likely to be called something along the lines of:

```
Crocodile and hippopotamus management in the Lower Shire /
prepared by Felix Kalowekamo, Development Alternatives,
Inc., in association with Development Management
Associates. - Blantyre, Malawi: Community Partnerships for
Sustainable Resource Management in Malawi, [2000]
```

In fact *Don't put socks on the hippopotamus* is a book about management in general, and has nothing at all to tell you about hippopotamuses. Apart from the illustration on the cover, the hippopotamus content is nil; the title is entirely whimsical. It is typical of the many cases where titles of books are not helpful in indicating content, and sometimes can be downright misleading. This is more likely to happen with books in the social sciences and humanities, particularly the latter, where authors often delight in producing amusing or intriguing titles, using wordplay such as puns, or quotations, rather than titles which convey a sense of the book's subject. Good examples include:

Feathers and the horizon (a book of Arab poetry)

Four-foot cucumbers, juvenile delinquents & frogs from the sky! (a social history of nineteenth century Canada)

Magic of polyurethane (a dull study about marketing plastic)

Romance of a nose (a book about Cleopatra)

In order to be confident about the real subject of a book, we need to examine it carefully for clues. Be observant when handling the book because information can be discovered in all sorts of places.

The subtitle

Although the title of a book may itself be misleading, the author, having enjoyed his literary reference or clever joke, often helps the reader by explaining it. *The beast in the boudoir* is a good example of this; without the subtitle we could imagine it to be something quite other than a book about the history of pets:

```
The beast in the boudoir: petkeeping in nineteenth-century
Paris / Kathleen Kete. - Berkeley: University of California
Press, 1994
```

The dust jacket and covers

A rapid examination of the external parts of the book can also help you to identify aspects of the content that aren't immediately apparent from the title page. For example, a title such as *Saints: the chosen few* suggests from the wording that it is a book about Christianity, but the description on the dust jacket indicates that the work deals with a whole range of religions, and should be described as a more general work on world faiths. Information on dust jackets, including the publisher's blurb, is also useful in revealing intended audiences for the book.

Inside the book: the contents page and beyond

Not everything that you have to catalogue will still have the dust jacket intact, and, if you are still in doubt about the subject of a book, it may be necessary to look beyond the title page for further clues. The contents page can provide you with a detailed list of the topics covered, and can clarify matters considerably; other sources can be the preface, introduction, first chapter or even the index with its list of key concepts. Look at this example:

```
The Fellowship: the story of a revolution / by John
Gribbin. - London: Allen Lane, 2005
```

The title gives very little indication of the subject of this book, nor does the subtitle; if anything it suggests something political. The dust jacket suggests that it might be something to do with science.

Only an examination of the contents gives the first clue to the actual subject with chapters headed:

Scientific minds
The philosopher scientist
The roots of the Royal I: the Oxford connection
The roots of the Royal II: the King's men

In fact this book is a history of the origins of the Royal Society, the leading learned scientific society in the UK. However, the name 'Royal Society' isn't mentioned in the introduction, and doesn't occur until quite a long way into the text; if you did not know about its existence it might be very difficult to arrive at a correct decision.

Reference sources

If you are completely stumped as to the subject of a book – perhaps it has a scientific or technical content beyond your experience – it is perfectly legitimate to seek someone else's opinion. There is no reason why you should be expert in every field of knowledge before you can think about subject cataloguing. All libraries, if not the cataloguing department itself, should have a collection of reference works that will provide you with information about subjects, define terms, and explain the structure of disciplines.

Other catalogue records

Nowadays most large general libraries, as well as many special collections, have online catalogues where you can search for an existing catalogue record for your book. The work of a more experienced cataloguer can help you to see how the book could be handled. Even if a different system is being used you will probably be able to work out what's been done, and in many instances subject headings will give you a clear indication of the book's subject. Beginner cataloguers often think of this as cheating, but it is only a sensible strategy when you are at a loss for what to do, and it is common practice among professional cataloguers; you can even think of it as good practice to check your work with others from time to time. There's no need to feel obliged to reproduce exactly existing subject data – simply take what you need for your own purposes and situation.

Summary

- Examine the book carefully.
- Look at the title, but exercise caution.
- See if there are clues in the subtitle.
- Read the covers and jacket description.
- Look at the contents page, introduction, first chapter, or index.
- Consult works of reference if the subject is obscure.
- Seek confirmation from existing catalogue records if necessary.

Constructing the document description
What to include

Having examined the document closely, we can now start to construct a proper description of the document content. The object of the exercise is to create a concise statement of the document's content in a form that can be easily translated into a subject heading or headings. If you are applying a classification scheme as well, this statement can also function as the basis of a classmark or callmark. Such a statement is called by a variety of names: subject string, subject summary and concept analysis all mean the same thing. In the following pages you will see a number of examples of such objects.

Identifying the main subject of the document

The first stage in creating a document description is to decide on the broad subject area to which the book belongs. If you are using a classification scheme as well as subject headings, this is absolutely unavoidable because the book must be physically located somewhere, but it can also be relevant to subject headings, as it helps you to think about who the user might be. Most of the time there won't be any difficulty about this. Consider this book:

```
A field key to four hundred common mushrooms and toadstools
/ by F. B. Hora. - Reading, Berkshire: Reading and
District Natural History Society, 1950
```

This is a book about mushrooms and toadstools, and it belongs in the biological sciences, under fungi; there isn't any other reasonable option. It is going to be of interest to naturalists and botanists (if fungi can still be considered as plants).

Here are further examples of relatively straightforward titles, with no ambiguity about the general subject matter:

```
Concise encyclopedia of metallurgy / A. D. Merriman. –
London: MacDonald and Evans, 1965

The Sumerians: their history, culture, and character /
Samuel Noah Kramer. – Chicago; London: University of
Chicago Press, 1970
```

There is not much doubt that the first book is about metallurgy, and the second about ancient history, more specifically the Sumerians. Sometimes the general subject of a book is less obvious, or the likely end-user needs specific consideration. A book about vegetables, for example, might be aimed at gardeners, farmers, botanists or cooks. The mushroom book above was for naturalists, but they are not the only people interested in mushrooms; cooks and toxicologists also need information about fungi.

In other cases the subject may be a combination of two different disciplines, and both need to be acknowledged if the description is to be accurate:

```
The use of computers in the study of ancient documents /
edited by A. K. Bowman and Marilyn Deegan. – [Oxford]:
Oxford University Press, 1997
```

A computer scientist and a classicist might perceive this book to belong to two different disciplines, but in fact it is about both computing, and the study of ancient documents. This kind of conjunction is quite common, and it is important to recognize complexity in the analysis of content.

Exercise 6.1

What alternative general subject areas might be appropriate for the following titles?

1   *Health education through biology teaching*
2   *Archimedes: new studies in the history and philosophy of science and technology*
3   *Scots law for journalists*
4   *Big ears: listening for gender in jazz studies*
5   *How to manage a law school library*
6   *Parrots, macaws, and cockatoos: the art of Elizabeth Butterworth*
7   *Terpsichore: study of the dance in ancient Greece*
8   *Britain's cathedrals and their music*

Significant concepts

Having established the general subject area of the book, the next task is to identify the important *specific* concepts contained in its subject. By this I mean those concepts which:

- best describe the content
- a user is most likely to search for.

The idea of *sought concepts* is very important since there's no point at all in identifying concepts that no one will look for. You should always remember to keep the readers in mind when you are cataloguing, and continually ask yourself who is likely to find the document useful, and what of the content they might be looking for.

Let us look at some examples to illustrate this:

```
Gold was the mortar: the economics of cathedral building /
Henry Kraus. - London; Boston: Routledge & Kegan Paul, 1979

Flights of fancy: early aviation in Battersea and
Wandsworth / by Patrick Loobey. - London: Wandsworth
Borough Council, Recreation Dept., 1981
```

In the first example there are several topics for which a reader could be searching. 'Economics' and 'cathedrals' are obviously important concepts, as is 'building'; anyone wanting information on any of these topics could find this book useful. Although it doesn't appear as such, the title also includes the notion of the medieval period since this was when most cathedrals were built (and certainly the period covered in this book), and similarly 'Europe' is where the building went on. Synonyms like 'architecture' and 'fund-raising' might also be included in the description. It is often necessary to translate *terms* from a title into more general *concepts* in this way. Again, try to keep in mind what will be looked for. In this case 'gold' and 'mortar' are not likely to be search terms.

At this stage we want just to identify the important concepts, and we could therefore list those as:

cathedrals
architecture
construction
costs
economics
Middle Ages
Europe

In the second example there are some useful key words: 'aviation', 'Wandsworth' and 'Battersea'. The term 'early' has a ring of history about it, so we can include that as well. But terms such as 'flights of fancy' don't really say anything about the subject, and nobody is very likely to choose this as a phrase to search for. (This is in fact another good example of an unhelpful title.) Our final selection might therefore be something like:

> aviation
> history
> Wandsworth
> Battersea

Common categories of terms
Place and time

In the examples above, in addition to the subjects of brewing and aviation, we have included some terms to do with place (England, Battersea, Wandsworth), and some to do with period (history, medieval). Places and periods occur very commonly in the subjects of books. *Flights of fancy* is not just of interest to students of aviation, but would also be relevant for someone searching for the history of Wandsworth and Battersea. You should therefore always include any indication of place or time in your subject summary.

Be aware that place does not mean just political or administrative place, like France, New York or Lancashire; it also includes physiographic regions, climatic zones and other sorts of spatial concepts (mountains, temperate regions, north and so on). Similarly time covers broad chronological terms (medieval, renaissance), specific dates (1920s, 9/11) and other temporal concepts (post-war, nocturnal):

```
Teenage pregnancy in Scotland, 1985-1995. Health briefing
no. 97/04. - National Health Service in Scotland,
Information & Statistics Division, 1997
```

Concepts: pregnancy
> teenagers
> Scotland
> 1985–1995

```
English costume of the later Middle Ages / Iris Brookes. -
London: A. & C. Black, 1963
```

Concepts: costume
           Middle Ages
           England

Form

Another type of term which is very common relates to the form of presentation of the book or document. Form is not really a part of the subject of a book, but it can be a useful thing for the reader to be aware of, and most systems make some provision for expressing form. Form comes in two varieties:

- the physical format of the document: book, video, three-dimensional object, digital object, website and so on
- the form in which the information is presented: encyclopedia, bibliography, table, conference paper, textbook and so on.

These are sometimes referred to as 'outer form' for the first group and 'inner form' for the second. In some indexing systems inner form can be extended to include the language in which the document is written:

```
Nineteenth international seaweed symposium / M.
Friedlander; [edited by] Michael A. Borowitzka. - New York:
Springer, 2009
```

Concepts: seaweed
           conference proceedings

```
The dictionary of sodium, fats, and cholesterol / by
Barbara Kraus. - New York: Grosset & Dunlap, [1974]
```

Concepts: food
           sodium
           fats
           cholesterol
           dictionary

Note that a document could have both forms of presentation at once, for example, a digital encyclopedia, or an online bibliography.

You should remember that forms can also occur as subjects in their own right. For example:

```
The Oxford English dictionary 2nd ed. / prepared by J.A.
Simpson and E.S.C. Weiner. - Oxford: Clarendon Press;
Oxford; New York: Oxford University Press, 1989
```

```
Caught in the web of words: James A.H. Murray and the
Oxford English dictionary / K.M. Elisabeth Murray; with a
pref. by R.W. Burchfield. - New Haven: Yale University
Press, 1977
```

The first of these two examples is the dictionary itself, so dictionary is the *form*. The second example is a book about the Oxford English Dictionary, and there, dictionary is the *subject*.

Persons

The example *Teenage pregnancy in Scotland* includes a *persons* concept – that of 'teenagers' or 'adolescents'. Persons are another frequently occurring idea, and their types can range across gender, age, ethnicity, nationality and other diverse characteristics, for example:

```
Breast cancer in women of African descent / edited by
Christopher Kwesi O. Williams, Olufunmilayo I. Olopade and
Carla I. Falkson. - Dordrecht: Springer, 2006
```

Concepts: cancer

breast

women

Africans

```
Images of older people in Western art and society /
Herbert C. Covey. - New York: Praeger, 1991
```

Concepts: portraits

older people

western world

A variation on the idea of the person as part of the subject is the idea of the person for whom the book is intended. Women and children are the most frequently encountered 'audiences', with titles of the type *Modern basketball for women*, and *Human anatomy for children* being relatively common. Subjects for particular sorts of occupations are also quite frequent:

```
Concepts of mathematics for students of physics and
engineering: a dictionary / Joseph C. Kolecki. - Hanover,
MD: NASA Center for AeroSpace Information, 2003
```

```
Tropical medicine for nurses / A. R. D. Adams. - Oxford:
Blackwell Scientific, 1980
```

With books of this kind, you should remember that the main content is the subject (mathematics, tropical medicine), not the audience (physics, engineering, nursing). Usually such books are simply general or introductory books on the subject, aimed at a group that requires some basic knowledge. For this reason, the audience is often not included in the subject description, the general exception being books for children. Be aware that a book like the following is very different:

```
Clothes for children: making new from old / Maureen
Goldsworthy. - London: B.T. Batsford, 1980
```

Here, the subject is 'children's clothes', a particular *kind* of clothing defined by the wearer, and so part of the subject.

Ordering the subject string

When compiling the subject description, it is a good idea to get into the habit of thinking about the order of concepts. The order in which concepts are listed is referred to as citation order, or occasionally combination order. The theory of citation order arose initially within the context of classification systems, and the physical organization of collections, although it is implicit in almost all tools for subject organization even from a very early period.

In a physical collection it is very important to get the citation order right, because it affects the way in which documents are grouped on the shelves. For example, if you have a large number of books about literature in different languages (such as French poetry, English novels and Italian drama), you can arrange these in two different ways: either you can keep together all the books on a particular language, and then divide each group into literary forms (a citation order of 'language – form'), or you can do the reverse, bringing all the poetry books and all the novels together, and then sub-dividing these by language (a citation order of 'form – language'). Which you will choose will largely depend on the interests and expectations of the users of the collections.

Whatever system is adopted, some related items will be scattered (for example, in the first option above, the novels will be dispersed among the different languages; these are known as 'distributed relatives', and users will depend on the subject index to find them). In the case of subject headings, a similar situation affects any compound subject, as a decision must be made about which aspects of the subject take priority. This is usually decided by the designers of the system, and the rules written in, as we shall find with LCSH. The important thing is that the rules are applied consistently, so that the treatment is logical and predictable for the end-user.

Try to place the most important concepts first (or what you think are the most important concepts). In other words, you should try to introduce some sense of the best citation order for the subject. You won't always be able to carry this through, because the vocabulary you are applying may not allow you to do exactly what you want, but in some systems there are alternative treatments available, and you need to think about how the subject is structured.

Summary

- Write down the important subject terms – remember to think about what users might be searching for.
- Are there any place or time concepts?
- Are there any concepts relating to persons?
- Is the document in any particular form?
- Is it intended for a particular audience?
- Put the concepts into order with the most significant first.

Now you should be able to begin to create document descriptions for yourself. Exercise 6.2 is provided for practice.

Exercise 6.2

Create subject strings for the following titles:

1 *Rules for the construction of boilers of locomotives*
2 *Illustrated history of the United States mint*
3 *Bibliography of Texas spiders*
4 *The early days of the American cocker spaniel in the United Kingdom*
5 *Problems of pig production in the tropics*
6 *Vocational training in the Belgian textile industry*
7 *Jewish women philosophers of first century Alexandria*
8 *Knitted pirates, princesses, witches, wizards and fairies*
9 *Pirates of the Caribbean: buccaneers, privateers, freebooters and filibusters, 1493–1720*
10 *Autonomous weeders for Christmas tree plantations*
11 *Antarctic meteorite research*
12 *Geographical dictionary of ancient and medieval India*
13 *Catalogue of an exhibition of water-colour drawings of old world gardens*

14 *Early Renaissance architecture in England*
15 *The art of rhinoceros horn carving in China*
16 *Studies for the advanced teaching of the oboe*
• •

• •
Answers to exercises

Remember the first law of subject cataloguing: there are no 'right answers'. The following are suggested answers to the exercises, and are meant to provide guidance. If you have a different answer but understand how you arrived at it, and have good reasons for your decision, you can count that as correct.

Exercise 6.1

What do you think is the main subject, or subjects, of the following titles?

1 *Health education through biology teaching*
   Health, education, teaching, biology
2 *Archimedes: new studies in the history and philosophy of science and technology*
   History, philosophy, science, technology
3 *Scots law for journalists*
   Law, journalism, Scotland
4 *Big ears: listening for gender in jazz studies*
   Music, gender studies
5 *How to manage a law school library*
   Management, librarianship, law resources, education
6 *Parrots, macaws, and cockatoos: the art of Elizabeth Butterworth*
   Birds, ornithology, pets, watercolours, scientific illustration
7 *Terpsichore: study of the dance in ancient Greece*
   Dance, ancient history, mythology, classics
8 *Britain's cathedrals and their music*
   Religion, architecture, history, music

Exercise 6.2

Create subject strings for the following titles:

1 *Rules for the construction of boilers of locomotives*
   Locomotives – boilers – construction – regulations
2 *Illustrated history of the United States mint*
   Coinage – production – United States – history – illustrated works

3 *Bibliography of Texas spiders*
 Spiders – Texas – bibliography
4 *The early days of the American cocker spaniel in the United Kingdom*
 American cocker spaniel – history – United Kingdom
5 *Problems of pig production in the tropics*
 Pigs – husbandry – tropics
6 *Vocational training in the Belgian textile industry*
 Textile industry – training – Belgium
7 *Jewish women philosophers of first century Alexandria*
 Philosophy – first century – Alexandria – women – Jewish
8 *Knitted pirates, princesses, witches, wizards and fairies*
 Knitting – toys – story tales
9 *Pirates of the Caribbean: buccaneers, privateers, freebooters and filibusters, 1493–1720*
 Piracy – Caribbean – 16th century
10 *Autonomous weeders for Christmas tree plantations*
 Christmas trees – cultivation – weeding – machinery
11 *Antarctic meteorite research*
 Meteorites – Antarctic – research
12 *Geographic dictionary of ancient and medieval India*
 India – geography – ancient and medieval period – dictionary
13 *Catalogue of an exhibition of water-colour drawings of old world gardens*
 Water-colour drawing – gardens – exhibitions – catalogues
14 *Early Renaissance architecture in England*
 Architecture – England – 16th century
15 *The art of rhinoceros horn carving in China*
 Carving – rhinoceros horn – China
16 *Studies for the advanced teaching of the oboe*
 Oboe – technique – studies

7 Assigning main headings

Because LCSH is such a complicated system, we will start by looking at how you can apply the headings exactly as they are published in the lists, either printed or online. In lots of cases the subjects of documents can be very well expressed simply by using one or more headings, without any further effort. In later chapters we will consider how to add subdivisions to these main headings, and how to create new headings where this is permitted. If you have access to Cataloguers' Desktop, it would useful to read the Introduction to the Subject Headings Manual at this stage. [Note: I have used the expression 'main headings' to indicate the headings as they occur in the published list of headings, and to differentiate these from subdivisions, and combinations of headings and subdivisions.]

Content analysis and LCSH

It is important that you go through the process of analysing the content of the document and establishing its subject before you begin to decide which headings to use. Remember that content analysis has two main objectives: to make a concise summary of the document's subject; and to identify any topics that users may be trying to retrieve. In the first case, the concept analysis should state the general subject of the document, which may be very broad (economic theory, the postal service, archaeology), or quite specific and complicated in nature (American films of the 1930s, manuscript illumination in Medieval Germany, laser excision of epithelial tumours). Your objective then is to try and find a heading, or set of headings, that will represent all the significant parts of the document's subject.

Analytical cataloguing

Most conventional library cataloguing and indexing stops at that point. The document is located physically alongside other documents with similar and related topics, and it has sufficient data in the subject field of the catalogue record to retrieve it according to its content. In other environments the practice of analytical indexing or cataloguing aims to provide subject information about the detailed content of a document; individual chapters or sections are indexed, and there is much more information about very precise topics.

For example, a collection of conference papers may share a broad subject, but individually tackle very diverse subjects. A good example is the recent *Twentieth International Seaweed Symposium*, the general subject of which is 'seaweed'. Individual papers addressed (among other things) 'climate change and seaweeds', 'pathogen and herbivore resistance', 'hydrocolloids and seaweed extracts', 'seaweed resources and biomass' and so on. Most libraries will classify and subject catalogue the collection according to its broad subject of seaweed, but documentation centres, digital libraries and subject specialist information services may also index the individual papers.

For general library use (and certainly for book cataloguing), you should be aiming at the first objective. But sometimes it seems useful to indicate some more specific content, particularly if it is the only information about that topic that you have. For instance, a chapter about snakes in a general book about British wild animals is worth indicating on the catalogue if you have no other books about British snakes.

The Library of Congress *Subject Headings Manual* provides some guidance on how far you should go in doing this, with a general recommendation that any topic should constitute at least 20% of a book before it warrants its own subject heading.

Summary
- Before you begin to select headings, make an independent analysis of the document's subject.
- Remember that your aim is to represent the overall subject of the document.
- Topics within the document should only be included if there is some special reason for this.
- Library of Congress guidelines suggest that only topics which represent at least 20% of the content should be included.

Finding appropriate headings
Because LCSH is such an enormous vocabulary, the biggest problem for you as a beginner is simply finding your way around it. The novice

usually has no sense of what headings might be available or any idea of the LCSH conventions in the way in which headings are formed. The situation is further complicated for British users by the presence of many American terms and expressions which are unfamiliar. The only answer to this is to launch yourself on the uncharted waters, and you will soon discover that there are some navigational aids. Each heading is accompanied by a set of cross-references, which help to put it in context, and also alert you to other headings in the same subject area.

Preferred headings

Let us look at a section from the list of LCSH (note that this is not complete, and represents a selection of headings):

Banana
>   USE **Bananas**

Banana, Abyssinian
>   USE **Ensete**

Banana aphid (May Subd Geog)
>   [QL527.A64 (Zoology)]
>>   UF   Pentalonia nigronervosa [Former heading]
>>   BT   **Pentalonia**

Banana black-end disease (May Subd Geog)
>>   BT   **Bananas--Pests and diseases**

Banana, Dog
>   USE **Pawpaw**

Banana farmers
>   USE **Banana growers**

Banana flour
>>   BT   **Flour**

Banana growers (May Subd Geog)
>>   UF   Banana farmers
>>   BT   **Fruit growers**

Banana splits (May Subd Geog)
>>   UF   Splits, Banana
>>   BT   **Cookery (Bananas)**
>>   **Desserts**
>>   RT   **Ice cream, ices, etc.**

The headings in bold type are the ones that you use; these are sometimes called authorized headings. The 'headings' in lighter type are not valid headings; they are simply there because they are words or phrases that cataloguers or users might look up, normally because they are synonyms or near synonyms of the valid headings. The USE instruction tells the cataloguer to use a different or 'preferred' heading. For example, in this section we can see that the valid headings are **Banana aphid**, **Banana black-end disease**, **Banana flour**, **Banana growers** and **Banana splits**, but that 'Banana', 'Banana, Abyssinian', 'Banana, Dog' and 'Banana farmers' are not the preferred forms of heading for these subjects, and that others should be used instead. The preferred headings reflect the vocabulary control conventions discussed in Chapters 4 and 5, such as the use of plurals, uninverted phrases and non-technical language.

In *Classification Web* the cross-references to valid headings are hypertext links so that the cataloguer can click on them and jump straight to the correct heading. You will also see under **Banana aphid** a reference to the classmark for banana aphids in the Library of Congress classification schedules, which online would be an active link. The printed versions also contain these classification cross-references.

Summary

- Preferred (valid, or authorized) headings are in bold type.
- Entries not in bold are non-preferred forms, and should not be used as headings.
- These entries will always have USE references to the correct form of heading.
- The online version of LCSH provides hypertext links from non-preferred to preferred forms.

Cross-references
Thesaural references

The codes used with cross-references given are of the kind employed in thesauri, although LCSH is not a thesaurus, and these references have been added retrospectively over the course of time. Note that the conventional T (for term) is retained, even though the references are to headings rather than terms. There are two kinds of thesaurus-type references: those that indicate preferred headings (USE and UF) and which we have touched on above, and those that refer to other headings elsewhere in the list (BT, RT, and NT).

The latter group function as navigational aids, providing a way of working up and down the implicit hierarchies in LCSH. In a practical sense they point cataloguers towards a range of headings that may be more appropriate than their original choices, or supplement them in some way. Those may be more general headings, more specific headings, or headings that are related in some other less tangible manner.

USE and UF references

In the section on vocabulary control in Chapter 5 we looked at the idea of preferring one form among headings that mean the same, or roughly the same, and how this improves retrieval. Non-preferred forms are still included in the list because they may well be looked for, but they all carry a USE tag, which directs the cataloguer to the preferred form:

Walking a dog
    USE Dog walking
Scratch-and-sniff books
    USE Scented books
Perukiers
    USE Wigmakers

Because these are all non-preferred headings, they will have no other notes or references attached to them. As with the classmarks, the electronic LCSH allows you to link to the preferred heading. The preferred headings have the reciprocal reference tag 'UF', meaning Use For:

Wigmakers
    UF   Perukiers
Dog walking
    UF   Walking a dog

It is not unusual for a heading to equate to more than one non-preferred heading. In that case they are listed in alphabetical order:

Apple brandy
    UF   Apple jack
        Calvados
Umbrellas
    UF   Bumbershoots
        Umbrellas and parasols

BT, NT and RT references

These are the standard cross-referencing tags used in thesauri to indicate broader terms (BTs), narrower terms (NTs) and related terms (RTs). Because of the lack of a strong structural basis to LCSH, the cross-references are not used with the precision that they would be in a well constructed thesaurus, but nonetheless you should find them very useful. Their purpose is to reveal those relationships that are dispersed in an alphabetical list, and to bring together headings in the same subject area. They are the principal means by which the cataloguer can navigate the headings, and they are essential for discovering a bigger range of options among the headings.

From these cross-references you can choose a more general, or a more specific, heading if you think that might be a more accurate indication of the subject. Cutter's *Rules* restricted the use of cross-references to downward links or NTs, but today LCSH uses the upward, or BT, link as well.

BT and NT relationships are what might elsewhere be called hierarchical relationships. This means that in a BT–NT relationship, one topic is a sub-class of the other: it is wholly contained by the other. For example:

Bears
>   BT   **Carnivora**
>   RT   **Cookery (Bear meat)**
>   NT   **Ailuropoda**
>   **Bear cubs**
>   **Little Smokey (Bear)**
>   **Problem bears**
>   **Samson (Bear)**
>   **Smokey Bear**
>   **Sun bear**
>   **Tremarctos**
>   **Ursus**
>   **Winnipeg (Bear)**

You can see here that the class **Bears** is part of the bigger class of **Carnivora**, whereas all the NTs are sub-classes of **Bears** being species of bear, general types of bear, or individual named bears. The heading about cooking bears is included as having something to do with bears, but is obviously not a kind or part of a bear, so is labelled RT.

You should note that, as in the thesaurus, the broader and narrower term references take only one step up or down the hierarchy. As a result, the heading **Problem bears** will not have a link to the heading **Carnivora** two levels up. The hierarchical structure of LCSH is not necessarily complete, so you may well find references between very general and very specific classes, but the general one-step principle is nevertheless adhered to.

LCSH is not very precise in distinguishing between NT and RT, and usually prefers to use NT, even when the headings referred to are clearly not NTs:

Potatoes		Pets	
BT	**Solanum**	BT	**Domestic animals**
RT	**Cookery (Potatoes)**	RT	**Household animals**
NT	**Frozen potatoes**	NT	**African bullfrogs as pets**
	Potato peeling		**Astrology and pets**
	Seed potatoes		**Ducks as pets**
			Pet shows
			Tadpoles as pets
			Worms as pets

In these examples of **Potatoes** and **Pets**, we can see that **Potato peeling** is not a kind of potato, nor are **Astrology and pets** or **Pet shows** kinds of pets. These should be RT and not NT. But, although they may look very odd to anyone used to the more rigorous structure of the thesaurus, and they may offend against your idea of what is correct, it really makes not one jot of difference to the business of identifying them as potential alternative headings.

A few years ago several papers were written in which the writers attempted to create a hierarchy or classification of subject headings in a particular subject area by using the BT–NT relationships to generate the systematic structure. LCSH wasn't constructed in this way and any such exercise is bound to be full of oddities, but it really doesn't matter from the point of view of applying the headings, so it is better not to worry about these structural imperfections.

Despite these criticisms, the cross-references are still absolutely essential to navigating LCSH, which would be very difficult to use without them. You would have to guess all the time about any other headings that you might use, and spend a long time searching for them. They also perform a vital function in helping you achieve the correct level of specificity in subject description.

Summary

- A system of cross-references allows you to locate other headings relevant to the topic.
- They use standard thesaurus tags of USE, UF, BT, NT and RT.
- USE and UF indicate the preferred forms of headings.
- BT, NT and RT tags point the cataloguer to more general, more specific, or otherwise related headings.
- BT and NT references are only to headings one level up or down the hierarchy.
- In LCSH the tags are not used very precisely.
- Nevertheless, they are an essential feature for finding your way round LCSH.

Selecting headings

Sometimes, in the case of an item with a very simple subject, a single main heading may be sufficient to represent the subject, for example:

```
Famous stamps of the world / by Max Hertsch. - Berne:
Hallwag, [1968]
```

```
The world of elephants / Lisa Lawley. - New York, NY:
Friedman/Fairfax Pub., c1994
```

In the Library of Congress catalogue these two books are given the single headings **Postage stamps** and **Elephants** respectively. Nothing more is needed because those headings represent the subject succinctly and specifically.

On the theme of specificity, a mistake that beginners often make is to assign headings that are too broad. The best description of content is normally an exact description. Both Cutter and Dewey recommended that the subjects of books should always be represented precisely. Cutter's first example of subject entry in *Rules for a Dictionary Catalogue* is this:

```
The cat, its history and diseases/ Mary Cust. - London:
Groombridge, 1856
```

which he refers to as 'Lady Cust's book on cats' and which he says should be given the subject heading 'Cat', and not 'Zoology', 'Mammals' or 'Domestic animals'.

On a practical level, searchers are usually fairly exact in their use of search terms; someone wanting information about cats will not routinely use 'animals', 'zoology' or 'domestic animals' when formulating a search.

At least one of Dewey's reasons was that the cataloguer would never need to return to the book if it had been described accurately in the first place. Cutter's concerns were with the effect on the catalogue of overloading it with unhelpful information, as the following example shows:

```
Book about bees / Edwin Way Teale. - New York: Dodd, Mead,
[1959?]
```

The main subject of this document can only be 'Bees', and this is the heading that the Library of Congress assigns to it. You might imagine that it would be helpful to the reader to add some extra headings such as **Insects** or **Entomology**, but in fact the reverse is true, and it is usually misleading to do so.

Imagine that you have a collection of a thousand documents on the subject of insects. Some of them will be general books on insects, but most will be about dragonflies, insect-borne diseases, the genetics of the fruit fly, bee-keeping, the butterflies of chalk downlands, and so on. You decide to attach to each book the appropriate subject heading, plus one for insects. Now imagine that you are carrying out a search for books on bee-keeping. This shouldn't give you any particular problems; you will retrieve all the books with the bee-keeping heading on the record. Now try and search again for all the general books on insects. What do you think will happen? Of course, the computer will give you a list of all the thousand books in the collection, rather than just those which are at a general level. If you add overly broad headings in this way, you swamp the indexes with them and you make accurate searching much more difficult.

··

Exercise 7.1

Try and select appropriate headings for the following titles:

1   Biology of grasshoppers / edited by R. F. Chapman and A. Joern. - New York: Wiley, 1990

2   Global trends in library and information science / edited by Subhas C. Biswas. - New Delhi: Gyan, 1995

3   Basic basket making: all the skills and tools you need to get started / Linda Franz, editor; Debra Hammond, basket weaver and consultant; photographs by Alan Wychek. - Mechanicsburg, PA: Stackpole, 2008

4   The art of juggling / Ken Benge. - New York: Brian Dube, 2006

5   One-leg resting position (Nilotenstellung), in Africa and

```
elsewhere / by Gerhard Lindblom. - Stockholm: Statens
etnografiska museum, 1949
```
· ·

A parallel problem occurs with headings that are too specific. We considered briefly the question of analytic cataloguing, and whether you should try to indicate the detailed content of a document. For most library purposes the answer is no: the object of the exercise is to indicate the overall subject of the work.

Some novice cataloguers struggle with this idea, and it probably arises from having examined a book too closely in order to determine its subject, taking note of the various chapter headings and so on. A nice example, which I use in class, is:

```
Apples: [the story of the fruit of temptation] / Frank
Browning. - New York: North Point, 1998
```

This is a fiendish book with chapters on the Garden of Eden, the history of the apple, the apple in mythology, pomiculture, apple varieties, cider making, apple recipes and so on. Despite this profusion of content, the subject of the book is 'apples', and not anything more specific.

Summary

- Try to select headings that match the subject of the document as closely as possible.
- You should try to represent the broad, overall subject of the document.
- Headings that are too general overload the indexes and make searching more difficult.
- In most situations it isn't necessary to indicate individual topics contained in the item.

Selecting multiple headings

One of the first rules to remember when selecting headings is to match as closely as possible the subject of the document. LCSH is plain about this: the heading that most nearly represents the subject of the document should be the one chosen. Here is an example:

```
The world in your cup: a handbook in the ancient art of
tea leaf reading / Joseph F. Conroy and Emilie J. Conroy.
- Eagleville, PA: DNA Press, 2006
```

This is a book about telling fortunes from tea leaves. Although there are headings for **Tea** and **Fortune-telling**, they should be disregarded, and you should select instead the heading which exactly matches the content, that is **Fortune-telling by tea leaves**. Having matched the heading precisely to the subject of the book, no more headings should be considered, and in fact Library of Congress uses only the one subject heading for this title.

It is possible that this is not the most helpful approach for users. An interesting heading is **Extrasensory perception in animals**, which is used routinely on the Library of Congress catalogue for a number of books about unexplained powers of pets. In theory no other headings need to be used, but the heading seems to me a phrase that would not naturally occur to the majority of searchers, who might instinctively look for something involving pets or animal psychology. So it is a matter of judgement whether to include some additional heading simply to provide alternative routes to the item. Note that this is not quite the same as using broader headings or those that reflect particular content.

Some items, such as those dealing with psychic pets, may require only one heading, but often a pair or a group of headings is needed to express all the parts of the content analysis.

Example
```
Knit your own royal wedding / Fiona Goble. – Kansas
City, MO: Andrews McMeel, 2011
```

A concept analysis for this book might be 'Knitting--royal weddings'. Both of these concepts have an appropriate heading: **Knitting** and **Royal weddings**. Note that you *cannot* combine the two headings into one. We shall look in the next chapter at the ways in which more complicated headings can be constructed, but adding headings together is not one of them. The headings must be listed separately, thus:

Knitting
Royal weddings

Using more than one heading like this is very common, and it gets round the problem of being unable to represent the whole subject of the document in a single heading. In this respect LCSH is more flexible in representing subject content than a classification system since you can add headings to represent all the aspects of a complicated subject. LCSH recommends that you shouldn't use more than six headings for one document, but this is usually more than enough to meet your needs, and if, on occasion, it really isn't, then rest assured that the Library of Congress exceeds its own limit from time to time. You should use your concept analysis of a document as a basis for deciding which headings to use, making sure that each component of the analysis is represented in a heading.

Example

> The dragon in art in medieval East Christian and Islamic art / Sarah Kuehn. – Leiden; Boston: Brill, 2011

This might be analysed as 'Dragons – art – Christian – Islamic – medieval', for which the following headings would cover all the various elements:

Dragons in art
Islamic art and symbolism
Christian art and symbolism--Medieval, 500–1500

Since there is so much pre-coordination of terms in LCSH, you won't necessarily use a separate heading for every single part of the concept analysis. Here there is no need to have a separate heading for 'art', or for 'medieval'.

....
Exercise 7.2
Find appropriate headings for the following titles:

1 Principles of indexing and filing / Laura Cadwallader. – Baltimore: H. M. Rowe, 1958

2 The world of butterflies and moths / Umberto Parenti. – New York: Putnam, 1978

3 Top-rated azaleas and rhododendrons and how to use them in your garden. – New York: Golden Press, 1983

4 Knitting for babies: from the archives of the Lindberg press: complete instructions for 36 sweaters, dresses, rompers, and other projects / edited by Sondra R. Albert. – New York: Dover, 1981

5 Keys to painting. Fruit and flowers / edited by Rachel Rubin Wolf. – Cincinnati, OH: North Light Books, 2000
....

Summary

- You should use the heading that most closely reflects the subject of the document.
- LCSH suggests that if one heading matches exactly, no others should be used.
- In practice, it may be useful to provide alternative ways of finding the book.
- In most cases more than one heading will be needed to represent the subject.
- Try to ensure that each element of the concept analysis is covered by one or more headings.
- Such headings must be listed separately and cannot be joined together.

Organizing headings on a record

When you have several headings attached to each document, you will need to think about how to arrange them. The Library of Congress advises you to put first the heading that approximates most closely to the subject, but otherwise there is no order of preference. Many libraries (although not all) number the headings on the catalogue record, and it is also common practice to put a full stop (period) at the end of each heading.

You also need to pay careful attention to the layout and construction of the headings. Mostly, you have only to copy the heading, but it is surprising how many beginner cataloguers do this carelessly, without paying attention to the punctuation, capitalization and spelling. Most errors probably occur by reading the heading and then mentally rehearsing it as you type, forgetting about the punctuation and so on. Even experienced cataloguers occasionally make mistakes, as you can easily see on the Library of Congress subject indexes where there are such entries as:

PostScript (Computer program language)   34 records
PostScript (Computer programming language) 1 record

Errors here can cause misfiling, poor collocation of records and consequently poor levels of retrieval. Because LCSH is a standard and internationally used, one of its great advantages is as a search tool within merged catalogues; if it is not used accurately that advantage is compromised, and users are confused by the variations. Strictly speaking, US spelling should be observed, but it seems likely that many British libraries adopt UK spelling in order not to confuse users.

Although you should always refer to the published list when copying out the heading, there are some common conventions to help you:

1 Capital letters are used at the beginning of headings, for example:

Parties for dogs
Varmint hunting
Submarines on postage stamps

2 In a structured heading (which we will encounter in the next chapter), each element starts with a capital letter, for example:

Snowmobiling--Law and legislation
Astrology and gardening--Periodicals

3 In an inverted heading, the word after the comma (the original lead word) has a capital letter, as do words after a bracket, for example:

Zoology, Economic
Evidence, Expert
Quasiparticles (Physics)
Snoopy (Fictitious character)

4 Otherwise, capitals are only used where one would always use them (for proper nouns, etc.), for example:

Lone Ranger films
Submarine topography--Pacific Ocean

Summary

- List multiple headings with the one closest to the subject of the document first.
- Otherwise there is no recommended order.
- Use any local conventions such as numbering or terminal full stops.
- Remember to reproduce accurately any capital letters, spaces or punctuation contained in the heading.
- Speakers of British English should look carefully for variations in spelling.

The biggest difficulty that most novice cataloguers will have in applying LCSH to a document is simply finding their way round the headings. However well you understand the principles of LCSH, knowing which headings to pick can often be a time-consuming guessing game at first. In this situation the most sensible thing you can do is look at what someone else has done. Very many OPACs now have LCSH on their records, and the biggest and most authoritative catalogue, that of the Library of Congress itself, is freely available online. Not only can you check the Library of Congress's records, but you can also browse the subject indexes, and check the Library of Congress authority files for further information about LCSH.

You don't have to take the Library of Congress's decisions as authoritative if your situation requires a different treatment, and you will soon become aware that the catalogue is not free of errors; there are lots of examples of misspelt headings. However, the Library of Congress records can give you a starting point and suggest headings that you might not otherwise have thought of for yourself.

Answers to exercises

Exercise 7.1

Try and select appropriate headings for the following titles:

1   Biology of grasshoppers / edited by R. F. Chapman and A. Joern. – New York: Wiley, 1990
    Grasshoppers
2   Global trends in library and information science / edited by Subhas C. Biswas. – New Delhi: Gyan, 1995
    Library science
3   Basic basket making: all the skills and tools you need to get started / Linda Franz, editor; Debra Hammond, basket weaver and consultant; photographs by Alan Wychek. – Mechanicsburg, PA: Stackpole, 2008
    Basket making
4   The art of juggling / Ken Benge. – New York: Brian Dube, 2006
    Juggling
5   One-leg resting position (Nilotenstellung), in Africa and elsewhere / by Gerhard Lindblom. – Stockholm: Statens etnografiska museum, 1949
    One-leg resting position

Answers to Exercise 7.2 overleaf

Exercise 7.2

Find appropriate headings for the following titles:

1 Principles of indexing and filing / Laura Cadwallader. –
   Baltimore: H. M. Rowe, 1958
   Indexing
   Filing systems

2 The world of butterflies and moths / Umberto Parenti. –
   New York: Putnam, 1978
   Butterflies
   Moths

3 Top-rated azaleas and rhododendrons and how to use them
   in your garden. – New York: Golden Press, 1983
   Azaleas
   Rhododendrons

4 Knitting for babies: from the archives of the Lindberg
   press: complete instructions for 36 sweaters, dresses,
   rompers, and other projects / edited by Sondra R. Albert.
   – New York: Dover, 1981
   Knitting
   Infants' clothing

5 Keys to painting. Fruit and flowers / edited by Rachel
   Rubin Wolf. – Cincinnati, OH: North Light Books, 2000
   Flowers in art
   Fruit in art
   Drawing
   Painting

8 Structured headings

In the previous chapter we looked at how to select individual headings for an item. Nearly all of the headings were pre-coordinated combinations of two or more concepts such as **Chocolate factories** or **Equine dentistry**, and indeed it can be hard to find headings that represent only simple concepts. Even so, in the case of more complex subjects, a series of headings is usually necessary to cover all the various aspects of the subject. In many cases complicated subjects can be expressed more elegantly by structured or composite headings rather than by a list of individual headings.

The nature of structured headings

Although cataloguers cannot invent headings, they can build extended headings using subdivisions provided as part of LCSH. (In *Classification Web* the subdivisions are held in a separate database from the main headings, and can be searched for independently.) The subdivisions are added to the main headings, subject to certain rules and constraints. These extended headings may be referred to as structured headings since they consist of more than one component or element. Like many other features of LCSH, structured headings can only be created according to the LCSH rules, and you should not be tempted to invent new ones by analogy.

For the most part, structured headings of this kind are not routinely included in the published LCSH, although you will come across some examples. This means that there are very many potential headings that individual cataloguers can create as needed.

Sometimes structured headings can become very complicated, with five or six elements, although a combination of two or three is more common. Typical examples of structured headings are:

Bells--Collectors and collecting
Cosmetics--Additives
Morse code--Problems, exercises, etc.

Organometallic chemistry--Nomenclature--Handbooks, manuals, etc.
Parapsychology and crime--Case studies
Perpetual calendars--Belarus--Periodicals
Books and reading--England--Northumbria (Region)--History
--To 1500--Sources

It feels somehow more satisfying to express a compound subject with a compound heading, and a single heading of this type seems to me essentially better than a list of unconnected headings, since it provides a succinct statement of the content of a document.

The structured headings also help the overall organization of the catalogue by bringing together the different aspects of a subject in one place. The subdivisions are effective in breaking down and organizing a long sequence of items in the catalogue or index, just as sub-classes in a classification make long shelf runs more manageable. Although it was originally intended to make browsing a card catalogue easier, you can also observe this phenomenon in the subject indexes of an online catalogue like that of the Library of Congress. Using the 'Basic search' option, select 'Subject browse' and type a subject word into the search box. The search will take you into the complete list of subject headings used in the catalogue at the point where your search word occurs.

Example
Artichokes
Artichokes--Breeding--Congresses
Artichokes--California
Artichokes--Congresses
Artichokes--Diseases and pests
Artichokes--Fiction
Artichokes--France
Artichokes--Marketing--Statistics--Periodicals
Artichokes--Poetry
Artichokes--Prices--France
Artichokes--Storage
Artichokes--Therapeutic use

This index, or list of headings, constructed by the cataloguers for particular documents, and using combinations of main headings and subdivisions, is obviously very much larger than the list of LCSH main headings. You can test this by comparing the published LCSH with the list of headings in the Library of Congress catalogue, where you will find there are many thousands of structured headings not present in LCSH itself. The subject index is thus a very useful resource for beginner cataloguers, who can use it to confirm the correctness of structured headings they have created. Browsing such indexes is also a very convenient way to make subject searches of collections, although many end-users will be unaware of their existence, and tend to rely on keyword searching instead.

The format of structured headings

You may have noticed that the elements of these structured headings are separated by double dashes. This is a convention used by the Library of Congress to show that the heading is a structured one, and to distinguish it from headings containing a hyphenated word, for example:

Sugar--Bacteriology
Sugar--By-products
Sugar-beet leaf-beetle

Wood--Density
Wood--Permeability
Wood-carvers
Wood-cutting tools
Wood-pulp

Although there is no reason why individual libraries must copy the Library of Congress, this seems a sensible practice and one to be recommended. You will see that this is the custom in most online catalogues.

You might also spot that each new part of the structured heading begins with a capital letter. Again, this is just a convention, but it is another way of emphasizing the structure of the heading, and recognizing the separate parts.

Categories of subdivisions

You might see that some of the subdivisions in the examples above are concepts that could occur within a whole range of subjects. Form subdivisions (**--Congresses, --Catalogs, --Dictionaries** and so on) are very common, as are a number of rather general subject subdivisions such as **--Study and teaching, --Law and legislation, --Maintenance and repair** and **--Religious aspects**. Geographic terms are also extremely frequent. Other subdivisions are more closely related to the particular main heading (**Cosmetics** and --**Additives,** for example), and do not appear to have such general applicability. Headings in this last category are usually referred to as topical, or subject, subdivisions.

Subdivisions can therefore usefully be divided into three broad categories:

- topical (or subject) subdivisions
- geographic subdivisions
- free-floating subdivisions.

The *Subject Headings Manual* considers four types of subdivision, adding chronological subdivisions and form subdivisions to the topical and geographic categories rather than free-floating subdivisions. This is useful in considering the order of combination (or citation order) between these various elements when more than one type of subdivision is needed. It is also reflected in the first attempts to rationalize the headings in the FAST Project (see Chapter 18). In order to incorporate free-floating subdivisions as a distinct entity, in this book form is treated as a special case of free-floating subdivisions, and chronological headings and subheadings are addressed in Chapter 13.

Topical subdivisions are attached to main headings, and displayed 'underneath' them in the published lists. (You may remember, in the section on format and display, the warning not to confuse them with the cross-references.) These subdivisions are either particularly common or important subdivisions of the main heading, or subdivisions that are peculiar to that heading. Chronological subdivisions for the history of individual countries are a good example of the latter:

Scotland
    --**History**
        --**James VI, 1567-1625**
        --**Malcolm IV, 1153-1165**
        --**Mary Stuart, 1542-1567**
        --**Revolution of 1688**
        --**Robert I, 1306-1329**

Geographic subdivisions allow for the expression of place concepts. There is no official list of geographic subdivisions, but there are rules for how they are arrived at, and the Library of Congress catalogue can be used to check whether you have got them right.

The free-floating subdivisions are those subdivisions that are not attached to any particular main heading but can be used more generally. Some can be combined with any heading while others are restricted to certain groups of headings (such as parts of the body, musical instruments, chemicals and so on). Because of this, there is some duplication of topical and free-floating subdivisions, but this does not matter for practical purposes.

In the next three chapters we will look at these different kinds of subdivisions and how to apply them.

9 Topical subdivisions

Presentation of topical subdivisions

Topical subdivisions are those subdivisions which are attached to a particular main heading, and listed under it. They come after the thesaural cross-references, and are identified by a double dash preceding the subdivision:

Folk songs (May Subd Geog)
    UF   Folksongs
    BT   **Folk literature**
           Folk music
           Songs
    RT   **Ballads**
    NT   **Lays**
           Yodels
    --Accompaniments
    --Criticism, Textual
    --Instrumental settings

Topical subdivisions are usually more closely related to the main heading than are the free-floating subdivisions such as '--Management' or '--Bibliography'. In this example, --**Accompaniments** and --**Instrumental settings** are obviously peculiar to music, although it should be stressed that this is not invariably the case.

Example

Ocean bottom (May Subd Geog)
    UF   Bottom of the ocean
           Ocean floor
           Sea bed
    BT   **Submarine topography**

> NT   **Abyssal zone**
> --**Law and legislation**

Here, --**Law and legislation** is very general, but it is also very important as a subdivision under this particular heading. If a particular subdivision is likely to be heavily used in conjunction with a given heading, it is helpful to provide it as a topical subdivision, which brings it more immediately to the attention of the cataloguer.

Just as in the case of the main headings, valid topical subdivisions are given in bold type. Subdivisions in ordinary type refer the cataloguer to some alternative form which should be used in preference:

Moon
> UF   Earth--Satellite
>   Selenology
> BT   **Satellites**
> RT   **Lunar transient phenomena**
> NT   **Fra Mauro Crater (Moon)**
>   **Lunar limb**
>   **Selenodesy**
>   **Space flight to the moon**
>
> --**Anecdotes**
> --Artificial satellites
>   USE **Artificial satellites--Moon**
> --**Atmosphere**
> --**Brightness**
> --Craters
>   USE **Lunar craters**
> --**Crust**
> --Eclipses
>   USE **Lunar eclipses**

Hence, **Moon** can have subdivisions --**Anecdotes**, --**Atmosphere**, --**Brightness**, and --**Crust**, but not --Artificial satellites, --Craters, or --Eclipses. This approach is somewhat inconsistent, and it scatters moon-related topics in the subject index. Recently there is some evidence that noun phrases like **Lunar craters** are gradually being replaced by structured headings.

Forming the structured heading

Remember to distinguish between the cross-references to other headings (accompanied by thesaurus tags such as UF, NT and so on), and the topical subdivisions (introduced by the double dashes). This is one of the commonest errors made by beginners, and causes them to create silly headings.

Topical subdivisions are added directly to the subject heading. When creating the structured heading, it is necessary to include both parts of the composite heading the main heading itself and the subdivision. This may seem extremely obvious, but it is another area where beginners often go astray, so is worth stressing. This is best shown by an example:

Cholera (May Subd Geog)
    UF   Asiatic cholera
    BT   **Vibrio infections**

    --Diagnosis
    --Homeopathic treatment
    --Immunological aspects
    --Vaccination

Here, the correct full forms of the heading with subdivisions are as follows, and these are what should be entered on the catalogue record:

Cholera--Diagnosis
Cholera--Homeopathic treatment
Cholera--Immunological aspects
Cholera--Vaccination

If you've muddled up the cross-references with the topical subdivisions, you may produce unlikely (and incorrect) headings such as:

Cholera--Asiatic cholera
Cholera--Vibrio infections

Do therefore take great care to look carefully and find the correct part of the entry. If you are using *Classification Web* this isn't a problem, as the heading plus subdivision is listed in the correct full version.

Example

Cholera (May Subd Geog)
    [RA644.C3 (Public health)]

[RC126-134 (Internal medicine)]

UF Asiatic cholera Cholera, Asiatic [Former Heading]
BT Vibrio infections

Cholera--Diagnosis (May Subd Geog)

Cholera--Homeopathic treatment (May Subd Geog)
[RX226.C5]

Cholera--Immunological aspects

Cholera--Preventive inoculation
USE Cholera--Vaccination
Cholera--Vaccination (May Subd Geog)

··

Exercise 9.1

Create structured LCSH using topical subdivisions for the following titles:

1   Victorian myths of the sea / by Cynthia Fansler Behrman.
    - Athens: Ohio University Press, 1977

2   Silage fermentation / by Michael K. Woolford. - New York:
    Dekker, 1984

3   Croquet: its history, strategy, rules and records / by
    James Charlton and William Thompson, with Roger,
    Katherine, and Andrew Adler. - Lexington, Mass.: S.
    Greene, 1988

4   Modified straw bale method for cucumbers / West of
    Scotland Agricultural College. - Auchincruve: The College,
    1977

5   Teaching children gymnastics / by Peter H. Werner. -
    Champaign, IL: Human Kinetics, 2004

6   Macramé: a Golden hands pattern book. - New York: Random
    House, 1974

7   Animal babies: a habitat-by-habitat guide to how wild
    animals grow / by Steve Parker. - Emmaus, Pa.: Rodale
    Press, 1994

8   On station: a complete handbook for surveying and mapping
    caves / by George R. Dasher. - Huntsville, Ala.: National
    Speleological Society, 1994
··

Sometimes there is more than one level of hierarchy shown: there are subdivisions of subdivisions:

Marriage (May Subd Geog)
    UF   Married life
           Matrimony
           Wedlock
    BT   **Love**
    RT   **Betrothal**
           Courtship
           Family

    --Annulment
    --Parental consent
    --Religious aspects
    ----Buddhism
    --Sermons

When this happens, all the levels of hierarchy must be included in the structured heading. Here, the correct forms would be:

Marriage--Annulment
Marriage--Parental consent
Marriage--Religious aspects
Marriage--Religious aspects--Buddhism
Marriage--Sermons

But not:

Marriage--Buddhism

Again, the *Classification Web* format manages this for the cataloguer, so that there is no chance of confusion.

Summary

- Composite, or structured, headings can be created by the cataloguer as needed by adding subdivisions.
- This allows more specific subject description than the use of the subject headings alone.
- Subdivisions fall into three main categories: topical, geographic and free-floating.
- Topical subdivisions are to be found listed under the relevant subject heading.

- Care should be taken not to confuse topical subdivisions with cross-references to other headings.
- Topical subdivisions must be attached to a main heading and cannot be used alone.
- If more than one level of hierarchy is shown, all the levels must be included in the structured heading.

Exercise 9.2

Write out all the valid combinations of main heading and topical subdivisions for this extract:

Singing

UF   Singing and voice culture
        Vocal culture
BT   **Music--Performance**
RT   **Throat singing**
NT   **Bel canto**
        Crooning
        Yodeling

--Auditions
--Breath control
--Diction
--Expression
        USE Singing--Interpretation (Phrasing, dynamics, etc.)
--Instruction and study
-- --Juvenile
--Interpretation (Phrasing, dynamics, etc.)
--Intonation
--Methods
-- --Group instruction
-- --Juvenile
-- --Self-instruction
--Religious aspects

Pattern headings

As we have seen above, some topical subdivisions are relevant only to a particular heading, but others could apply to lots of headings in the same subject area. For example, subdivisions such as --**Diagnosis** and --**Epidemiology** are relevant to all sorts of disease, and --**Pests and diseases** and --**Varieties** are common under headings for plants. For categories of heading where there is likely to be a long list of topical subdivisions, it makes sense to list these only under one or two typical examples of that category, and allow cataloguers to 'borrow' the subdivisions for other examples.

Such a model for a group of headings is known as a pattern heading and LCSH has a number of them. They are listed in the *Subject Headings Manual* and at the front of each volume in the print version. The existence of pattern headings is not at all apparent in *Classification Web*, so you must know what they are in order to make use of them if you are using the electronic version.

Here are some examples of the categories, with the relevant pattern heading(s):

Animals	Cattle, Fishes
Chemical substances	Copper, Insulin
Composers	Wagner
Diseases	Cancer, Tuberculosis
Industries	Construction industry, Retail trade
Languages	English language, French language
Literary authors	Shakespeare
Musical compositions	Operas
Musical instruments	Piano
Parts of the body	Heart, Foot
Plants and crops	Corn
Religious and monastic orders	Jesuits
Religions	Buddhism
Sacred works	Bible
Wars	World War, 1939-1945

Obviously the topical subdivisions are specific to each category. For example **Piano** has musical subdivisions such as --**Chord diagrams** and --**Fingering**, whereas **Copper** has --**Isotopes** and --**Oxidation**.

The number of subdivisions under a pattern heading may be very extensive. This is just a selection of the plant subdivisions enumerated under **Corn**, which numbered 330 at the time of writing:

Corn
- --Abnormalities
- --Analysis
- --Anatomy
- --Biotechnology
- --Breeding
- --Cladistic analysis
- --Microbiology
- --Milling
- --Molecular genetics
- --Planting time
- --Pollen management
- --Postharvest diseases and injuries
- --Seeds
- --Water requirements

As with the other topical subdivisions, there are occasional further levels of hierarchy, with some subdivisions having subdivisions of their own:

Corn
- --Pollen
- -- --Morphology
- --Roots
- -- --Anatomy
- -- --Diseases and pests

And, just as before, these should be written out in full as:

Corn--Pollen--Morphology
Corn--Roots--Anatomy
Corn--Roots--Diseases and pests

Pattern headings are one of the very few examples of where headings can be inferred on the basis of analogy. You must also infer the existence of the pattern heading. For example, the heading **Cattle** provides the pattern for all animals, but the other individual headings for animals don't tell you to use the pattern. And you must not only be aware of the pattern heading, but also be able to decide that a particular heading fits the category.

Having decided that another heading is in the same category, you can transpose all the subdivisions of the pattern heading to its counterpart. For example, these subdivisions of **Cattle**:

Cattle
Cattle--Behavior
Cattle--Breeding
Cattle--Diseases
Cattle--Exercise
Cattle--Feeding and feeds
Cattle--Grooming
Cattle--Handling
Cattle--Parasites
Cattle--Pedigrees
Cattle--Showing
Cattle--Vaccination

can all be applied to headings such as **Sheep, Wallabies, Budgerigar** or
Australian stumpy tail cattle dog:

Australian stumpy tail cattle dog
Australian stumpy tail cattle dog--Behavior
Australian stumpy tail cattle dog--Breeding
Australian stumpy tail cattle dog--Diseases
Australian stumpy tail cattle dog--Exercise
Australian stumpy tail cattle dog--Feeding and feeds
Australian stumpy tail cattle dog--Grooming
Australian stumpy tail cattle dog--Handling
Australian stumpy tail cattle dog--Parasites
Australian stumpy tail cattle dog--Pedigrees
Australian stumpy tail cattle dog--Showing
Australian stumpy tail cattle dog--Vaccination

Although most of the topical subdivisions of a heading that can draw on
a pattern will be derived from the pattern, you may also come across topical subdivisions which are peculiar to a non-pattern heading. For example,
Cats and **Dogs** can be combined with all the topical subdivisions from **Cattle,** but cats and dogs also have some topical subdivisions of their own.
LCSH contains structured headings such as:

Dogs--Obedience trials--Novice classes
Cats--Toilet training

which have clearly not been transposed from **Cattle,** but only apply to cats
and dogs.

Similarly, some combinations of main headings and topical subdivisions may be included to allow for downward references to be made to very precise subjects. In such cases, topical subdivisions borrowed from the pattern heading are spelled out. An obvious instance is the cross-referencing of topics peculiar to particular species of animal, hence:

Horses--Equipment and supplies
>[SF285.4]
>>NT   **Horse blankets**
>>   **Horse collars**
>>   **Horseshoes**
>>   **Saddle blankets**

Other examples are fairly numerous and include the many instances of medical subdivisions necessary to accommodate the substantial medical terminology of LCSH:

Leg--Muscles
>NT   **Hamstring muscle**
>   **Quadriceps muscle**
>   **Vastus lateralis**

Bones--Diseases (May Subd Geog)
>[RC930-931]
>>NT   **Achondroplasia**
>>   **Fibrous dysplasia of bone**
>>   **Osteoporosis**
>>   **Osteosclerosis**
>>   **Rickets**

Summary

- Pattern headings exist to provide topical subdivisions for particular subject categories of headings (plants, animals, authors, musical instruments, etc.).
- One example of the category is chosen to display the complete range of subdivisions.
- These may be transposed to other members of the category as necessary.
- Pattern heading subdivisions are comparable to other topical subdivisions, e.g. they need to be written out carefully including all the levels of hierarchy.
- Some pattern heading subdivisions have cross-references to other subject specific headings.

On the whole, topical subdivisions are very easy to use, because you have only to copy out what is in front of you; but you should take care not to confuse the subdivisions with cross-references, and to reproduce all the levels of hierarchy.

Pattern headings are slightly more complicated since you have to know that the patterns are there, and then transfer the subdivisions to another heading.

Answers to exercises

Exercise 9.1

Create structured headings using topical subdivisions for the following titles:

1   Victorian myths of the sea / by Cynthia Fansler Behrman.
    - Athens: Ohio University Press, 1977
    Subject heading: Ocean--Mythology

2   Silage fermentation / by Michael K. Woolford. - New York:
    Dekker, 1984
    Subject heading: Silage--Fermentation

3   Croquet: its history, strategy, rules and records / by
    James Charlton and William Thompson, with Roger,
    Katherine, and Andrew Adler. - Lexington, Mass.: S.
    Greene, 1988
    Subject heading: Croquet--Rules

4   Modified straw bale method for cucumbers / West of
    Scotland Agricultural College. - Auchincruive: The
    College, 1977
    Subject heading: Cucumbers--Artificial growing media

5   Teaching children gymnastics / by Peter H. Werner. -
    Champaign, IL: Human Kinetics, 2004
    Subject heading: Gymnastics for children--Coaching

6   Macramé: a Golden hands pattern book. - New York: Random
    House, 1974
    Subject heading: Macramé--Patterns

7   Animal babies: a habitat-by-habitat guide to how wild
    animals grow / by Steve Parker. - Emmaus, Pa.: Rodale
    Press, 1994
    Subject heading: Animals--Infancy

8   On station: a complete handbook for surveying and mapping
    caves / by George R. Dasher. - Huntsville, Ala.: National
    Speleological Society, 1994
    Subject heading: Caves--Surveying

Exercise 9.2

Write out all the valid combinations of main heading and topical subdivisions for
this extract:

Singing
>   UF   Singing and voice culture
>   Vocal culture
>   BT   **Music--Performance**
>   RT   **Throat singing**
>   NT   **Bel canto**
>   **Crooning**
>   **Yodeling**
>
>   **--Auditions**
>   **--Breath control**
>   **--Diction**
>   --Expression
>   USE Singing--Interpretation (Phrasing, dynamics, etc.)
>   **--Instruction and study**
>   **-- --Juvenile**
>   **--Interpretation (Phrasing, dynamics, etc.)**
>   **--Intonation**
>   **--Methods**
>   **-- --Group instruction**
>   **-- --Juvenile**
>   **-- --Self-instruction**
>   **--Religious aspects**

Singing--Auditions
Singing--Breath control
Singing--Diction
Singing--Instruction and study
Singing--Instruction and study--Juvenile
Singing--Interpretation (Phrasing, dynamics, etc.)

Singing--Intonation
Singing--Methods
Singing--Methods--Group instruction
Singing--Methods--Juvenile
Singing--Methods--Self-instruction
Singing--Religious aspects

10 Geographic subdivisions

The most superficial examination of a library, bookshop or other collections of documents will reveal that the idea of place is a very common element in the subjects of books. Titles abound such as:

Agro-climatology of the highlands of East Africa
Black country tramways
Day trips from Milwaukee
Industries of Croydon
Inkas: last stage of stone masonry development in the Andes
Orchestral music in Salzburg, 1750-1780
Referendum on independence and presidential election in Uzbekistan

It is therefore vital that any system of subject cataloguing enables us to express these geographic aspects. LCSH does this through the medium of geographic subdivisions.

When to use geographic subdivisions

The great majority of headings are accompanied by the legend (May Subd Geog), standing for 'May Subdivide Geographically', which tells the cataloguer that the name of a place can be added to the heading.

Example
Bagpipe reeds (May Subd Geog)
Carpal tunnel syndrome (May Subd Geog)
Dance for older people (May Subd Geog)
Entrance halls (May Subd Geog)
Lumholtz's tree kangaroo (May Subd Geog)
Mutilated coins (May Subd Geog)
Underbalanced drilling (Petroleum engineering) (May Subd Geog)

Where there is no such instruction, you should assume that geographic subdivision is not permitted, and sometimes, in case you were in doubt, there is a specific injunction not to subdivide.

Example

Chess on postage stamps
Cigarette paper
Filmstrips in religious education
Proverbs

Chevrolet vans (Not Subd Geog)
Dead animals in art (Not Subd Geog)
Golf stories (Not Subd Geog)
Prisoners' writings (Not Subd Geog)
Wilgefortis (Legendary saint) (Not Subd Geog)

This is usually because such subdivision would be unnecessary, the topic being already limited geographically, as with names of places, or because alternative headings make provision for local specification, as in **Prisoners' writings, Bulgarian** or **Prisoners' writings, Chinese**. That is not always the case, however, and in some cases it is very hard to see why geographic subdivision is forbidden. Some general types of headings seem always to be debarred from geographic subdivision: for example, names of families, names of fictitious and legendary characters, and headings of the type **Brooms and brushes in art**, **Bureaucracy in motion pictures** or other similar combinations.

The format of geographically subdivided headings

Geographic subdivisions form structured headings in just the same manner as the topical subdivisions, using the double dash:

Drinking vessels--Greece
Jellyfishes--South Pacific Ocean
Snail farming--Indonesia
Tall people--Asia
Vegetable oil industry--Canada

What constitutes place

Generally speaking, geographic subdivisions in LCSH consist of named places: names of continents, countries, administrative subdivisions, towns and villages, and other named regions or groupings, for example the European Union or Scandinavia. Geographic features such as mountains, lakes, seas and rivers can also be used as geographic subdivisions, but these too are normally named examples.

Example

    Sea birds--South Atlantic Ocean

    Mountain life--Blue Ridge Mountains

    Desert plants--Sahara

General geographic concepts such as 'mountains', 'cities', 'moorland', 'temperate zones' or 'developing countries' cannot be added. If faced with a document on such a topic, you must try and find it embedded in a pre-coordinated main heading, for example **Mountain animals, Urban climatology, Coastal forests, Grassland ecology, Maritime anthropology**. These cannot be attached to another main heading, so should be added to any list of subject headings on the catalogue record.

Example

```
The ecology of stray dogs; a study of free-ranging urban
animals / by Alan M. Beck. - Baltimore: York Press, 1973
```

Subject headings: Dogs--Behavior

                       Urban animals

                       Dogs as carriers of disease

Place authorities and the form of geographic names

LCSH normally uses the current name of a place, even where the content of a document may be historical, or the title uses an older version.

Example

```
Drama kings: players and publics in the re-creation of
Peking opera, 1870-1937 by Joshua Goldstein. Berkeley:
University of California Press, c2007
```

Subjects: Mei, Lanfang, 1894-1961.

            Theater--China--Beijing--History.

            Operas, Chinese--China--Beijing--History.

This may not seem very sensible, particularly if the title of the document uses the older name, but it is only a specialized kind of synonym control, and it ensures that searches will retrieve everything about a particular place. For browsing purposes, all the information about one place is kept together in the subject index, even when the name has been changed.

Where there is no equivalent modern place, names of ancient places are provided for, as in the case of **Assyria** and **Gaul**. Where a different modern place has the same name, the original may be qualified, as in **Troy (Extinct city)**. But **Athens (Greece)** or **London (England)** implies both the modern and the historic city.

The official names of places are dealt with under the Library of Congress Authorities http://authorities.loc.gov, where the authority record for the name of a place can be seen. This will show the authorized form of the geographic name for use in catalogue records (including LCSH) as well as all the variant forms of the name which are not to be used. The history of name changes is also included, as well as boundary changes which have affected the named area. Reference to external authorities is frequently made, particularly the US Board of Geographic Names (BGN), which is the Library of Congress' main source of official names. As with other authority records for subjects, some evidence for the use of the name in published sources is often included, for example, in the authority record for Mercia:

> LC Control Number: n 85068448
> HEADING: Mercia (Kingdom)
> Geographic Subdiv. usage: England Mercia (Kingdom)
> Found in: Dresher, B. E. Old English and the theory of phonology, 1985
> Enc. Brit., 1978 (Mercia, kingdom of Anglo-Saxon England)

Summary

- Place concepts are a common element in many complex subjects.
- LCSH allows most headings to have a geographic subdivision added.
- This is indicated by the instruction 'May Subd Geog'.
- The current name of the place is to be used except for ancient places that have no modern equivalent.
- The correct form of a name can be found in the Library of Congress Authority files, which themselves draw on external reference sources.

Forming the geographic subdivision
Direct subdivision

When adding a geographic subdivision for a country, or for some larger area, the name of the place is added directly to the subject heading. This is referred to as direct subdivision, for example:

Pickpockets--Japan
Soap factories--Germany
Dandelions--Himalaya Mountains Region
Icebergs--South Pacific Ocean

There are some exceptions to this rule, where smaller administrative units are added directly. The first of these exceptions concerns US States, for example:

Picnic grounds--California
Christmas lights--Illinois
Sports sponsorship--Florida

The provinces of Canada are also attached to main headings directly, as are the constituent countries of the UK:

Bison industry--Saskatchewan   **Gnomes--England**
Recreation areas--Manitoba   **Home rule--Scotland**
Mammal populations--Quebec   **Witchcraft--Wales**

This rule also applies to a small number of cities: Vatican City, Jerusalem, New York, and Washington, D.C.:

Bronze doors--Vatican City
Automobile parking--Jerusalem
American newspapers--New York
Gentrification--Washington (D.C.)

The only other situation where administrative units smaller than a country are added directly is that of territories, colonies, and islands which are distant from the ruling nation, for example:

Historic ships--Falkland Islands
Low income housing--Guam
Metamorphism--Queen Maud Land
Sacred vocal music--Azores

Summary

- Names of countries or larger regions are added directly to the main heading (direct subdivision).
- This includes geographic regions as well as administrative ones.

- There are some exceptions to this rule: US states, Canadian provinces and the countries of the UK may also be added directly to a heading, as may the cities of New York, Washington, Jerusalem and Vatican City.
- Islands, territories and colonies distant from the ruling nation may also be added directly.

Exercise 10.1

Create structured headings for the following titles, using direct geographic subdivision:

1 Oriental horses of Pakistan / by Pervaiz Amir; foreword by Farooq Ahmad Khan Leghari. - Islamabad: Asianics Agro-Dev. International, 1997

2 Digging for bird-dinosaurs: an expedition to Madagascar / by Nic Bishop. - Boston: Houghton Mifflin, 2000

3 Egyptian revenge spells: ancient rituals for modern payback / by Claudia R. Dillaire. - Berkeley, Calif.: Crossing Press, 2009

4 British lighthouses / by John Poland Bowen. - London: Longmans, 1947

5 So you're going to wear the kilt / by J. Charles Thompson; with a foreword by Andrew MacThomas of Finegand. - Arlington, VA: Heraldic Art, 1982

6 American patchwork quilts / by Lenice Ingram Bacon. - New York: Bonanza, 1973

7 Haunted Ireland: her romantic and mysterious ghosts / by John J. Dunne. - Belfast: Appletree, 1977

8 Egg marketing manual: for guidance of producers, wholesalers, and retailers, and for the consumer's protection in buying eggs. - Okla. City: Marketing Division, Oklahoma State Board of Agriculture, 1979

Indirect subdivision

In every other case a unit smaller than a country must be added as a second order subdivision after the containing country. These may be administrative divisions (counties, states, towns, cities) or geographic features such as rivers and mountains. For example:

Boxing--Germany--Berlin
Trees in cities--Brazil--Brasilia
Sunshine--Greece--Olympus, Mount
Floods--Italy--Tiber River

There is no need to include a complete hierarchy of administrative levels; only the name of the country is necessary. So, for example:

> **Excavations (Archaeology)--England--Ipswich**
> and not: Excavations (Archaeology)--England--Suffolk--Ipswich

The above example also demonstrates that the direct subdivision 'exceptions', such as US States, Canadian provinces, countries of the UK, and so on, act as the first level subdivision where their smaller units are concerned. The other exceptions follow the same pattern:

> **Riot control--Nevada--Las Vegas**
> **Police misconduct--Scotland--Glasgow**
> and not: Riot control--United States--Las Vegas
> Police misconduct--United Kingdom--Glasgow

Independent bookstores--Utah--Salt Lake City
Railroad bridges--Quebec (Province)--Montreal
Synagogues--Jerusalem--Yemin Moshe
Portuguese poetry--Azores--Sao Jorge Island

The correct form of a geographic subdivision can be found not only in the subject indexes to the Library of Congress catalogue, but also in the Library of Congress authorities. If you look up the authority record for a given place, it will include the geographic subdivision form. For instance:

> **LC Control Number:** n 97090797
> **HEADING:** Lachute (Quebec)
> **Geographic Subdiv. usage:** Quebec (Province) Lachute
> **Found in:** Repertoire des pierres tombales du Cimetiere catholique de Lachute, 1880-1995: t.p. (Lachute) p. 1 (Lachute, Quebec) p. 3 AMICUS, 10-16-97 (Lachute (Quebec))

This means that a heading involving the town of Lachute should take the form:

Inscriptions--Quebec (Province)--Lachute

Note that the double dashes are not represented in the authority record, so you need to think carefully about where they should go; you can use the subject indexes to help you here.

Summary

- For a smaller geographic subdivision, the name of the country should precede it in the heading (indirect subdivision).
- This applies to both administrative units and geographic features.
- There is no need to include any intermediate administrative levels.
- The exceptions to the direct subdivision rule (US states, Canadian provinces, and so on) act as the 'first-level' subdivision rather than country.

· ·

Exercise 10.2

Create structured headings for the following titles, using indirect geographic subdivisions (don't worry about anything other than the main headings and geographic subdivisions):

1   A statistical essay on the libraries of Vienna and the world / by Adriano Balbi; translated by Larry Barr and Janet L. Barr. – Jefferson, N.C.: McFarland, 1986

2   London bridges / by Sir Henry Percy Maybury. – London: HMSO, 1925

3   Paris restaurants / by Robert Burnand. – London: Bles, 1924

4   Bird pageant; field studies of some East Anglian breeding birds. – London: Batchworth, 1954

5   Geology of the Western Cordillera of northern Peru / by E. J. Cobbing. – London: H.M.S.O., 1981

6   Breton folktales / translated from the German by Ruth E. K. Meuss. – London: Bell, 1971

· ·

Using more than one geographic subdivision

If the subject of a document has more than one geographic concept, two or more separate headings must be used. Each structured heading can only contain one geographic subdivision.

Example

Rise and fall of abacus banking in Japan and China / Yuko
Arayama. - Westport, Conn.: Quorum, 200

Subject headings: Banks and banking--China

Banks and banking--Japan

Wild orchids of Arizona and New Mexico / Ronald A.
Coleman. - Ithaca: Comstock, 2002

Subject headings: Orchids--Arizona

Orchids--New Mexico

Inner city poverty in Paris and London / Charles Madge. -
London; Boston: Routledge Kegan Paul, 1981

Subject headings: Inner cities-- England--London

Inner cities--France--Paris

Poor--England--London

Poor--France--Paris

Exercise 10.3

Construct appropriate subject headings with geographic subdivisions for the
following titles:

1   The flight of the dragon, an essay on the theory and
practice of art in China and Japan, based on original
sources / Laurence Binyon. - New York: Grove, 1961

2   Birds of the Cornish coast, including the Isles of Scilly
/ by R. D. Penhallurick. - Truro: Barton, 1969

3   Hydrography. Deep-sea soundings. Atlantic and Pacific
oceans and Caribbean Sea, 1919 and 1922. - Washington:
Government Printing Office, 1923

4   The artist and social reform; France and Belgium, 1885-
1898 / by Eugenia W. Herbert. - Freeport, N.Y.: Books for
Libraries, 1971

Geographic subdivisions with topical subdivisions

If geographic subdivision is allowed where there is also a topical subdivision, you must be careful to put the geographic part in the right
place. Sometimes only the main heading can be subdivided geograph-

ically, but on other occasions the topical subdivision itself can also be qualified by place. Very occasionally a topical subdivision can have its own geographic subdivision where the main heading cannot. As a rule of thumb, you should insert the place subdivision exactly where you see (May Subd Geog).

Example

> **Cricket** (May Subd Geog)
> **--Batting**
> **--Betting** (May Subd Geog)
> **--Bowling**
> **--Coaching** (May Subd Geog)
> **--Rules**
> **--Societies, etc.**
> **--Tournaments** (May Subd Geog)

This allows you to construct such headings as:

> **Cricket--Australia**
> **Cricket--Batting**
> **Cricket--Betting**
> **Cricket--Australia--Betting**
> **Cricket--Betting--Australia**
> **Cricket--Australia--Betting--England**
> **Cricket--Australia--Bowling**
> **Cricket--Coaching**
> **Cricket--Coaching--England**
> **Cricket--Australia--Rules**
> **Cricket--Australia--Societies, etc.**
> **Cricket--Australia--Tournaments**
> **Cricket--Australia--Tournaments--England**

but not:

> Cricket--Rules--England

nor:

> Cricket--Societies, etc.--Australia

If you think carefully about the differences, you should see that **Cricket--Australia--Tournaments** would be used for competitions involving

Australian cricket teams, whereas **Cricket--Tournaments--England** means competitions taking place in England. However, if the distinction escapes you, you can take comfort from the fact that research has shown that most end-users and some librarians fail to appreciate these nuances of meaning.

Main headings with geographic elements

The great majority of headings for geographic content will be formed by the cataloguer following the May Subd Geog instruction, but there is also some apparent provision for expressing geographic and national concepts through the main headings. Typical examples include **Canadian clubs**, **African cooperation**, **Australian wit and humor** or **Brazilian fiction**.

You will notice that many of these could be referring to language or culture rather than place. For example, **Chinese newspapers** may be intended to mean newspapers in the Chinese language rather than newspapers in China. You should therefore be very careful about how you interpret these headings.

It is more common for headings of this kind to take the inverted form, as with **Catechisms, German, Folksongs, Ukrainian** or **Architecture, French**. In many cases these 'cultural' headings can themselves be subdivided geographically, which makes it clear that the main heading is not precisely geographic in nature. For example:

> **Art, Chinese--Czechoslovakia**
> **Children's stories, Portuguese--Brazil**
> **Manuscripts, French--Germany**
> **Prisoners' writings, Polish--Soviet Union**

Geographic names as main headings

Geographic terms occur as main headings in their own right, as well as subdivisions of headings for other subjects. Names of places that occur as main headings are dealt with in more detail in Chapter 14.

· ·

Answers to exercises

Exercise 10.1

Create structured headings for the following titles, using direct geographic subdivision:

```
1   Oriental horses of Pakistan / by Pervaiz Amir; foreword
```

by Farooq Ahmad Khan Leghari. – Islamabad: Asianics Agro-Dev. International, 1997

Subject heading: Horses--Pakistan

2 Digging for bird-dinosaurs: an expedition to Madagascar / by Nic Bishop. – Boston: Houghton Mifflin, 2000

Subject heading: Dinosaurs--Madagascar

3 Egyptian revenge spells: ancient rituals for modern payback / by Claudia R. Dillaire. – Berkeley, Calif.: Crossing Press, 2009

Subject heading: Magic--Egypt

4 British lighthouses / by John Poland Bowen. – London: Longmans, 1947

Subject heading: Lighthouses--Great Britain

5 So you're going to wear the kilt / by J. Charles Thompson; with a foreword by Andrew MacThomas of Finegand. – Arlington, VA: Heraldic Art, 1982

Subject heading: Kilts--Scotland

6 American patchwork quilts / by Lenice Ingram Bacon. – New York: Bonanza, 1973

Subject heading: Patchwork quilts--United States

7 Haunted Ireland: her romantic and mysterious ghosts / by John J. Dunne. – Belfast: Appletree, 1977

Subject heading: Ghosts--Ireland

8 Egg marketing manual: for guidance of producers, wholesalers, and retailers, and for the consumer's protection in buying eggs. – Okla. City: Marketing Division, Oklahoma State Board of Agriculture, 1979

Subject heading: Eggs--Oklahoma

Exercise 10.2

Create structured headings for the following titles using indirect geographic subdivisions (don't worry about anything other than the main headings and geographic subdivisions):

1 A statistical essay on the libraries of Vienna and the world / by Adriano Balbi; translated by Larry Barr and Janet L. Barr. – Jefferson, N.C.: McFarland, 1986

Subject heading: Libraries--Austria--Vienna

2 London bridges / by Sir Henry Percy Maybury. – London: HMSO, 1925

Subject heading: Bridges--England--London

3 Paris restaurants / by Robert Burnand. – London: Bles, 1924

Subject heading: Restaurants--France--Paris

4 Bird pageant; field studies of some East Anglian breeding birds. – London: Batchworth, 1954

Subject heading: Birds--England--East Anglia

5 Geology of the Western Cordillera of northern Peru / by E. J. Cobbing. – London: H.M.S.O., 1981

Subject heading: Geology--Peru--Cordillera Occidental

6 Breton folktales / translated from the German by Ruth E. K. Meuss. – London: Bell, 1971

Subject heading: Fairy tales--France--Brittany

Exercise 10.3

Construct appropriate subject headings with geographic subdivisions for the following:

1 The flight of the dragon, an essay on the theory and practice of art in China and Japan, based on original sources / Laurence Binyon. – New York: Grove, 1961

Subject headings: Art--China

                       Art--Japan

2 Birds of the Cornish coast, including the Isles of Scilly / by R. D. Penhallurick. – Truro: Barton, 1969

Subject headings: Birds--England--Cornwall (County)

                       Birds--England-- Isles of Scilly

3 Hydrography. Deep-sea soundings. Atlantic and Pacific oceans and Caribbean Sea, 1919 and 1922. – Washington: Government Printing Office, 1923

4 Subject headings: Deep-sea soundings--Atlantic Ocean

                       Deep-sea soundings--Pacific Ocean

                       Deep-sea soundings--Caribbean Sea

5 The artist and social reform; France and Belgium, 1885-1898 / by Eugenia W. Herbert. – Freeport, N.Y.: Books for Libraries, 1971

Subject headings: Art and society--France

Art and society--Belgium

••

11 Free-floating subdivisions

Free-floating subdivisions are non-geographic concepts that can be added to headings. Until 2003, they were contained in the green *Subject Headings Manual*, but they are now included in the red books; they are also available in a separate print publication, *Free-floating Subdivisions: an alphabetical index*, and they are searchable as a separate database within the online LCSH. The print version is now in its 23rd edition (2011), and unfortunately this will be the last.

We saw in Chapter 6 on content analysis that some varieties of concept occur very frequently in the subjects of documents: concepts such as place, time, form and persons, the last often as the intended readership. In classification systems these very common ideas are usually contained in special auxiliary tables, represented by codes which can be attached to classmarks, sometimes using particular symbols or facet indicators to indicate that an auxiliary concept is present. In LCSH a similar purpose is served by the free-floating subdivisions. The idea of the free-floating subdivision is that it can be used without any specific instruction, and attached to main headings as required. Some can be added to any heading, whereas others are restricted to particular types of heading, such as those for individual authors which are used to specify the different texts and editions and secondary publications associated with an author.

Free-floating subdivisions are added to main headings using the double dash in exactly the same way as topical and geographic subdivisions. Conveniently, the dashes are included in the subdivisions as they are displayed in the alphabetical list in *Classification Web*. The subdivisions are also accompanied by copious notes explaining the way in which individual subdivisions are to be used:

--Classification
   Use as a form subdivision under classes of persons and topical

headings for works that consist of a systematic breakdown of a subject into its constituent categories or subtopics

--Editions, Curious
Use as a topical subdivision under uniform titles of sacred works

--Kings and rulers
Use as a topical subdivision under names of countries, cities, etc., and ethnic groups

--Semantics
Use as a topical subdivision under individual languages and groups of languages

The *Subject Headings Manual* identifies five major groups of free-floating subdivisions, mainly on the basis of which kinds of headings they are used to subdivide:

- form or topical subdivisions that are generally applicable
- subdivisions applicable to classes of persons
- subdivisions applicable to individual bodies, persons, or families
- subdivisions for place names
- subdivisions controlled by pattern headings.

Within these categories the free-floating subdivisions comprise a variety of concepts; a large number are concerned with the form of the document (**--Encyclopedias, --Specifications, --Biography**), some refer to particular classes of persons (**--Women authors, --Juvenile fiction**) and others make provision for chronological treatment (**--History--16th century**).

Most deal with common subject, or topical, subdivisions (**--Law and legislation, --Salaries, --Songs and music, --Research**), or with topical subdivisions for a particular class of headings, such as Military services, Languages, Persons, Families and so on. The latter types overlap with the pattern headings to some extent, although the pattern headings are more limited in number. (These subdivisions with restricted application are covered in more detail below.) The headings to which a free-floating subdivision can be applied are clearly explained in notes attached to each subdivision, so you should not be confused about this.

You may be confused about finding your way through the free-floating subdivisions. As in the case of the headings themselves, it can be difficult to determine what free-floating subdivisions there are, as you initially have to guess which terms have been used. I think this is a particular difficulty for British users, as some of the American terminology may not naturally spring to mind. There is not much that can be done about this problem, except to use the cross-references, and be comforted by the fact that familiarity improves the situation.

The scope and range of free-floating subdivisions

Although some subdivisions are limited to certain categories of heading, for the time being we will consider only the more generally applicable types of subdivisions. These include form, presentation, time (although there are very few of these), place (to a more limited extent) and also many frequently needed subject subdivisions.

Form and presentation

These are perhaps the most obvious uses of free-floating subdivisions, and there are many examples to be found. You will find that form subdivisions are usually clearly indicated:

--Dictionaries
> Use as a form subdivision under subjects

--By-laws
> Use as a form subdivision under names of individual corporate bodies
> and under types of corporate bodies...

--Pictorial works
> Use as a form subdivision under names of countries, cities, etc.,
> individual persons, families, and corporate bodies...

Form as subject

Although strictly speaking form is not part of the subject of a document, it is often helpful to include it in the subject description, and it is commonly provided for in subject indexing systems. You may remember from Chapter 6 that you should take care to distinguish between form and subject as aspects of the document. For example, *The Encyclopedia of Science Fiction* is in the form of an encyclopedia, but its subject is science fiction, whereas Herman Kogan's book *The Great EB: the story of the Encyclopædia Britannica* is a work where encyclopedia is the subject, but the form is a monograph or book.

Example

```
The encyclopedia of science fiction: an illustrated A to
Z/edited by Peter Nicholls et al. - London: Granada, 1979
```

Subject headings: Science fiction--Dictionaries

                              Science fiction--Encyclopedias

```
The great EB; the story of the Encyclopaedia Britannica/by
Herman Kogan. - Chicago: University of Chicago Press, 1958
```

Subject headings: Encyclopedias and dictionaries

                              Encyclopedia Britannica

You will usually be able to determine the difference by asking yourself: is this an *example* of a dictionary (atlas, manuscript, recording, etc.) or is it *about* dictionaries (atlases, manuscripts, recordings, etc.)?

Exercise 11.1

Say whether the underlined word in the following titles is the subject of the document, or its form:

1   Dictionary of American resurrectionists, 1865-- 1990 / by Edward T. Janas. - Chicago, Ill.: E. T. Janas, 1991

2   Harvard concise dictionary of music and musicians / edited by Don Michael Randel. - Cambridge, Mass.: Belknap, 1999

3   Digital resources and librarians: case studies in innovation, invention, and implementation / edited by Patricia O'Brien Libutti. - Chicago, Ill.: Association of College and Research Libraries, 2004

4   Catalogue of the positions and proper motions of 4292 stars / by Frank Schlesinger. - New Haven: The Observatory, 1943

5   Music of the Beatles [sound recording] / Cincinatti Pops Orchestra. - Cleveland, Ohio: Telarc, 2001

6   Rules for a dictionary catalog / by Charles A. Cutter. - Washington, D. C.: Government Printing Office, 1904

7   Digital stamp album [electronic resource]: a multimedia tour of US postal treasures. - Walnut Creek, CA: Walnut Creek CDROM, 1996

LCSH has substantial provision for form as a subject, for example **Illustrated books, Jungle television programs, Planet of the Apes**

films, as well as **Encyclopedias and dictionaries.** In the recently restructured *Classification Web* a number of form and genre terms are now held as a separate database. It is important to understand that these are main headings, and not form subdivisions, and they are all replicated in the main subject heading list.

Inner form and outer form

Form in a non-subject sense can be understood in two different ways: what is sometimes referred to as outer form, the 'physical' format of the document, and inner form, which is the structure, organization and presentation of the content. Physical format includes concepts such as books, ephemera, microfilms, multimedia and electronic resources (although the last two are not physical, it is difficult to find any comprehensive term to cover these ideas of external form). Examples of inner form include biography, dictionary, catalogue, periodical, statistics and so on. You may find it easier to grasp the distinction if you consider how an item may display both inner and outer form; for example, electronic journals, miniature encyclopedias.

LCSH is far from exhaustive in its coverage of physical formats, which are usually represented in other parts of the catalogue record. So, for example, there is no subdivision for electronic information sources as a form, but there are subdivisions:

--Blogs
--Databases

Subdivisions are to be found for visual formats and other non-text media, but they tend to be sporadic, and, like the electronic formats, do not allow for everything one might expect:

--Designs and plans
--Manuscripts
--Maps
--Photographs
--Pictorial works
--Remote-sensing images

By contrast, inner form is very well catered for, and there are numerous headings for form of presentation, bibliographical formats, literary forms, and so on:

--**Bibliography**
--**Catalogs**
--**Fiction**
--**Periodicals**
--**Poetry**

There is a great variety of more unusual form subdivisions to be found: --**Anecdotes**, --**Autographs**, --**Exercises for dictation**, --**Longitudinal studies**, --**Manufacturers' catalogs**, --**Maps for the blind**, --**Non-commissioned officers' handbook**, --**Private bills**, --**Vocal scores with harp**, and so on. The novice's problem with this abundance is that, as usual, it is very hard to predict what might be included, but the problem will be overcome with practice and familiarity.

Summary

- The form of a document is commonly expressed using free-floating subdivisions.
- Care should be taken not to confuse this with form as the subject, for which main headings are available.
- Form may refer to the external format (print, electronic, and so on).
- It may also mean the internal structure and organization of the content (catalogue, encyclopedia, and so on).
- In some cases, these may both be used (electronic journals).
- LCSH has a huge variety of form subdivisions, some general, and some associated with particular subjects.

Exercise 11.2

Construct headings using free-floating subdivisions of form for the following titles:

- *Accordionist's encyclopedia of musical knowledge*
- *Autobiography of a geisha*
- *The greatest weddings of all time (with illustrations)*
- *Chimpanzee: a topical bibliography*
- *Book of Merlin: insights from the first Merlin conference*
- *Journal of the Society of Parrot Breeders and Exhibitors*
- *The Dead Sea scrolls catalogue*

Time and date

Period, or time, subdivisions are not very numerous. Chronological aspects of a subject are more usually dealt with through main headings containing periods and dates (see Chapter 13); and period in the free-floating subdivisions is limited to the broad concept 'History' with some century subdivisions, and occasional types of history, usually as inverted headings, for example:

History--16th century
History--19th century
History, Local
History, Military

It is not usually possible to express narrower date ranges through the use of free-floating subdivisions, so the structured headings will necessarily be inexact.

Example

```
British fiction in the 1930s: the dispiriting decade / by
James Gindin. - New York: St. Martin's Press, 1992
```

Subject headings:
    Literature and society--Great Britain--History--20th century
    Great Britain--Social life and customs--1918-1945

Period subdivisions in a few cases use only the century numbers (**--16th century,--19th century,** and so on). These are restricted to art and art forms, languages and literatures, groups of literary authors, and musical compositions.

Example

```
Dog painting, 1840-1940: a social history of the dog in
art, including an important historical overview from
earliest times to 1840 when pure bred dogs became popular
/ by William Secord. - Woodbridge, Eng.: Antique
Collectors' Club, 1992
```

Subject headings: Dogs in art
                    Painting, Modern--19th century
                    Painting, Modern--20th century

Exercise 11.3

Find appropriate period subdivisions for the following titles (do not worry about geographic subdivision for this exercise):

1   *A history of school buses*
2   *The sacred history of knitting*
3   *Legacies of twentieth-century dance*
4   *Food in the United States, 1820s to 1890*
5   *Roman woodworking*
6   *Watches, 1850-1980*
7   *Angels in the early modern world*

Combining free-floating and geographic subdivisions

Although geographic subdivisions are managed as described in Chapter 10, and they do not form part of the free-floating subdivisions, some free-floating subdivisions may themselves be subdivided geographically, so place may be an element in some subdivisions. For example:

--**Catalogs and collections** (May Subd Geog)
--**Diseases** (May Subd Geog)
--**Government policy** (May Subd Geog)

Geographic subdivisions are added in exactly the same way as they are with main headings, and the same rules for direct and indirect subdivision apply.

Example

```
Targets for family planning in India: an analysis of policy
change, consequences, and alternative choices. - New Delhi:
POLICY Project (Futures Group International), 1998
```

Subject heading: Family planning--Government policy--India

Exercise 11.4

Construct headings for the following titles:

1   *Sheep breeding in the People's Republic of Bulgaria*
2   *The remarkable story of Great Ormond Street Hospital*
3   *Nigerian musical instruments: a definitive catalogue*
4   *Annotated compendium of wheat diseases in India*
5   *Women's words: a select list of books written by, for, and about women* (Birmingham Public Library)

Care must be taken, when combining these subdivisions with a heading that itself can be subdivided geographically, that the geographic subdivision goes in the right place in the sequence. The geographic subdivision will qualify (limit) the concept that it follows. The first of the next two examples indicates an Australian catalogue of fossils from many different places; the second refers to a catalogue of fossils from the USA:

```
Catalogue of a collection of fossils in the Australian
museum, with introductory notes. - Sydney: Australian
Museum, 1883
```

Subject heading: Fossils--Catalogs and collections--Australia

```
Catalogue of type specimens of trilobites in Field Museum
of Natural History / by Matthew H. Nitecki and Julia
Golden. - [Chicago], 1970
```

Subject heading: Fossils--United States--Catalogs and collections

Summary

- Period can be indicated in a fairly general way using free-floating subdivisions for History.
- This can only be done at the level of centuries, and there is no way to express more precise periods or individual dates.
- Periods of time greater than a century require multiple headings, one for each century.
- Period is more commonly managed in LCSH through the use of pre-coordinated main headings.
- Place can be added to free-floating subdivisions where the instruction (May Subd Geog) appears.
- Care should be taken to put the geographic subdivision in the correct place in the structured heading.

Persons

Persons are patchily covered, and there is no systematic way to subdivide a main heading by the readership or audience, or to indicate persons as part of the subject. Persons might therefore be reasonably omitted from this chapter, but since such concepts regularly feature in documents, it seems appropriate to consider here how they can be managed.

Persons as audience are principally denoted in pre-coordinated headings, and many of the prepositional phrase headings, such as **Etiquette for women** or **Bodybuilding for children,** can be brought into use here. Resources for children may be denoted by a range of subdivisions using the term 'juvenile', such as --**Juvenile fiction, --Juvenile films, --Juvenile literature** and --**Juvenile poetry,** but this is the only regularly occurring example of a specific audience.

Common categories of persons as subject also tend to appear as part of pre-coordinated headings, again in a relatively random and unpredictable manner. This can be frustrating for the cataloguer because it results in unevenness of coverage, and inconsistency in handling of comparable topics.

Persons by gender

Representation of gender is perhaps the best known example of inconsistency, largely because the lack of parity between male and female has been so frequently criticized for its apparent political incorrectness. For example, women may be denoted as:

Women accordionists
Women alcoholics
Women explorers
Women mathematicians
Women murderers
Women priests
Women soldiers
Women test pilots

There are no male equivalents of these headings. A logical explanation may be that historically it has been more unusual for women to follow these occupations, and that there is consequently an associated literature for which headings are needed. This theory is supported by the occurrence of comparable headings (without female equivalents) for unusual male occupations, such as:

Male child care workers
Male models
Male nurses
Male prostitutes

Nevertheless, there are numerous 'women' headings for professions in which women are common, or even dominant (**Women kindergarten teachers, Women librarians, Women volunteers in social service**), so this hypothesis cannot be pushed too far.

In fairness, there are many headings where both genders are specified (**Male artists** and **Women artists, Male musicians** and **Women musicians, Male teachers** and **Women teachers**), and many where neither are (**Business analysts, Golf course managers, Hospital consultants, Secretaries, Underprepared college students**).

Some difficulties in interpretation may be caused by fine nuances in similar headings. What is the difference, for example, between **Women journalists** and **Women in journalism**, or **Women and journalism**? Usually scope notes will make the distinction clear, but this is not always the case, and a local policy may need to be imposed.

There are many headings where 'women' or 'men' appear qualified by some other characteristic and these are almost invariably presented as pre-coordinated compounds in main headings:

Lesbian rabbis
Older Hispanic American women
Overweight women in art
Women marine mammalogists
Women poets, Bolivian
African American male college students
Male authors, Russian
Male feminists
Photography of men
Working class men

Persons by ethnicity or sociological characteristics

Like gender, ethnicity, in common with other sociological attributes, is mainly represented in the main headings rather than through subdivisions, and there is no systematic means of indicating that a document refers to a particular ethnic group other than by including appropriate main headings for that group. For example:

British Americans
Kurdish diaspora
Romanies

Similar kinds of headings are available for personal attributes such as disability, social class, and sexual orientation:

Deaf gay men
Learning disabled teenagers
Upper class on television
Working class families

As with gender, ethnicity is often pre-coordinated with other personal characteristics in main headings:

Asian American bisexuals
Chinese American grocers
Jewish anarchists
Working class African Americans

Although the free-floating subdivisions don't allow for subdivision of a topical main heading by gender, ethnicity, or other personal attributes, they do provide for topical subdivision where personal attributes occur in main headings. For example:

Deaf children--Education (Elementary)
Mexican American agricultural laborers--Employment
Social workers--United States--Job stress

Summary

- There is no systematic way to represent persons through the free-floating subdivisions.
- The free-floating subdivisions include occasional examples of persons mainly in combination with other concepts.
- Persons as audience are not very well represented, other than children, using form subdivisions including the term 'juvenile'.
- Persons as subject are normally expressed through main headings.
- These are not very consistent, particularly in their treatment of gender.

Common subject subdivisions

These are by far the most common category of free-floating subdivisions, and they include all kinds of commonly occurring concepts. In the notes they are often, perhaps confusingly, referred to as 'topical subdivisions' although they are not quite the same as 'topical subdivisions' special to particular headings. 'Topical subdivision' is just the LCSH way of expressing 'subject subdivision'.

Example

--Ability testing
> Use as a topical subdivision under topical headings

--Chiropractic treatment
> Use as a topical subdivision under individual diseases and types of diseases

--Church history
> Use as a topical subdivision under names of countries, cities, etc.

--Dynamics
> Use as a topical subdivision under individual land vehicles and types of land vehicles

--Psychological aspects
> Use as a topical subdivision under topical headings

This may cause you to wonder how these topical subdivisions relate to the topical subdivisions described in Chapter 9. The subdivisions dealt with in that chapter are mostly subdivisions peculiar to a specific main heading and only used in combination with that heading. A good example is the use of very precise chronological subdivisions associated with the history of individual countries and not relevant to any others.

The topical free-floating subdivisions have wider application, either to all main headings or to particular kinds of headings, such as authors, languages, animals, wars and so on. It is true to say that there is some overlap between these two kinds of topical subdivision, particularly those limited to particular categories. The latter are usually given both as topical subdivisions of the pattern heading within the main list, and as topical free-floating subdivisions within the free-floating subdivisions database. It is also sometimes the case that combinations of a main heading and a free-floating subdivision can be found in the main database. You should therefore not read too much into the placing of subdivisions in the respective lists, but follow the notes carefully when applying them.

Free-floating subdivisions with limited application

As we have already noted, some of the free-floating subdivisions are restricted to particular categories of heading. For example, we find:

--Armenian authors
>   Use as a topical subdivision under individual literatures

--Homes and haunts
>   Use as a topical subdivision under names of individual persons, families, and performing groups, classes of persons, and ethnic groups...

This means that the subdivision **--Armenian authors** cannot be used in combination with headings generally, but only with headings such as **Russian literature,** and that **--Homes and haunts** is to be restricted to headings for individuals and various groups of people.

It is extremely hard to group these subdivisions in any meaningful way, but there are some obvious categories. Many free-floating subdivisions of this kind will be found to equate with the pattern headings. For instance, if we look at the heading **Cattle,** we see a large number of topical subdivisions as in the following examples:

Cattle--Abnormalities
Cattle--Anatomy
Cattle--Behavior
Cattle--Diseases
Cattle--Diseases--Genetic aspects
Cattle--Endocrinology
Cattle--Feeding and feeds

All of these topical subdivisions also appear as free-floating subdivisions, with the instruction 'Use as a topical subdivision under animals and groups of animals'.

Another common example is the group of subdivisions intended for organizing works of and about important individuals, encompassing such delights as **--Autographs, --Comic books, strips, etc., --Death mask, --Homes and haunts, --Knowledge and learning, --Mental health, --Palaces, --Spiritualistic interpretations,** and so on.

Other regularly occurring examples include subdivisions for use with particular countries or regions, with art and art forms, languages and literatures, and ethnic groups. More unexpected categories include 'bodies of water', 'land vehicles', 'military services', 'monastic orders', 'navies', 'occupational groups', 'parts of the Bible' and 'programmed texts'. Any type of heading, it seems, where some economy can be achieved by not having to repeat subdivisions under individual headings is likely to be included.

Exercise 11.5

Which categories of heading do the following free-floating subdivisions apply to?

--**Canonical criticism**

--**Color**

--**Fake books**

--**Fluid capacities**

--**Homonyms**

--**Hormone therapy**

--**Reconnaissance operations**

--**Recycling**

More complicated uses of free-floating subdivisions
Structured free-floating subdivisions

Just as the main headings themselves may be structured, some subdivisions exhibit levels of hierarchy, or are otherwise compound. (We have seen a special example of this above, where some free-floating subdivisions can be qualified by geographic subdivisions.) These structured subdivisions should be taken exactly as they stand and added directly to a main heading. For example:

--**Music--History and criticism**

--**History of Biblical events--Art**

--**Diseases--Genetic aspects**

Example

He was singin' this song: a collection of forty-eight traditional songs of the American cowboy, with words, music, pictures, and stories. – Orlando, Fla.: University Presses of Florida, 1981

Subject heading: Cowboys--Music--History and criticism

Between the text and the canvas: the Bible and art in dialogue / edited by J. Cheryl Exum and Ela Nutu. – Sheffield: Phoenix, 2007

Subject heading: Bible--History of Biblical events--Art

Congenital heart disease: molecular diagnostics / edited by Mary Kearns Jonker. – Totowa, N.J.: Humana, 2006

Subject heading: Heart--Diseases--Genetic aspects

Exercise 11.6

Add structured free-floating subdivisions as appropriate to create headings for the following titles:

1   *A comparative study of World War casualties from gas and other weapons [1931]*
2   *Union list of chemical periodicals in Cincinnati libraries*
3   *Finger fun for the little piano beginner*
4   *Grass seed production and harvest in the Great Plains*
5   *Radio control for model cars*
6   *My fat dog: ten simple steps to help your pet lose weight for a long and happy life*
7   *Senior church appointments: a review of the methods of appointment of area and suffragan bishops, deans, provosts, archdeacons, and residentiary canons: the report of the Working Party established by the Standing Committee of the General Synod of the Church of England*

Compound headings of this kind can only be used as they are published in the list of free-floating subdivisions. You must not add two subdivisions together to create new examples. If two aspects of a subject are not represented by a structured subdivision, they must be added separately, as described below.

Adding more than one free-floating subdivision to a heading

Occasionally, you may need to use more than one free-floating subdivision with a main heading. You should not add the subdivisions together, but repeat the main heading in combination with each individual subdivision (in just the same way as the geographic subdivisions). For example:

```
Zwei Kulturen der Wissenschaft / edited by Jost Halfmann
and Johannes Rohbeck. - Weilerswist: Velbruck Wissenschaft,
2007
```

Subject headings: Science--Classification
                       Science--Philosophy
                       Social sciences--Classification
                       Social sciences--Philosophy

```
Notes on the anatomy of Macrochirichthys macrochirus
(Valenciennes), 1884: with comments on the Cultrinae
(Pisces, Cyprinidae) / by G. J. Howes. - London: British
Museum, 1979
```

Subject headings: Fishes--Anatomy
                       Fishes--Classification

This happens fairly regularly with historical studies which span more than one period, and the same principle applies.

Example

```
Anthology of Baroque music: music in Western Europe, 1580-
1750 / edited by John Walter Hill. - New York: Norton,
2005
```

Subject headings: Music--History and criticism

                                Music--17th century

                                Music--18th century

You do, however, need to exercise some judgement about how far to take this. For example, the title *Music in the Western Tradition*, which deals with the history of western music from ancient times through to the twentieth century, could conceivably be given the headings:

Music--To 500

Music--500-1400

Music--15th century

Music--16th century

Music--17th century

Music--18th century

Music--19th century

Music--20th century

But the broad subject of the book is perhaps more accurately represented by a single period subdivision:

```
Music in the Western tradition / by Claire Detels. -
Mountain View, Calif.: Mayfield, 1998
```

Subject heading: Music--History and criticism

••

Exercise 11.7

Find appropriate headings with free-floating subdivisions for the following titles:

1 *The fast set: the world of Edwardian [horse] racing*

2 *What philosophy can tell you about your cat*

    ```
[Eighteen essays investigate philosophical aspects of the
feline mind and the world of cats, illustrated by
anecdotes about cats the authors have known.]
```

3 *The artful teapot*

[Exhibition of fine art teapots from private collections
held May 16-Sept. 2, 2002, at COPIA: the American Center
for Wine, Food, and the Arts, Napa, Calif. and other
locations.]

Answers to exercises

Exercise 11.1

Say whether the underlined word in the following titles is the subject of the document, or its form:

1 Dictionary of American resurrectionists, 1865-- 1990 / by
Edward T. Janas. – Chicago, Ill.: E. T. Janas, 1991
Form

2 Harvard concise dictionary of music and musicians / edited
by Don Michael Randel. – Cambridge, Mass.: Belknap, 1999
Subject

3 Digital resources and librarians: case studies in
innovation, invention, and implementation / edited by
Patricia O'Brien Libutti. – Chicago, Ill.: Association of
College and Research Libraries, 2004   **Subject**

4 Catalogue of the positions and proper motions of 4292
stars / by Frank Schlesinger. – New Haven: The
Observatory, 1943   **Form**

5 Music of the Beatles [sound recording] / Cincinatti Pops
Orchestra. – Cleveland, Ohio: Telarc, 2001   **Form**

6 Rules for a dictionary catalog / by Charles A. Cutter. –
Washington, D. C.: Government Printing Office, 1904 **Subject**

7 Digital stamp album [electronic resource]: a multimedia
tour of US postal treasures. – Walnut Creek, CA: Walnut
Creek CDROM, 1996   **Form**

Exercise 11.2

Construct headings using free-floating subdivisions of form for the following titles:

1 *Accordionist's encyclopedia of musical knowledge*
Accordion--Dictionaries

2 *Autobiography of a geisha*
Geishas--Biography

3   *The greatest weddings of all time* (with illustrations)
    Celebrity weddings--Pictorial works
4   *Chimpanzee: a topical bibliography*
    Chimpanzees--Bibliography
5   *Book of Merlin: insights from the first Merlin conference*
    Wizards in literature--Congresses
6   *Journal of the Society of Parrot Breeders and Exhibitors*
    Parrots--Periodicals
7   *The Dead Sea scrolls catalogue*
    Dead Sea Scrolls--Catalogs

Exercise 11.3

Find appropriate period subdivisions for the following titles (do not worry about geographic subdivision for this exercise):

1   *A history of school buses*
    School buses--History
2   *The sacred history of knitting*
    Knitting--History
3   *Legacies of twentieth-century dance*
    Dance--History--20th century
4   *Food in the United States, 1820s to 1890*
    Food--History--19th century
5   *Roman woodworking*
    Carpentry--History--To 1500
6   *Watches, 1850-1980*
    Clocks and watches--History--19th century
    Clocks and watches--History 20th century
7   *Angels in the early modern world*
    Angels--History--16th century
    Angels--History--17th century

Exercise 11.4

Construct headings for the following titles:

1   *Sheep breeding in the People's Republic of Bulgaria*
    Sheep--Breeding--Bulgaria
2   *The remarkable story of Great Ormond Street Hospital*
    Children--Hospitals--Great Britain

3   *Nigerian musical instruments: a definitive catalogue*
    Musical instruments--Catalogs and collections--Nigeria
4   *Annotated compendium of wheat diseases in India*
    Wheat--Diseases and pests--India
5   *Women's words: a select list of books written by, for, and about women*
    (Birmingham Public Library)
    Women--Books and reading--Great Britain

Exercise 11.5

Say which categories of heading the following free-floating subdivisions apply to:

--**Canonical criticism**	Sacred works
--**Color**	Plants and animals
--**Fake books**	Musical compositions
--**Fluid capacities**	Land vehicles
--**Homonyms**	Languages
--**Hormone therapy**	Diseases
--**Reconnaissance operations**	Individual wars
--**Recycling**	Chemicals and materials

Exercise 11.6

Add structured free-floating subdivisions as appropriate to create headings for the following titles:

1   *A comparative study of World War casualties from gas and other weapons [1931]*
    World War, 1914-1918--Casualties--Statistics
2   *Union list of chemical periodicals in Cincinnati libraries*
    Chemistry--Periodicals--Bibliography
3   *Finger fun for the little piano beginner*
    Piano--Studies and exercises--Juvenile
4   *Grass seed production and harvest in the great plains*
    Grasses--Seeds--Harvesting
5   *Radio control for model cars*
    Automobiles--Models--Radio control
6   *My fat dog: ten simple steps to help your pet lose weight for a long and happy life*
    Dogs--Diseases--Diet therapy
7   *Senior church appointments: a review of the methods of appointment of area and*
    suffragan bishops, deans, provosts, archdeacons, and residentiary canons: the
    report of the Working Party established by the Standing Committee of the General

Synod of the Church of England
Church of England--Clergy--Appointment, call, and election

Exercise 11.7

Find appropriate headings with free-floating subdivisions for the following titles:

1   *The fast set: the world of Edwardian* [horse] *racing*
    Horse racing--England--History--19th century
    Horse racing--England--History--20th century
2   *What philosophy can tell you about your cat*
    [Eighteen essays investigate philosophical aspects of the
    feline mind and the world of cats, illustrated by
    anecdotes about cats the authors have known.]
    Cats--Philosophy
    Cats--Psychology
3   *The artful teapot*
    [Exhibition of fine art teapots from private collections
    held May 16-Sept. 2, 2002, at COPIA: the American Center
    for Wine, Food, and the Arts, Napa, Calif. and other
    locations.]
    Teapots--Exhibitions
    Teapots--History
    Teapots--Private collections
    Teapots--Design--History

12 More complex headings: combining the different kinds of subdivisions

The great majority of headings that are either included in the published lists or constructed by cataloguers are relatively simple. Most will consist of a main heading alone or a main heading in combination with a topical subdivision, a geographic subdivision or a free-floating subdivision. Hence, most structured headings consist of no more than two or three elements. If you look at the subject index to the Library of Congress catalogue you will see that this is the case.

However, there is potential to have headings that are more complicated than this. In the preceding chapters we have considered how to add the various kinds of subdivision, but only in situations where one sort is added at a time. Although you cannot add together more than one of each kind of subdivision, the different sorts can be used in combination with each other, and in this chapter we will examine the rules that govern the construction of such headings.

You will not need to make a complicated heading very often, but they are extremely useful when you want to express a complex subject precisely.

Geographic subdivisions combined with free-floating subdivisions

Free-floating subdivisions that are generally applicable can be attached to any heading that has already been subdivided geographically. The usual order of things is:

Main heading--Geographic subdivision--Free-floating subdivision

---

Example

```
Doin' Arizona with your pooch: Eileen's directory of dog-
friendly lodging & outdoor adventures in Arizona / by
Eileen Barish. - Scottsdale, Az.: Pet-Friendly
Publications, [1996]
```

Subject heading: Dogs--Arizona--Handbooks, manuals, etc.

```
Sensitive issues in the workplace: a practical handbook /
Sue Morris. - London: Industrial Society, 1993
```

Subject heading: Problem employees--Great Britain--Handbooks,
                       manuals, etc.

The general rules for indirect geographic subdivision apply here:

```
The secret history of Guernsey marmalade: James Keiller &
Son Offshore, 1857-1879 / W.M.Mathew. - St.Peter Port,
Guernsey: La Société Guernesiaise, 1998
```

Subject heading: Marmalade industry--Channel Islands--Guernsey--
                       History

```
Gifts from the ancestors: ancient ivories of Bering Strait
/ edited by William W. Fitzhugh, Julie Hollowell and Aron
L. Crowell; with contributions by Robert E. Ackerman... [et
al.]. - Princeton: Princeton University Art Museum; New
Haven, Conn.; London: Yale University Press [distributor],
c2009
```

Subject heading: Ivories, Ancient--Alaska--Bering Strait Region--
                       Exhibitions

In some instances the free-floating subdivision may itself be compound
(for example '--History--19th century'), and this will introduce an additional element to the heading:

```
The origins of croquet in America, 1859-1873: a
presentation before The Certain Conditions Club, 13 March
2001, Washington, D.C./ by George G. Herrick. - Washington,
DC: G.G.Herrick, c2001
```

Subject heading: Croquet--United States--History--19th century

You should also be careful to remember the general rules about not adding
two subdivisions of the same kind together, and ensure that separate
headings are made when this situation arises:

```
British teapots & tea drinking, 1700-1850 / Robin Emmerson;
illustrated from the Twining Teapot Gallery, Norwich Castle
Museum. - London: HMSO, 1992
```

Subject headings: Tea making paraphernalia--England--History--18th
                       century
                       Tea making paraphernalia--England--History--19th
                       century

Occasionally, a free-floating subdivision can be subdivided geographically. Examples of where there may be geographic limits to the subdivision include --**Law and legislation** (May Subd Geog), --**Government policy** (May Subd Geog), --**Catalogs and collections** (May Subd Geog) and --**Museums** (May Subd Geog). These are fairly clear candidates for further arrangement by place, but there are a number of other less obvious examples, such as --**Blunt trauma** (May Subd Geog), --**Galvanomagnetic properties** (May Subd Geog), and --**Biodegradation** (May Subd Geog).

Clearly, in these examples, the geographic element follows the free-floating subdivision. **Law and legislation** is very often an element in a compound free-floating subdivision, such as --**Examinations--Law and legislation**, --**Finance--Law and legislation**, and --**Employees--Pensions--Law and legislation**, all of which can themselves be subdivided by place. There shouldn't be any confusion about the sequence of elements here, as you simply follow the prescribed order.

Example

Reasons for reducing the tax on tobacco. – Washington: Joseph L. Pearson, 1868

Subject heading: Tobacco industry--Taxation--Law and legislation--United States

Ethics in mental health research: principles, guidance and cases / James M. Dubois. – Oxford; New York: Oxford University Press, 2008

Subject heading: Psychiatry--Research--Law and legislation--United States

Horse power: the politics of the turf / Christopher R. Hill; with a foreword by the Rt. Hon. Viscount Whitelaw. – Manchester, UK; New York: Manchester University Press; New York, N.Y., U.S.A.: St. Martin's Press, c1988

Subject heading: Horse racing--Betting--Law and legislation--England

Summary

- Headings may be constructed that incorporate both geographic and free-floating subdivisions.
- The sequence of elements is usually: geographic subdivision--free-floating subdivision.

- The rules affecting geographic subdivisions generally (such as those for direct and indirect subdivision) apply here.
- Similarly, where more than one geographic or free-floating subdivision is involved, separate headings must be created for each.
- If the free-floating subdivision may be subdivided geographically, the order should follow that instruction.

Topical subdivisions combined with geographic subdivisions

A heading with a topical subdivision can often be further qualified by a geographic subdivision, although you should make certain of this by looking for the instruction (May Subd Geog):

> **Underwater archaeology**
>   **--Law and legislation** (May Subd Geog)

This means that that you can construct headings such as:

> **Underwater archaeology--Law and legislation--England**
> **Underwater archaeology--Law and legislation--France**

The situation with combinations of topical and geographic subdivisions is more complicated than that of geographic and free-floating subdivisions, since the order of combination can vary, and you need to take care that the geographic subdivision goes in the correct place. As a general rule of thumb, you can put a geographic subdivision wherever the instruction (May Subd Geog) stands. The main heading may have such an instruction, and be followed by topical subdivisions, in which case the geographic part goes between them:

> **Birds** (May Subd Geog)
>   **--Anatomy**
>   **--Embryology**
>   **--Folklore**

This means that you can create headings on the pattern:

> **Birds--South America--Anatomy**
> **Birds--Australia--Embryology**
> **Birds--Japan--Folklore**

Example

```
Pterylography; the feather tracts of Australian birds with
notes and observations / by F.E.Parsons. - Adelaide:
Libraries Board of South Australia, 1968
```

Subject heading: Birds--Australia--Anatomy

```
Birds of Ireland: facts, folklore & history / Glyn
Anderson. - Cork: Collins, 2008
```

Subject heading: Birds--Ireland--Folklore

Alternatively, the (May Subd Geog) can follow the topical subdivision, in which case it goes right at the end of the structured heading:

Insulin

    --Antagonists

    --Decontamination

    --Secretion (May Subd Geog)

    --Technological innovation (May Subd Geog)

In this example the main heading **Insulin** cannot itself be geographically subdivided, but some of its topical subdivisions can, hence the possible headings:

Insulin--Secretion--Philippines

Insulin--Technological innovation--Germany

Example

```
Congenital hyperinsulinism in the Finnish population /
Hanna Huopio. - Kuopio: Department of Public Health,
University of Turku, 2002
```

Subject heading: Insulin--Secretion--Finland

```
Technology in Indian insulin industry: a status report
prepared under the National Register of Foreign
Collaborations. - [New Delhi]: Govt. of India, Dept. of
Scientific & Industrial Research, Ministry of Science and
Technology, [1990]
```

Subject heading: Insulin--Technological innovations--India

In theory it is possible to have a geographic subdivision qualifying both the main heading and the topical subdivision, although in practice this is rarely found:

Birds (May Subd Geog)
   --Breeding (May Subd Geog)
   --Collection and preservation (May Subd Geog)

So, theoretically (although the Library of Congress catalogues suggest this hasn't happened in practice), headings could be created of the type:

Birds--Europe--Breeding--British Isles
Birds--Arctic--Collection and preservation--North America

In such cases you should think carefully about what the subject actually is. In the first example above the heading implies a work about European birds breeding in the British Isles. A work about British birds breeding in Europe would have the heading:

Birds--British Isles--Breeding--Europe

This interpretation is by no means intuitive, so don't worry if you find it difficult to see. It may be helpful to think of the heading in 'stages'; for example, **Birds--British Isles** suggests the subject of British birds, and **Birds--British Isles--Breeding**, their breeding activities. The addition of a further geographic subdivision allows you to specify where this is taking place. Alternatively, you can consider the main heading and the topical subdivision, and their respective geographic qualifications separately; ask yourself whether the birds are British (or European), and whether the breeding is in Europe (or the British Isles).

The general rules that apply to geographic subdivision, such as those for indirect subdivision, also apply here, allowing further elements to be added to the heading; for example:

Birds--Southern Europe--Breeding--England--Suffolk

This also includes the rule that if two or more places qualify the same part of the structured heading, then separate headings must be made for each place; hence a document about European birds breeding in Norfolk and Suffolk would have the headings:

Birds--Southern Europe--Breeding--England--Norfolk
Birds--Southern Europe--Breeding--England--Suffolk

Note that this isn't the same as the situation above, where the two places are attached to different parts of the same heading.

Summary

- Headings may be constructed which combine geographic subdivisions with topical subdivisions.
- You should take care only to add geographic subdivisions where instructed.
- The geographic subdivision may apply to either the main heading or the topical subdivision.
- Add the geographic subdivision in the position where the instruction (May Subd Geog) appears.
- Occasionally both heading and topical subdivision may be qualified geographically.
- If two different places are involved, think carefully about which place belongs to which element of the heading.
- If the two different places both qualify the same part of the heading, then two separate headings must be constructed.

Topical subdivisions combined with free-floating subdivisions

In the same way, free-floating subdivisions can be attached to a main heading with a topical subdivision:

Planets (Not Subd Geog)
    --Atmospheres
    --Brightness
    --Ephemerides
    --Magnetospheres
    --Orbits

Planets--Atmospheres--Research
Planets--Brightness--Measurement
Planets--Ephemerides--Bibliography
Planets--Orbits--Data processing

Example

```
Computus ecclesiasticus. [Ephemerides compendiosae ad
sciendum in quo signo zodiaci planetae sint. De ortu &
occasu syderum ex libris VI Fastorum P. Ovidij Nasonis.
Extracta ex libro Georgicorum Virgilij Maronis. Ortus
stellarum fixarum & occasus.]. - [not before 1583]
```

Subject heading: Planets--Ephemerides--Early works to 1800

> Astrocycles: how to make the major planetary cycles work
> for you / Vivian B. Martin. – New York: Ballantine, 1991
>
> Subject heading: Planets--Orbits--Miscellanea

Note that, unlike geographic subdivisions, there is no option to place the free-floating subdivision between the main heading and the topical subdivision, so it will usually be placed at the end.

Just as geographic subdivision sometimes requires more than one element, the free-floating subdivisions may be compound, and this too gives rise to a more complex structure, such as:

Planets--Ephemerides--Bibliography--Exhibitions

where '--Bibliography--Exhibitions' is a compound, free-floating subdivision.

Example

> Planetary atmospheres. – Washington, D.C.: Scientific and
> Technical Information Division, National Aeronautics and
> Space Administration; Springfield, Va.: [Available from the
> Clearinghouse for Federal Scientific and Technical
> Information], 1965–

Subject heading: Planets--Atmospheres--Bibliography--Periodicals

---

Combinations of topical, geographic, and free-floating subdivisions

In theory, it is possible to have combinations of main headings with topical subdivisions, geographic subdivisions, and free-floating subdivisions, although it is fairly hard to find real examples of these. For the most part, the order of combination will follow the pattern:

Heading--Topical subd.--Geographic subd.--Free-floating subd.

Where there is indirect geographic subdivision, and/or compound free-floating subdivisions, this structure can become much more involved:

Heading--Topical--Country--Local place--Free-floating 1--Free-floating 2

If both the main heading and the topical subdivision may be subdivided geographically, the number of elements in the heading can in theory be as high as seven or eight, and compound free-floating subdivisions can further complicate things.

Example

Mammalian biology in South America: a symposium held at the Pymatuning Laboratory of Ecology, May 10-14, 1981 / edited by Michael A. Mares, Hugh M. Genoways. - Linesville, Pa.: Pymatuning Laboratory of Ecology, University of Pittsburgh, 1982

Subject heading: Mammals--Research--South America--Congresses

Handbook for timber and mule deer management co-ordination on winter ranges in the Cariboo Forest Region / H.M. Armleder, R.J. Dawson, R.N. Thomson. - Victoria, B.C.: Information Services Branch, Ministry of Forests: Queen's Printer Publications [distributor], c1986

Subject heading: Mule deer--Habitat--British Columbia--Cariboo
                      (Forest Region)--Handbooks, manuals, etc.

The important thing here is to keep calm, and think carefully about the subject and how to represent it. In the normal course of events, the sequence of the four elements 'main--topical--geographic--free-floating' is only disturbed where geographic subdivisions can be put in more than one place, but the instructions for this are usually clear.

Subdivisions with more than two parts, such as indirect geographic subdivisions and compound free-floating subdivisions, are always kept intact, and their elements should never be separated. Hence, although they make the final heading look complicated, they really do not add to the complexity of constructing the heading.

Remember, too, that such headings are uncommon, and are needed only when you have a complicated subject that you want to represent precisely. If you look at the subject index to the Library of Congress catalogue you will see that almost all headings consist of just two or three parts. Although there is some satisfaction in making a heading that encompasses all the aspects of a very specific subject, if you don't feel confident about doing this, you can always resort to using a series of simpler headings to cover all the parts of your subject.

Finally, be aware that the cataloguers at the Library of Congress itself occasionally do strange things, that some headings are very old and not necessarily accurate, and do not worry if you find headings that do not seem to follow the rules.

13 Chronological headings and subdivisions

Like place, period is commonly found as an element in the subjects of books. This is not limited to the discipline of history, but occurs in the great majority of subjects. Period can be expressed as specific periods, actual dates, or in broader and more general ideas of time:

French social cinema of the nineteen thirties
On lutes, recorders and harpsichords: men and music of the baroque
October nineteenth, seventeen eighty-one: victory at Yorktown: the story of the last campaign of the American Revolution
Studies in ancient Indian law and justice
Science in the Spanish and Portuguese Empires, 1500-1800
Post-medieval archaeology in Britain
The royal pardon: access to mercy in fourteenth century England
Aldus Manutius: printer and publisher of renaissance Venice

Since period is such a common element of compound subjects you might expect that time subdivisions would be provided for in the same way as geographic subdivisions, but that is not the case. There is a very limited selection of periods available within the free-floating subdivisions, and time is usually expressed through various kinds of main heading. This means that you cannot create headings with dates, as you created headings with places, but are restricted to those dates and times that are specified. It is rather difficult to predict how any individual heading will be dealt with, but it is possible to discern some general approaches.

Free-floating subdivisions for history

There is some provision for very basic historical arrangement of a topic, using the subdivision '--**History**', which is further qualified by century divisions for the 16th, 17th, 18th, 19th, 20th and 21st centuries. LCSH uses numbers here in preference to words and the subdivisions are written as, for example:

History--16th century
History--20th century

The 'History' part must always be included, and these subdivisions may be applied to any topic:

Cathedral libraries--History--18th century
Crossword puzzles--History--20th century

--To 1500 is available for history before the modern period, but there is no means of expressing the medieval period more precisely using the free-floating subdivisions.

It is sometimes permitted to use just the century, but you should follow the guidelines laid down in the scope notes for these subdivisions. You will find that they are restricted to the creative arts, and often further limited to art and art forms, language and literary topics, or musical compositions:

Miniature painting--19th century
Concertos (Oboe)--16th century

Otherwise, period is either an intrinsic element of the heading, or is expressed as a subdivision usually peculiar to that heading.

Main headings with period aspects

There are five main categories of chronological headings:

- headings for particular time periods *per se*, i.e. where a specific date or period is the main subject
- headings in which the time element is implicit
- headings containing general descriptive period terms in the form of adjectival qualifiers such as 'Ancient'
- headings containing dates, e.g. **World politics 1945--**
- chronological subdivisions of particular headings which may take various forms, e.g.:
  — headings with periods and dates, e.g. **Christian art and symbolism--Medieval, 500-1500**
  — headings with century subdivisions e.g. **Italian poetry--15th century**.

There are also a number of headings where a specific date or period is the main subject.

There is a good deal of overlap between these different varieties of heading, and they are given here principally as a guide to the possible formats that period headings may take, rather than as a set of distinct and mutually exclusive options. A number of them replicate the free-floating subdivisions and there is often no useful distinction to be made between a main heading with period topical subdivisions and the same main heading with free-floating subdivisions. The topical subdivisions are often much more precise than the free-floating ones, but that isn't always the case.

In these headings precise dates, whether topical subdivisions or qualifiers, and century subdivisions are usually expressed as numerals. Broad periods, or headings where the date or time is the main subject, tend to be given verbally.

Headings for named periods, dates and times

A group of headings exists where the period or date is the main subject, rather than being a subdivision of some other topic. It is likely that the majority of these are historical in nature. They cannot usually be subdivided geographically, so they should only be used where there is no particular place involved:

Middle Ages
Fourteenth century
Nineteen twenties

Sometimes very precise dates can be expressed:

Two thousand, A.D.
Nineteen sixty four, A.D.
International Polar Year, 2007-2008

There is also provision for recurrent dates, feasts and festivals and annual events. These are more useful for accommodating materials on customs and folklore rather than history:

Fourth of July
Mother's Day
April Fools' Day
Saint Patrick's Day

In addition to all of these specific dates and times LCSH includes headings for general time concepts such as **Summer, Midnight, Morning,** months of the year, e.g. **November, April,** and occasional headings like **Week**. Apart from the months these are random in nature; there is no heading for 'Afternoon', for instance, or 'Weekend', or for days of the week.

Headings with adjectival qualifiers

Verbal headings exist for broad periods such as 'ancient', 'medieval', 'renaissance', 'baroque' and 'modern'. These are almost invariably expressed as inverted headings, for example:

> **Choir stalls, Renaissance**
> **Textile fabrics, Ancient**
> **Hebrew language, Medieval**
> **Naval history, Modern**

This serves the standard purpose of bringing together in the index all the documents about textile fabrics or Hebrew language, and gives prominence to the topic over the date.

You may occasionally discover what appears to be an exception to this rule, but on closer inspection these headings usually turn out to be established names of topics such as **Modern dance**. The only real departure from the inversion rule is the use of 'Classical' to refer to Greek and Roman culture, as in **Classical antiquities** or **Classical literature**. Nevertheless, there are plentiful examples of where this is not the case, for instance, **Marble sculpture, Classical** and **Verse satire, Classical,** so it is not possible to lay down any general principle.

Main headings with date qualifiers

These last examples also show how dates are frequently used to qualify or define events in the same way that they are used to define headings for persons:

> **Sino-Japanese War, 1894-1895**
> **New Deal, 1933-1939**
> **Great Plague, London, England, 1664-1666**
> **San Francisco Earthquake and Fire, Calif., 1906**
> **Actium, Battle of, 31 B.C.**

Main headings with chronological subdivisions

A great number of headings for history, particularly those for the history of specific countries, contain dates, normally expressed as numerals. There are several different sorts of these, some of them containing dates, some with period descriptors as well as dates, and some with simple century subdivisions. This is a very sensible way to organize material about countries since the significant periods for a given country are normally peculiar to it and wouldn't be useful in a more general sense. A very common way to subdivide history is by reigns:

Norway--History--Oscar I, 1844-1859
Norway--History--Oscar II, 1872-1905

Dates of monarchs may similarly be used to further subdivide the topical subdivision --**Politics and government,** and regimes and governments can provide an alternative approach:

Great Britain--Politics and government--1830-1837
Great Britain--Politics and government--1837-1901
Great Britain--Politics and government--1901-1910

Germany--Politics and government--1918-1933
    UF Weimar Republic, Germany, 1918-1933
Germany--Politics and government--1933-1945
    UF Third Reich, 1933-1945

Main headings containing periods and dates

This type of heading is closer in nature to one with a free-floating subdivision, except that the date element is usually provided as a topical subdivision, rather like the date range subdivisions for the history of particular places.

It is particularly common in association with headings for artistic subjects, and there are only a few very broad periods used:

Christian art and symbolism--Renaissance, 1450-1600
Dutch drama--Early modern, 1500-1700
English drama--Early modern and Elizabethan, 1500-1600

It is not altogether clear why these subjects are not represented by the more common inverted format without dates, such as 'Christian art and symbolism, Renaissance', but possibly the headings here are preferable where the date range is more exact.

Another instance is where named periods are also defined by dates, rather like the specific events discussed above. This class of heading tends to be limited to historical subdivisions of place headings, such as:

Finland--History--Revolution, 1917-1918
Great Britain--History--Commonwealth and Protectorate, 1649-1660
Aragon (Spain)--History--Interregnum, 1410-1412

Headings with century subdivisions

Century subdivisions are fairly common as topical subdivisions, more so in the case of culture and the arts. It is also possible to find century subdivisions among the free-floating subdivisions, but these too are mostly limited to kinds of art and artistic topics. The use of topical century subdivisions occurs frequently with different kinds of history as well:

Authors, Mexican--17th century
Civilization, Arab--19th century
Drawing--16th century
Music--20th century

Brazil--Economic conditions--19th century
England--Intellectual life--18th century
Europe--Social life and customs--18th century

Summary

- There is no systematic means of subdividing a main heading topic by period, as there is with place.
- A few free-floating subdivisions are provided for centuries of the modern period.
- Period is mainly represented through chronological elements in main headings.
- Some broad period subdivisions occur in verbal form.
- Some headings contain very specific dates, either as topical subdivisions or qualifiers, expressed as numbers.
- There are also headings for particular dates and times as subjects in their own right.

14 Name headings

Apart from the structured headings constructed from the elements of the main headings and various kinds of subdivisions, there is only one kind of heading that can be created by the cataloguer: the name heading.

What constitutes a name heading?

Name headings are used when some person, place or entity with a proper name (a name beginning with a capital letter) occurs as the subject of a work. You need to make a careful distinction between the person or entity as the *subject* of the work, and the other ways in which they might be represented in different parts of the catalogue or metadata record; for example, a person may be author, editor or illustrator, and an organization could be a corporate author or a publisher. Only when the document is *about* the person or organization should a subject heading be made.

Because there are so many possibilities for name headings, LCSH does not routinely include these in the published list of headings, but expects the cataloguer to create them as needed, following certain rules and conventions for their construction. Notable exceptions include prominent historical figures and prolific authors and artists, the latter often serving as pattern headings for others in the same category. The Library of Congress Authorities database (http://authorities.loc.gov/) provides a useful check for practitioners as to the forms of names that have been used there, and can be searched freely online.

There are several different categories of things that can have name headings. I have taken a fairly liberal view of what constitutes a name heading, and Library of Congress would regard some of these technically as title headings (which are used for created works such as works of art or literature). My general policy has been to embrace all those unique persons or objects for which headings can be developed by the cataloguer where they do not exist in the published list; it seems important to address the situation where a heading for such an entity isn't available, and the cataloguer wonders what to do about it. Everything in this chapter, therefore, is indicative of the kinds of subjects where cataloguers can adopt an innovative stance and exercise their own judgement in 'making up' a heading, using comparable examples as a model. Needless to say, the Library of Congress authorities contain thousands of examples of such headings, and only occasionally will a cataloguer not find an existing record there.

The most obvious type of heading required is for an individual person occurring as the subject of a biography or history, or, in the case of a creative individual, in writings of criticism, analysis or interpretation of their works. We might therefore need headings for persons such as:

Milton, John, 1608-1674
Buffalo Bill, 1846-1917
Umberto II, King of Italy, 1904-1983
Presley, Elvis, 1935-1977
Beckham, David, 1975-

Named organizations and institutions may also exist as subjects and they too can be found as subject headings at the Library of Congress:

Amnesty International
Apple Computer, Inc.
Ballets Russes
Dreamworks Pictures
English Folk Dance and Song Society
European Council for Nuclear Research
University of Cambridge

Another very large category of name headings that we have already touched upon is that for geographic names. These can be created for places of all kinds, and for geographic features:

Arizona
Brecon Beacons National Park (Wales)
Ile de la Cite (Paris, France)
Rio de Janeiro (Brazil)
Yangtze River (China)

Persons, organizations and places readily to spring to mind as examples of proper names, but there are other, less obvious, categories. We will consider in more detail the headings for created works in other chapters, but all sorts of unique documents, works of art, and created objects fall into this category. In the Library of Congress authorities some of these come more properly under the heading of title authorities, but for practical purposes they are handled in the same way:

Auld lang syne
Cutty Sark (Ship)
Domesday Book
Goon show (Radio program)
Lindisfarne Gospels
Star Trek (Television program)
Swan Lake (Choreographic work)
Wizard of Oz (Motion picture: 1939)

Another very substantial group of headings is that for named historical events, notably wars and battles, but also other significant happenings. These are more likely to be found in the published lists, but you may also add to them where necessary:

Boston Tea Party, 1773
Great Fire, London, England, 1666
Hundred Years' War, 1339-1453
Marengo, Battle of, Marengo, Italy, 1800
Punic wars
Reformation
World War, 1939-1945

In general terms, therefore, you can regard any unique person, group, organization, place, event or created entity as a legitimate candidate for a subject heading, where there isn't one already in the published LCSH or the Library of Congress authorities. There are various conventions and standards in place to help you in this process, and we shall now look at the various broad categories in more detail.

Personal names

Headings for persons as subjects can be created freely using the AACR2 rules for personal names as a guide. At the time of writing, a new standard for descriptive cataloguing, *Resource Description and Access* (RDA) has just been launched. Although this is different in conception to AACR2, it seems unlikely that it will make a substantial difference to the way in which the majority of personal names are handled. It is inany case unknowable how many libraries will implement RDA immediately, so the general guidelines here should still serve you well.

Names for persons should be those by which the persons are usually known. Most straightforward personal names are very easily managed. The general pattern for a heading is to invert the usual form of the name, so that entry is under the surname (or family name), followed by a comma, followed by the forename(s):

Brookner, Anita
Clegg, Nick
Minnelli, Liza
Obama, Barack
Part, Arvo
Suchet, David
Tarantino, Quentin

In the case of simple, unique names, this is enough to ensure identification of the individual, but names are more frequently shared than you might think, and in many cases something must be added to differentiate (or disambiguate) one person from another with the same name. Usually, this is the date of birth (NB the information in brackets is mine and not part of the heading):

Tennant, David, 1902-1968   [member of the English aristocracy]
Tennant, David, 1971-   [Scottish actor]

Blair, Tony   [performer]
Blair, Tony, 1953-   [British prime minister]

Apart from the need to disambiguate, it is common Library of Congress practice to add dates of birth and death for people no longer living, even where this seems not to be strictly necessary (again, it is surprising how many William Wordsworths, Charles Dickens and Isaac Newtons there have been); for example:

Chanel, Coco, 1883-1971
Christie, Agatha, 1890-1976
De Gaulle, Charles, 1890-1970
Elgar, Edward, 1857-1934
Picasso, Pablo, 1881-1973

Where persons are primarily known by initials, rather than full fore-names, these may be used instead, but it is usual to include the full version in brackets:

Auden, W. H. (Wystan Hugh), 1907-1973
Eliot, T. S. (Thomas Stearns), 1888-1965
Milne, A. A. (Alan Alexander), 1882-1956
Taylor, A. J. P. (Alan John Percivale), 1906-1990

Titles of honour and similar additions are usually placed after the name (although many name headings in the authorities are not so distinguished):

Benedict XVI, Pope, 1927-
Bstan-'dzin-rgya-mtsho, Dalai Lama XIV, 1935-
Disraeli, Benjamin, Earl of Beaconsfield, 1804-1881
Doyle, Arthur Conan, Sir, 1859-1930
Joan, of Arc, Saint, 1412-1431
Makarios III, Archbishop of Cyprus, 1913-1977

Fictional and legendary persons

Name headings for fictional characters are constructed exactly as if they were real people, with the addition of a qualifier to indicate that they are not:

Dumbledore, Albus (Fictitious character)
Holmes, Sherlock (Fictitious character)
Jones, Indiana (Fictitious character)
Lecter, Hannibal (Fictitious character)
Marlowe, Philip (Fictitious character)

Characters known only by their forenames may be qualified by the author's surname in the following manner:

Alice (Fictitious character: Carroll)

Legendary characters are distinguished from those in fictional works:

Aladdin (Legendary character)
Galahad (Legendary character)
Maid Marian (Legendary character)
Pied Piper of Hamelin (Legendary character)

There is some variation in the way these are handled in the Library of Congress catalogue, particularly where inversion is concerned. Most names of legendary characters do not lend themselves to inversion, but some that do are not consistently handled. It is sometimes difficult to know whether the second part of the name is truly a surname or rather a description. Titles may sometimes follow the name, as with real or fictitious persons:

Bean, Sawney (Legendary character)
John Henry (Legendary character)
Lionza, Maria (Legendary character)
Robin Hood (Legendary character)

Guenevere, Queen (Legendary character)
Finn, King of the Frisians (Legendary character)

As a matter of interest, despite the legendary status of Queen Guenevere, King Arthur is regarded by the Library of Congress as a real person.

Legendary religious figures are also specifically catered for:

Wilgefortis (Legendary saint)
Joan (Legendary Pope)

There are also a number of headings for those who, while dead, continue to be active. Spirit versions of real people merit headings in their own right, which stand alongside headings for the corporeal versions:

Diana, Princess of Wales, 1961-1997 (Spirit)
Garland, Judy (Spirit)
Hitler, Adolf, 1889-1945 (Spirit)
Kennedy, John F. (John Fitzgerald), 1917-1963 (Spirit)
Presley, Elvis, 1935-1977 (Spirit)--Songs and Music

Example

```
Life in the world unseen / Anthony Borgia; foreword by Sir
John Anderson. - Midway, UT: M.A.P., c1993
```
Subject headings: Benson, Robert Hugh, 1871-1914 (Spirit)
                                  Spirit writings

Non-humans

Numerous headings exist for well known animals, and there seems no reason why these can't be added to where there is literary warrant. There are current headings for several different kinds of animals, including ten individual elephants, four polar bears, and a giraffe, Daisy Rothschild. Race horses are particularly plentiful. Headings should be qualified by the kind of animal involved:

Greyfriars Bobby (Dog)
Little draggin' bear (Cat)
Lonesome George (Tortoise)
Red Rum (Race horse)

Fictitious animals require the same treatment as fictitious humans, although, unlike real animals, the kind of animal need not be indicated:

Felix the Cat (Fictitious character)
Scooby-Doo (Fictitious character)
Tweety Pie (Fictitious character)

As a point of interest, 'Pie' seems to be regarded as a surname, for we find a non-preferred version:

Pie, Tweety (Fictitious character) USE **Tweety Pie (Fictitious character)**

Non-Western names

The standard Western pattern of a personal name (forenames followed by surname or family name) may not hold good for some cultures, so it is difficult to establish which is which. Commonly, the family name may be cited first, so that the form of entry in a heading is to all intents and purposes the same as the form of the name in everyday use, for example:

Mao, Zedong, 1893-1976
Chiang, Kai-shek, 1887-1975

This is the norm for many Asian cultures, and also in Hungary, where the local form of the composer Zoltan Kodaly would be Kodaly Zoltan. While familiar names may be manageable, it can be much harder to be certain about the make-up of unfamiliar ones. In some Asian languages names consist of several parts, and the correct order for the purpose of a heading is even more difficult to establish. Unless you are expert in the conventions of the particular language it is probably wiser to make use of name authorities to confirm the correct version.

For names in non-Roman scripts, transliteration tables will need to be used in the interests of consistency. These may result in names that are rather different from the popular rendering, as in the case of the heading for Mao Tse-Tung above.

....

Exercise 14.1

Establish the correct form of a heading for the following persons:

1 Richard Starkey
2 P. D. James
3 Dan Brown
4 Richard Nixon
5 Walt Disney
6 Walter Raleigh
7 Ho Chi Minh
8 Stephen Fry
9 Alfred, Lord Tennyson
10 Sir Arthur Sullivan
11 Charlemagne
12 Ban Ki-Moon
13 Lara Croft
14 King Lear
15 King Charles I
16 Lassie

....

Summary

- Personal names are entered in the inverted form 'surname/family name, comma, forenames'.
- Where two or more people have the same name, they can be differentiated by using the date of birth.
- Dates of birth and death are commonly included for those no longer alive.
- Where persons are commonly known by their initials, the heading may reflect this, but the full version should be included in parentheses.
- Offices and titles of honour follow the name.
- Fictitious persons are treated in the same way as real persons, while headings for legendary persons use the normal form of the name.
- Non-western names may follow a different order of elements and should be checked against an authority to establish the correct heading.

Corporate names

Corporate names, or names of corporate bodies, should also be created as needed, and according to AACR rules. Corporate bodies comprise all kinds of institutions and organizations, public and private, such as government departments, companies, museums, charities, sports clubs, police authorities, professional bodies, learned societies and so on.

The Library of Congress has provided a very extensive list of categories of entities that constitute the different kinds of personal and corporate name heading (www.loc.gov/marc/ambiguous-headings.html), and some of those in the corporate name category are surprising. Grain elevators and herbariums feature, as do prisons and railway stations, and there is a large number of types of buildings, such as chapels, dance halls and public comfort stations. The inclusion of more general sites and spaces including cemeteries, bus terminals and resorts suggests that some of the ambiguity arises in the understanding of place and of organization. That does not necessarily cause practical difficulties in the construction of headings, but it is a distinction that students often find hard to appreciate, particularly in the case of a building in a particular location: is 'at school' or 'in hospital' a place? It is interesting that Library of Congress have recently made changes to some headings to move them from geographic to organization status (see below, page183).

As with personal names, there are very few corporate names in the published LCSH; although there are subject headings for general types of organizations, such as **Law firms, Prisoner of war camps, Tennis clubs** and **Veterinary hospitals**, named examples are rarely to be found. There are, however, many thousands of examples in the Library of Congress catalogue which you can use as authorities and models, for example:

Arsenal Football Club
Hallé Orchestra
Microsoft Corporation
Royal Flying Doctor Service of Australia

The general rule is that the name of the corporate body should be that by which it is normally known, rather than any official or legal form of the name:

British Telecom (rather than BT Group plc)
News Corporation (rather than News Corporation Limited)

Unesco (rather than United Nations Educational, Scientific, and Cultural Organization)

Unlike **Unesco,** most acronyms are spelled out in full:

London Symphony Orchestra
Museum of Modern Art (New York, N.Y.)
Royal Society for the Protection of Birds

Unlike geographic name headings, corporate name headings for organizations from non-English speaking countries have their names in the original language:

Association bourguignonne des socétiés savants
Berliner Bibliophilen Abend
Società astronomica italiana

These examples are all very simple ones, but there are a number of categories of corporate bodies whose names need some disambiguation, and where qualifiers are needed.

Names that are not unique

Just as some people may share the same name, corporate names are often not unique. Disambiguation here is usually achieved by adding a geographic qualifier:

National Academy of Sciences (India)
National Academy of Sciences (U.S.)

Geographic qualifiers are often used as well where the location of the organization is vague or unclear, even though it may be uniquely named:

Royal Festival Hall (London, England)
National Agricultural Library (U.S.)

Names that do not imply a corporate body

Often a corporate body will have the name of a person or persons, or some other unconventional title that on its own doesn't convey the idea of an organization. Names of this sort should be qualified by a descriptor indicating the nature of the organization:

Amazon.com (Firm)
Black Sabbath (Musical group)

Pegasus (Soccer team)
Peter Kiefer (Firm)
Rainbow Acres (Organization)
Royal de luxe (Theater group)

Subordinate bodies

Some potentially difficult choices need to be made when the corporate body is part of a larger body. AACR has quite complicated rules for this, and it is hard to give simple guidelines. Generally speaking, a body which is under the control of another should have a 'hierarchical' heading including the parent body. This is most clearly seen in the case of government organizations:

United States. National Aeronautics and Space Administration
Great Britain. Central Criminal Court

All types of ministries, government departments, legislative bodies, military services and so on should be treated in this way. Any name that includes a term such as 'division', 'section', 'committee' or 'department', which implies it is part of a larger body, should be dealt with similarly. Note that there is no need to specify a country as is the case with some geographic headings:

Manitoba. Child and Family Services Division
New South Wales. Dept. of Health
University of Cambridge. Faculty of Archaeology and Anthropology

Clearly, in these cases, the name of the subordinate body would not be significant on its own.

Names of bodies which are distinctive need not have the larger body included, so the University of Cambridge's history of science museum, and its polar studies department, can stand alone:

Scott Polar Research Institute
Whipple Museum of the History of Science

Geographic names

Names of places very frequently occur as main headings. Strictly speaking these are name headings, but they function as subject headings where place is the subject of the document. Names may be of both political jurisdictions and non-political entities, and the names of countries, large cities and named geographic features are all to be found in the authorized list of headings:

Appalachian Mountains
Cambodia
Danube River
Kalahari Desert
Nigeria
South Carolina
Vatican City

This should not be very surprising, as clearly there is an enormous body of literature on such geographic topics. What may be more unexpected is the provision for much smaller and more obscure places:

Sprogø (Denmark)
Suffolk Sandlings (England)
Tian'an Men (Beijing, China)
West Bank
Whalsay (Scotland)

Not every place is represented in the list of LCSH, but you are allowed to create a subject heading for a place as needed. You should be certain before you do this that the place is the main subject of the document, and not simply an aspect of it. In almost all cases a combination of a subject with a place should be represented by a main heading for the subject with a geographic subdivision.

Creating original geographic headings is a very convenient way of managing local literature or ephemeral material, as headings can be made for the smallest and most obscure places. Lots of headings for small and obscure American places are already to be found in the name authorities:

Broad Creek Memorial Scout Camp (Md.)
Little Cranberry Island (Me.)
Port Moller Hot Springs Village Site (Alaska)

and you can augment this with examples of your own.

There are headings for locations within towns and cities, and there seems to be no reason not to be absolutely specific, right down to the level of individual streets and buildings (although, as discussed above, it is not always entirely clear whether a building is strictly speaking a place, or if it should be regarded as an entity or an organization):

Hampstead Heath (London, England)
Princes Street (Dunedin, N.Z.)
Blackpool Pleasure Beach (England)
Broadway (New York, N.Y.)
Cimetiere de Montmartre (Paris, France)
Number 10 Downing Street (London, England)

Preferred form of geographic name headings

Some general conventions are observed in the preferred form of geographic name headings, which make sure they conform to the AACR rules for geographic headings. As with the geographic subdivisions:

- Use the English form of the name where there is one.
- Otherwise, prefer the vernacular (local) form of the place name.
- The current name of the place should always be used, whatever appears in the document.

The current name of the place should be used, even where the work to be catalogued refers to it under a different name. The Library of Congress name authorities are invaluable in providing a history of name changes, and variant forms of geographic names. (British readers should note that headings for many outdated names of administrative divisions in the UK seem to be retained alongside those for their current names.)

Headings should prefer the English version of a name where one exists, otherwise the vernacular, or local, form is used:

Dublin (Ireland)   not Baile Átha Cliath
Saint Petersburg (Russia)   not Leningrad, Petrograd, etc.

This policy is not universally adhered to; for example, the 'official' Library of Congress form for Timbuktu is now **Tombouctou**, the French name for that place, and local areas may also be expressed in the vernacular language:

Saint Mark's Square (San Francisco, Calif.)
Piazza San Marco (Venice, Italy)

Structure of geographic name headings

Many place names need disambiguation because they are not unique, as you can see in the examples above. This is rather like indirect geographic subdivision in reverse, and like indirect subdivision, there are some exceptions to the rules. Cities and towns should be qualified by country, and more specific places by city or town and country:

Azay-le-Rideau (France)
Gdansk (Poland)
P'ing-tung hsien (Taiwan)
Tubingen (Germany)

Golden Temple (Amritsar, India)
Jardin des Tuileries (Paris, France)

The exceptions are the UK, the USA and Canada, as might be expected, but also Australia and Malaysia. In these cases towns and cities are qualified by states or provinces, or by the constituent countries of the UK. Standard abbreviations for states and provinces are used:

Auchtermuchty (Scotland)
Halifax (England)
Halifax (N.S.)
Ipswich (England)
Ipswich (Mass.)
Montréal (Québec)

Bondi Beach (Sydney, N.S.W.)
Carnegie Hall (New York, N.Y.)
Chantry Park (Ipswich, England)

Note that the order of elements is the reverse of that in geographic subdivisions; for example, a work about a factory fire in Ipswich in Suffolk has the heading:

Fires--England--Ipswich (Suffolk)

For a geographic name heading there is no need to include more steps in the administrative chain, although occasionally some older catalogue records do include, for example, counties of England.

Where a specific locality needs to be qualified by a town or city and a country (or state, and so on), these are separated by a comma:

Notting Hill (London, England)
Madison Square Park (New York, N.Y.)
Montparnasse (Paris, France)

Royal Mile (Edinburgh, Scotland)

In practice, the Library of Congress will already have created subject headings for thousands of places, using their authorized form of such names. You can find these in the subject index to the Library of Congress catalogue, using the 'Subject browse' option within the Basic catalogue search. Remember that you can also look at the authority records to see the history of place names and literary warrant for them.

Imaginary places

Just as with personal names, provision is made for fictitious and legendary places. The expression 'imaginary place' is used rather than 'fictitious', but it normally refers to places in works of fiction:

Middle Earth (Imaginary place)
Narnia (Imaginary place)
Springfield (Imaginary place)

Where an imaginary place is situated in a real location it should be qualified in the usual manner for real places. The qualifier (Imaginary place) is appended to the geographic qualifier using a colon:

221B Baker Street (London, England: Imaginary place)
Barsetshire (England: Imaginary place)
Blandings Castle (England: Imaginary place)
Coronation Street (Manchester, England: Imaginary place)
Dawson's Creek (New England: Imaginary place)
Lake Wobegon (Minn.: Imaginary place)

Reflecting the difficulty of making accurate distinctions between institutions and the places where they exist, LCSH has recently introduced the qualifier (Imaginary organization), and a number of headings that were previously imaginary places have been reassigned:

Camel Club (Imaginary organization)
Greyfriars School (Imaginary organization)
King Street Kennels (Imaginary organization)
Sweet Valley High School (Imaginary organization)

Fictional places that are the names of television programmes tend to be designated as such, rather than as places:

77 Sunset Strip (Television program)

> **Dawson's Creek (Television program)**
> **Fawlty Towers (Television program)**
> **Smallville (Television program)**

(Dawson's Creek appears also as an imaginary place because of a novel based on the television series.)

Legendary places are the geographic equivalent of legendary characters, being mythical rather than fictitious in origin:

> **Atlantis (Legendary place)**
> **Camelot (Legendary place)**
> **Mel's Hole (Wash.: Legendary place)**

However, not all mythical places are qualified in this way. Some appear to have religious connotations (**Eden, Valhalla**), but this isn't exclusively so (**Cockaigne, El Dorado**).

....

Exercise 14.2

Find the correct forms of the following place names, according to the Library of Congress subject authorities:

1 Nanking
2 Byelorussia
3 Zaire
4 Eire
5 Moldavia
6 Bangalore
7 Dacca
8 Karl-Marx-Stadt
9 Bombay
10 Danzig
11 Huntingdonshire
12 Cumberland

....

Summary
- Main headings for place names can be created as needed.
- The headings should conform to AACR rules for geographic headings.
- Headings can be very specific, down to the level of individual streets or buildings.

- The current form of the name should be used, and, where possible, the place name as it is known in English.
- Nearly all place names need disambiguation.
- Add the relevant country to names of towns and cities as a qualifier.
- Towns and cities in the USA, Canada, Australia and Malaysia are qualified by states or provinces, and in the UK by constituent countries.
- The subject indexes and authorities of the Library of Congress catalogue can be used as a reference source.
- Headings can also be created for places in fiction, qualified as (Imaginary place) and for legendary places (Legendary place).
- Care should be taken to distinguish between imaginary places and imaginary organizations.
- Imaginary places set within real places should be qualified by country (or town plus country).

Named historical events

The published list of LCSH contains a large number of headings for historical events, many of them associated with wars, campaigns and battles, but there are also some for more peaceful happenings. Others occur as topical subdivisions of the history of a country, and it is likely that headings for internal events such as rebellions and wars of independence, will be found subordinated to the particular place:

> **Brazil--History--Naval Revolt, 1893-1894**
> **Knoxville (Tenn.)--History--Siege, 1863**
> **Finland--History--Club War, 1596-1597**
> **Sierra Leone--History--Civil War, 1991-2002**

While this approach has the advantage of keeping the history of a nation together, there are also lots of headings for individual events entered under their names, and it is slightly difficult to predict which option will be preferred. The creation of a name heading seems to be preferred where a specific personal or geographic name is already involved, but this is not carried through consistently:

> **Buckingham's Rebellion, England, 1483**
> **Frog Lake Massacre, Frog Lake, Alta., 1885**
> **Rakovica Rebellion, Croatia, 1871**
> **Titto Meer's Revolt, India, 1831**

but   **Zimbabwe--History--Chimurenga War, 1896-1897**
Ireland--History--Emmet's Rebellion, 1803

It is possible to create similar headings using the existing ones as a pattern, and, like headings for very specific locations, this is invaluable for dealing with publications about very local or obscure events.

Until recently many of these headings were in the form 'Battle of ...', or 'War of ...' but they have now been changed to bring the place name into the lead position:

Trafalgar, Battle of, 1805

The form of the heading should include the name of the battle, where relevant its geographic location, and the date:

Bosworth Field, Battle of, England, 1485
El Alamein, Battle of, Egypt, 1942
Marston Moor, Battle of, England, 1644
Waterloo, Battle of, Waterloo, Belgium, 1815

Other historical events are dealt with on the same pattern, using the familiar name of the event, place (where applicable), and date:

Argonaut Gold Mine Disaster, Jackson, Calif., 1922
Hurricane Katrina, 2005
Influenza Epidemic, 1918-1919
Izmit Earthquake, Turkey, 1999
Tay Bridge Disaster, Dundee, Scotland, 1879
US Airways Flight 1549 Crash Landing, Hudson River, N.Y. and N.J.,
   2009

You should be aware, when searching the Library of Congress subject indexes and authorities, that many headings have been created for literary texts, paintings, music and so on that depict historical events. These are essentially title headings, and they do not necessarily represent the event as it would be in a subject heading. The situation is further complicated by the fact that such title headings are not always qualified, so that it isn't clear that they represent created works:

Battle of Pavia (Tapestries)
Battle of Shaker Heights (Motion picture)

Battaglia di Marengo [An anonymous music manuscript]

Battle of the frogs and mice [A parody of an epic poem]

Checking the full authority records will usually clarify things, and often provide you with the correct form of the heading as a subject heading, for example:

Pavia, Battle of, Pavia, Italy, 1525
Marengo, Battle of, Marengo, Italy, 1800

Summary

- Headings can be created for named historical events, and for named artefacts.
- Many headings for specific events will already exist as topical subdivisions of the history of a place.
- Otherwise, the name by which the event is usually known should be used.
- The country where the event occurred and the date(s) should be included in the heading.
- Common forms, such as 'Battle of...', should take the inverted form.
- Care should be taken to avoid confusion with the names of, for instance, works of art which represent historical events; the names of these use the natural word order.

Named objects and entities

There are a number of name headings for individual created works and objects in LCSH. The systematic treatment of the works of authors, artists and musicians will be dealt with more fully in the next chapter, but the way in which other non-natural phenomena are handled is conveniently covered here. The categorization of these headings as *name, subject* or *title heading* is often ambiguous, as was the case with places and organizations. Those for created works are generally treated as title headings, but others may occur as name headings, subject headings or sometimes both.

As with the categories already discussed, we are in the territory of unique entities and the way in which they can be named. Anonymous (or corporate) texts and works of art, and historical objects, are obvious examples, and these unique and well known things need no qualification:

Bayeux tapestry
Holy Crown of Hungary
Magna Carta
Roman de la Rose
Stone of Scone

Others are occasionally qualified by place, particularly if they are in a specific location:

Esquiline Treasure (British Museum)
Great Pyramid (Egypt)
Sutton Hoo Ship Burial (England)

More unconventional artefacts may be qualified to indicate what they are; in these examples no attempt has been made to indicate geographic location, even where that is clearly fixed:

Big Ben (Tower clock)
Brandaris (Lighthouse)
Emerald Buddha (Statue)
Mary Rose (Ship)
Rocket (Steam locomotive)

All these are examples of headings created by the cataloguers at the Library of Congress, and none exist within the published standard itself.

As with the other categories, there is allowance for fictional and legendary artefacts:

Necronomicon (Imaginary book)
Rama (Imaginary space vehicle)
Olafs saga Helga (Legendary saga)

The small number of current headings here seems surprising, even if it is the result of literary warrant, as one imagines that there must be a substantial literature on imaginary space vehicles; there are after all very few actual ones. Despite that, there is clearly a precedent for the creation of such headings where needed.

Summary

- Names of well known artefacts may be used as headings without any qualification.
- Artefacts in particular places should be qualified by that place.
- Other artefacts may be qualified by the object type.
- Headings may also be made for fictitious objects using the qualifier (imaginary book, space vehicle, etc.).

....

Answers to exercises

Exercise 14.1

Establish the correct form of a heading for the following persons:

1	Richard Starkey	Starr, Ringo
2	P. D. James	James, P. D.
3	Dan Brown	Brown, Dan, 1964-
4	Richard Nixon	Nixon, Richard M. (Richard Milhous), 1913-1994
5	Walt Disney	Disney, Walt, 1901-1966
6	Walter Raleigh	Raleigh, Walter, Sir, 1552?-1618
7	Ho Chi Minh	Ho, Chi Minh, 1890-1969
8	Stephen Fry	Fry, Stephen, 1957-
9	Alfred, Lord Tennyson	Tennyson, Alfred Tennyson, Baron, 1809-1892
10	Sir Arthur Sullivan	Sullivan, Arthur, 1842-1900
11	Charlemagne	Charlemagne, Emperor, 742-814
12	Ban Ki-Moon	Pan, Ki-mun, 1944-
13	Lara Croft	Croft, Lara (Fictitious character)
14	King Lear	Lear, King (Legendary character)
15	King Charles I	Charles I, King of England, 1600-1649
16	Lassie	Lassie (Fictitious character) (where the document concerns Lassie in films or television programs, etc.) Lassie (Dog) (where the original animal who portrayed Lassie, also called Lassie, is the subject)

Exercise 14.2

Find the correct forms of the following place names, according to the Library of Congress subject authorities:

1	Nanking	Nanjing (Jiangsu Sheng, China)
2	Byelorussia	Belarus
3	Zaire	Congo (Democratic Republic)
4	Eire	Ireland
5	Moldavia	Moldova
6	Bangalore	Bangalore (India)
7	Dacca	Dhaka (Bangladesh)
8	Karl-Marx-Stadt	Chemnitz (Germany)
9	Bombay	Bombay (India)

10	Danzig	Gdansk (Poland)
11	Huntingdonshire	Huntingdonshire (England)
12	Cumberland	Cumberland (England)

15 Literature and the arts

In disciplines such as literature, music, and the visual arts, the material to be dealt with can be divided into two major groups: the works themselves, poems, novels, scores, recordings, and so on (primary sources); and works of interpretation and criticism (secondary sources).

In the arts, organization by subject content is seldom seen as the most useful means of arranging resources; arrangement by language, form, period, or genre (or rather, combinations of these) provides an easily understandable and non-contentious method, and is preferred at least for initial organization. It also reflects the way in which literature, for example, is commonly studied.

Although LCSH is not used to provide a systematic arrangement, this focus on attributes of language, form, period and genre is reflected in many of the headings for the creative arts:

English poetry
French drama
Landscape painting, Medieval
Modern dance music
Portrait miniatures, English
Sonatas (Bassoon and keyboard instrument)
Watercolor painting, Australian

Headings for literature
A great number of the headings for literature reflect this basic preoccupation with the three major facets of language, period and form, but LCSH has a considerable advantage for retrieval over its associated classification scheme (and indeed most other knowledge organization schemes in their treatment of literature). LCSH allows the cataloguer to express an unusually large range of attributes of literature, including very precise themes and topics, as well as literature specified by all sorts of social and

cultural characteristics. It can be very erratic in coverage and, as usual, very unpredictable in what is included and how it will be manifested, but you should find yourself able to express some very complex ideas through the different kinds of headings.

Headings for literature: language, period, and form

The examples at the beginning of this chapter demonstrate a degree of pre-coordination, which is a general characteristic of the headings for creative subjects, and this is certainly the case for literature. There is fairly comprehensive coverage of languages and forms in combination (e.g. **Swedish fiction, Urdu drama**) using headings of this general form. There is, however, a degree of inconsistency in the order in which form and language are combined; for very broad aspects, language is usually the lead term, whereas narrower concepts are likely to make language subordinate, for example:

> **Italian literature**
> **Italian drama**
> **Italian essays**
> **Italian fiction**
> **Italian poetry**

but: **Short stories, Italian**
> **Humorous poetry, Italian**
> **Novelists, Italian**
> **Odes, Italian**

and: **Sonnets, Italian**
> **Sonnets, Polish**
> **Sonnets, Portuguese**
> **Sonnets, Russian**
> **Sonnets, Swedish**

The overall result is that the broad divisions of literature are kept together in the alphabetical sequence by language, but that more specific aspects such as forms (in this instance) are collocated, with language as a secondary consideration. Headings can be found for very precise literary forms, and for various genres, either alone, or with language qualifications (e.g. **Farce, Limericks, One-act plays**, and **Masques, Chinese**).

Non-specific headings such as these are used for the cataloguing of general works about literature, focusing on period and form, and which cover a range of authors. There is also a large category of headings through which you can express the idea of literatures belonging not only to specific languages, but also to particular cultures and ethnic groups; these are the headings for various kinds of authors, for example:

African American authors
Muslim authors

As usual, both inverted and un-inverted forms are used, and it is hard to predict which will be preferred, although the inverted form is perhaps more common in the case of language:

Authors, Catalan
Authors, Hebrew
Authors, Latin

The same form of heading is used to represent literature of particular classes, genders, sexual orientations, disabilities, occupations and other similar concepts:

Catholic authors
Child authors
College teachers as authors
Deaf authors
Older authors
Working class authors

More highly pre-coordinated examples of this pattern of heading can also be found:

African American women authors
Young male authors

Further degrees of complexity can be achieved through the use of the free-floating subdivisions, where many subdivisions of the form '...**authors**' can be discovered:

--Foreign authors
--Minority authors
--Quaker authors

Attached to the main headings for language and form, they enable a sophisticated level of expression, reflecting very particular nuances of meaning in the subject:

> **South African literature (English)--Black authors**
> **Finnish poetry (Swedish)--Women authors**
> **French-American poetry--Creole authors**

The free-floating subdivisions can also be used to provide an alternative means of expressing period, and various subdivisions specific to literature can be found there. Note that this departs from the normal form of the free-floating subdivision (**--History--19th century**, etc.) and should only be used, as instructed, in the context of art, literature and music:

> **--18th century**
> **--20th century**

These subdivisions can be used with individual literatures and groups of literary authors to generate headings with three or four facets such as:

> **Male authors, Russian--19th century**
> **African fiction (French)--20th century**

Headings for literature: topics and themes in literature

Various literary styles, literary devices, and structural and linguistic elements can be expressed as subject headings (e.g. **Alliteration, Metalepsis, Metaphor, Plots (Drama, novel, etc.), Postmodernism, Rhyme, Romanticism**). A very small number of these occur as free-floating subdivisions applicable to language, so that it is possible to make occasional headings such as **Latin language--Metrics and rhythmics**, but these are very few and far between.

As well as literary concepts, LCSH makes extensive, if not very even, provision for particular subjects in literature, although doubtless the unevenness arises because of literary warrant. There are a great number of headings of the form 'x in literature', and while some of them represent common literary topics (for example, **Family secrets, Medical ethics, Mistresses, Political campaigns, Refugees, Traitors, War**), many others are rather unexpected:

> **Bees in literature**
> **Big Ben (Tower clock) in literature**
> **Contempt (Attitude) in literature**

Flowering cherries in literature
Glassware in literature
Implements, utensils, etc., in literature
Primogeniture in literature
Sepulchral monuments in literature
Shipbuilding in literature

Another way to achieve a similar expression of subject is to use the free-floating subdivisions for literary forms (such as --**Poetry** and --**Fiction**) in conjunction with main headings. For a long period of its history, the Library of Congress did not assign subject headings to works of fiction (as opposed to works of literature). That policy has changed recently, and now headings using the free-floating subdivisions are routinely applied to novels and collections of poetry. Here there is virtually no limit to what can be represented as the subject of literary output:

```
Habeas corpus / Jill McDonough. - Cambridge, UK: Salt, 2008
```

Subject headings: Capital punishment--United States--Poetry
                     Murder–United States–Poetry

```
The company of crows: a book of poems / Marilyn Singer;
illustrated by Linda Saport. - New York: Clarion, 2002
```

Subject heading: Crows--Poetry

Summary

- Literary works are usually represented through a combination of language, period, and form.
- LCSH contains a large number of headings that combine language and form that are useful for the cataloguing of general literary works.
- Language or form may take precedence in the heading.
- Headings for groups of authors provide a way of expressing literatures of various national, cultural, or social groups.
- Free-floating subdivisions allow for combination of these with literature by language, and for period subdivisions.
- The subjects of literary works can be expressed through the use of headings of the form 'subject x in literature', or by combining free-floating form subdivisions with main headings.

Headings for literature: works about individual authors

The headings for individual authors form the basis of another substantial group of headings in literature. You will not discover many entries for authors by looking in the published list of LCSH, but name headings for authors can be created in the way described in the previous chapter, using the inverted form of the name and, where necessary, dates of birth and death. Consulting the subject indexes and authorities of the Library of Congress will reveal a huge number of such headings devised by the cataloguers there, for example:

> Behn, Aphra, 1640-1689
> Cervantes, Saavedra Miguel de, 1547-1616
> Eliot, T. S. (Thomas Stearns), 1888-1965
> Goethe, Johann Wolfgang von, 1749-1832
> Ovid, 43 B.C.-17 or 18 A.D.

The heading for Shakespeare is included in the published list; it embraces a vast number of topical subdivisions and provides a pattern for other literary writers. The following is only a selection of these, taken from the early part of the record:

> Shakespeare, William, 1564-1616
>   --Adaptations
>   --Anecdotes
>   --Anniversaries
>   --Authorship
>   --Baconian theory
>   --Bibliography
>   --Folios
>   --Birth
>   --Characters
>   --Animals
>   --Clowns
>   --Falstaff
>   --Correspondence
>   --Criticism and interpretation
>   --Dramatic production
>   --First editions
>   --Bibliography
>   --Forgeries
>   --Illustrations

--Last years
--Manuscripts
    --Facsimiles
--Poetic works
--Quotations

You can see that these subdivisions allow you to index the whole range of Shakespeare studies, biographical and historical material, criticism, performance, bibliography and so on, and that it includes both scholarly and popular aspects. The topical subdivisions of Shakespeare can be applied to any other literary author, for example:

Dickinson, Emily, 1830-1886--Childhood and youth
Miller, Arthur, 1915-2005--Dramatic production
Tolkien, J.R.R. (John Ronald Reuel), 1892-1973--Film and video
    adaptations

Headings for literature: works by individual authors

The author's name heading also forms the basis for subject headings for primary works of literature. In this situation the title of the work is appended to the author heading, following a full stop (period), and omitting any initial articles, to form what is known as a name-title entry. The full stop is used to show that the title is a part of the main heading, and not a subdivision:

Shakespeare, William, 1564-1616. Cymbeline
Lewis, C. S. (Clive Staples), 1898-1963. Lion, the witch and the wardrobe
Stendhal, 1783-1842. Rouge et le noir

There is some variation in Library of Congress practice regarding the language of the title. In the Stendhal example above, headings exist for both the French and the English form of the title, and are applied irrespective of whether the text is in English or French. If this sort of thing is a regular occurrence, it would seem sensible to implement a local policy to ensure consistency.

Having formed the heading, free-floating subdivisions can be added to increase subject specificity. These are attached using the normal double dash:

Milne, A. A. (Alan Alexander), 1882-1956. Winnie-the-Pooh--
    Illustrations
Marlowe, Christopher, 1564-1593. Doctor Faustus--Sources

Ovid, 43 B.C.-17 or 18 A.D. Metamorphoses--Translations

Although general works of criticism for individual works are often catalogued using just the basic 'title' heading, it is possible to use free-floating
subdivisions to differentiate secondary works (of criticism) from primary
works (the texts themselves):

Eliot, T. S. (Thomas Stearns), 1888-1965. Four quartets--Criticism and
interpretation
Milton, John, 1608-1674. Paradise lost--Criticism, Textual

Non-literary texts

The same principles can be applied to significant texts in other disciplines,
where these are the subject of study. This is a fairly common occurrence
in Classics and Philosophy, but otherwise fairly unusual:

Aristotle. Metaphysics
Caesar, Julius. De bello Gallico
Darwin, Charles, 1809-1882. On the origin of species
Newton, Isaac, Sir, 1642-1727. Arithmetica universalis

Summary

- Works about individual authors are constructed using the name heading for the
  author.
- This is formed using the inverted form of the author's name, with dates of birth
  and death where necessary.
- A large number of topical subdivisions may be added to this heading using the
  entry for Shakespeare as a pattern.
- Works by individual authors are formed in a similar way, adding to the name
  heading the titles of individual works.
- These may be further qualified by free-floating subdivisions.
- Important non-literary texts can be treated in the same way.

Sacred texts

Sacred and religious primary sources present some problems in that they do not have
personal authors. The headings are therefore formed using the title. Free-floating
subdivisions can be added to differentiate works of criticism and interpretation from
the text itself, and the Bible acts as a pattern heading for this purpose. Here is a sample of the available topical subdivisions:

Bible
  --Abridgements
  --Antiquities
  --Authorship
  --Canon
  --Chronology
  --Commentaries
  --Concordances
  --Criticism, Form
  --Criticism, Textual
  --Devotional use
  --Evidences, authority, etc.
  --Hermeneutics
  --Sources
  --Versions

This allows the construction of analogous headings, such as:

Adi-Granth--Criticism, interpretation, etc.
Koran--Commentaries
Koran--Sources
Tripitaka--Concordances

In the case of the Bible, there are various other main headings and headings of the type 'Bible and subject x' or 'subject x in the Bible', which can only be guessed at, or discovered through the cross-references:

Bible and meteorology
Bible in numismatics
Books mentioned in the Bible
Hieroglyphic Bibles
Group decision making in the Bible
Homing pigeons in the Bible
Irony in the Bible

There are occasional analogous headings for other religions, such as **Koran stories, Plants in the Tripitaka** and **Bhagavadgita and science**, although there is nothing on the scale of those for the Bible.

Primary sources are dealt with in a way similar to the works of literary authors. Individual parts of the sacred text are separated from the overall title by a full stop:

> **Bible. O.T. Genesis**
> **Bible. O.T. Apocrypha. Bel and the dragon**
> **Koran. Surat al-Bagarah. 21**
> **Upanishads. Bhavanopanisad**

The same device is used to indicate a version in a particular language:

> **Bible. O.T. Genesis. Aramaic**
> **Upanishads. Bengali and Sanskrit**

Library of Congress seems to have no means of representing the Hebrew Bible, other than using the heading **Bible. O.T.** While this practice has the advantage of keeping all the items on, say, the book of Exodus together, it does feel biased and unacceptable. Of course, as these headings are created by the cataloguer, there seems no reason why a Hebrew studies library, for example, should not create its own headings of the form **Bible. Chronicles I** or **Bible. Isaiah**.

The individual sections of sacred works can themselves by qualified by the topical subdivisions from the pattern heading:

> **Bhagavadgita. Purusottamayoga--Commentaries**
> **Bible. O.T. Genesis--Criticism, Redaction**
> **Tripitaka. Abhidharmapitaka. Dharmaskandha--Criticism, Textual**

Headings for art

Headings for the visual arts very closely parallel those for literature, with the major proviso that there is no pattern heading for artists. Otherwise, the headings fall into roughly the same categories. As with literature, art is understood primarily in terms describing place, form and genre (if form is understood to embrace artistic media), and there are a large number of headings that combine these basic concepts. The broad headings for art combine medium with place (or nationality) in a compound term, and this is usually inverted:

> **Drawing, Chinese**
> **Painting, Flemish**
> **Sculpture, Italian**

The main headings can also be subdivided geographically, and there are examples of headings of the form 'Medium--Place' in the Library of Congress catalogue and also occasionally in the published LCSH:

Painting--Australia
Sculpture--Colombia

You should be aware that there is a subtle distinction between the meaning of the two headings (e.g. **Sculpture, Japanese** and **Sculpture--Japan**), and use them accordingly.

Example

```
Dutch and Flemish paintings from the Hermitage. - New York:
Metropolitan Museum of Art; [Chicago]: Art Institute of
Chicago; Distributed by Abrams, 1988
```

Subject headings: Gosudarstvennyi Ermitazh (Russia)--Exhibitions
                         Painting, Dutch--17th century--Exhibitions
                         Painting, Flemish--17th century--Exhibitions

---

This is a catalogue of an exhibition held in the USA of a collection of Dutch and Flemish paintings held in the Hermitage in Russia. Library of Congress has been unusually conservative in its use of subject headings, and the following could easily have been added:

Painting, Dutch--17th century--Russia--Exhibitions
Painting, Flemish--17th century--Russia--Exhibitions

As with literature, place is also subordinated to more specific form or medium, and the minor arts:

Engraving, English
Calligraphy, Irish
Watercolor painting, Dutch

Cultural concepts may take the place of nationality in headings such as **Goldwork, Celtic** or **Calligraphy, Arabic**.

There are various main headings incorporating period concepts, some of which are narrow in scope. Period free-floating subdivisions without the intervening 'History' are also applicable to art:

Embroidery, Tudor
Wood-carving, Baroque
Portrait drawing--20th century
Watercolor painting, Dutch--16th century

Art as the product of ethnic, cultural and social groups is represented through headings denoting different kinds of artists:

Artists with mental disabilities
Coal miners as artists
Deaf sculptors
Navajo artists
Shaker artists
Women potters

Subjects in art

Just as with literature, subject can be represented quite precisely in the arts. Headings exist for all the major genres and topics, with and without qualification by place:

Equestrian statues
Figure drawing
Landscape painting
Marine art, British
Narrative art, American
Portrait sculpture, Greek

There is also a great number of headings of the kind '**Subject x in art**', many of them quite as odd as their literary counterparts. Books requiring these headings are often very specific in scope, but they are normally not permitted to be qualified geographically and they seem always to appear on the catalogue record in the simple form, even where it might be expected that period subdivisions could be added:

Dentistry in art
Eggs in art
Fingerprints in art
Half-open door in art
Noise in art
Prickles in art

Example

The man who loved to draw horses: James Howe, 1780-1836 / A.D. Cameron. Aberdeen: Aberdeen University Press, 1986

Subject headings: Howe, James, 1780-1836--Criticism and
                       interpretation
                       Horses in art

Works about individual artists

LCSH contains only a few entries for specific artists, and headings for artists mostly have to be constructed following the general rules for personal names described in Chapter 14. It can be difficult to decide whether some components of names of early artists are family names or places of origin, and the personal names of some artists are not known at all, so we can identify them only by their works. The Library of Congress authorities have a useful part to play in providing guidance. These, and the subject index to the catalogue, are also a source of reference for the many more manageable artists' names that already exist there:

Picasso, Pablo, 1881-1973
Constable, John, 1776-1837
Hopper, Edward, 1882-1967
Hepworth, Barbara, Dame, 1903-1975

Michelangelo Buonarroti, 1475-1564
Leonardo, da Vinci, 1452-1519
Master of the Saint Bartholomew Altarpiece, 15th cent.

Unlike literary authors, artists will not usually have versions of their work held in a library, so the distinction between primary and secondary materials does not entirely hold good here. Nevertheless, there is a need to cater for documents about the artist and documents about individual works of art, and the headings for these are arrived at in a comparable manner.

Subdivisions for general aspects of an artist's life and work need to be derived from the free-floating subdivisions, as there is no pattern heading to follow. These are plentiful, however, and it is perfectly possible to generate a very good range of structured headings, for example:

Gauguin, Paul, 1848-1903
    --Catalogues raisonnés
    --Childhood and youth
    --Correspondence
    --Exhibitions
    --Friends and associates
    --Notebooks, sketches, etc.
        --Facsimiles
    --Portraits
    --Relations with painters

--Symbolism
--Travel
--French Polynesia

Headings for specific artistic works are created in exactly the same way as for literary works, using the name heading, and the title of the work following a full stop (period):

Gogh, Vincent van, 1853-1890. Starry night
Katsushika, Hokusai, 1760-1849. Thirty-six views of Mt. Fuji
Moore, Henry, 1898-1986. Large two forms
Uccello, Paolo, 1397-1475. Battle of San Romano

These headings can then be subdivided by appropriate free-floating subdivisions as necessary:

Raphael, 1483-1520. Sistine Madonna--Congresses
Leonardo, da Vinci, 1452-1519. Mona Lisa--Parodies, imitations, etc.--
   Catalogs
Turner, J. M. W. (Joseph Mallord William), 1775-1851. Fighting
   Temeraire, tugged to her last berth to be broken up, 1838--Exhibitions

Headings for performing arts and media

Dramatic works are largely covered by the headings for literature; the performance aspects of Shakespeare's plays, for example, are partially dealt with through the topical subdivisions of the pattern heading, for example:

Shakespeare, William, 1564-1616. Othello--Dramatic production
Shakespeare, William, 1564-1616. Romeo and Juliet--Musical settings

There are also headings for actors (and actresses) characterized in various ways, and a general heading for **Theatrical producers and directors**, although this has only a very small number of narrower terms. Headings for individual actors and directors can be created using the name heading rules. A few headings occur for different kinds of theatre, and there are a number of headings for specific aspects of acting, production, technical support and so on:

Actors with disabilities
Child actors
Gay actors
Teenage actors

Musical theater producers and directors

Amateur theater
Deaf, Theater for the
Workers' theater

There is a tiny number of headings for particular subjects in the theatre (**Pain in the theater, Violence in the theater,** etc.) presumably where these present a problem of representation on stage. Normally subjects in drama are dealt with using the '**Subject x in literature**' headings.

There is also a need to represent creativity and performance in the mass media, namely radio, television and cinema. LCSH provides headings for these very much on the pattern of literature and the visual arts. As these have been fairly thoroughly covered in the preceding pages, we shall just consider some examples here to demonstrate the similarity.

Actors and producers in all media are covered by the headings for motion pictures (LCSH's preferred term for cinema), radio and television. There are not many specific varieties of these, other than for US ethnic minorities. There are also headings for other kinds of professionals:

Chinese American motion picture actors and actresses
Radio actors and actresses
Gay motion picture actors and actresses
Television producers and directors

Radio writers
Screenwriters
Television journalists

Subject in the media is much more fully dealt with, with a large number of headings for both genres, and subject content. It is noticeable that the term 'films' is used here, rather than 'motion pictures':

Animal films
Disaster films
Horror films
Magazine format radio programs
Superhero television programs

Gay skinheads in motion pictures
Household employees in motion pictures
Invisibility in motion pictures

Nihilism (Philosophy) on television
Prehistoric peoples on television
Stamp collecting on television

Individual persons, films and programs

Headings for individuals in the media are created in the usual way. There are no pattern headings here, so the free-floating subdivisions should be used to improve specificity:

Gable, Clark, 1901-1960
Goldwyn, Samuel, 1882-1974
Pressburger, Emeric, 1902-1988

Burton, Richard, 1925-1984--Homes and haunts--Wales
Monroe, Marilyn, 1926-1962--Collectibles--Prices--United States
Truffaut, Francois--Appreciation--United States

Headings for specific films and programs are formed using title, presumably because it is difficult to assign individual personal responsibility. The heading should include the format in brackets:

Archers (Radio program)
Gone with the wind (Motion picture)
Buffy, the vampire slayer (Motion picture)
Buffy, the vampire slayer (Television program)
War of the worlds (Motion picture)
War of the worlds (Radio program)

Like persons with the same name, films which are remade can be distinguished by the inclusion of a date:

Cleopatra (Motion picture: 1963)
Henry V (Motion picture: 1944)
Wizard of Oz (Motion picture: 1939)

Series of television programmes can use the form 'Title x programs', presumably where there are variant versions of the programme in different series; this is a very fine distinction, and it seems doubtful that it is always made. Series of films can be expressed in the same way:

Star Trek films
Superman films
Big Brother television programs

Scooby-doo television programs

Individual films and programs can be further qualified using the free-floating subdivisions:

Harry Potter and the chamber of secrets (Motion picture)--Pictorial works

Pirates of the Caribbean, the curse of the black pearl (Motion picture)--Juvenile literature

Shrek 2 (Motion picture)--Computer games

Simpsons (Television program)--Comic books, strips, etc.

Star Trek (Television program)--Encyclopedias

Practical subject cataloguing in the arts

The way in which LCSH manages headings for subjects in the creative arts is complex and often inconsistent. Although there are identifiable categories of headings, and distinct patterns in their construction, there are no clearly and consistently applied rules and policies in operation. You should therefore not feel worried if you see headings that do not conform to the majority, or feel that you have misunderstood if some headings do not 'make sense'.

There will quite often be more than one way in which you can express the subject content of a particular item; for example, a compound phrase in inverted form may appear to mean very much the same as a simple concept with geographic subdivision. Try to think carefully whether there is any essential difference between the meanings of two such expressions, but don't let yourself be overburdened by the choice.

Many documents about the arts will be very complex with several facets. Make sure that you represent all the parts of your subject, but you will not usually be able to do this in a single heading. The great freedom of subject headings, certainly in comparison with classification systems, is that you can use as many as you need to in order to express the complete meaning of the subject.

16 Headings for music

Music is one of the richest and most complex subjects, with a very large literature. It embraces a great variety of traditions and genres, and the vocabulary required for music indexing is very considerable. There are no widely used specialist controlled vocabularies for music, and, apart from its use in general libraries, LCSH is probably the most substantial subject cataloguing tool available to music librarians.

Like those for the visual arts and media, music headings have close similarities to the headings for literature, and several of the sections below will parallel the literature chapter, although music is unusual in having a tripartite structure of books about music, works of music (scores and parts in printed music) and recordings. Music has some additional features; these include the need to represent musical forces – musical instruments, voices and ensembles – and their combination in headings for sheet music. These can become complex, apart from the representation of specific compositions, and there is also a substantial number of headings for material on individual instruments. Finally, the way in which named compositions are handled is more complicated than that for literary works.

Numbers of main headings exist for music theory, performance and criticism, such as **Arpeggios**, **Chords (Music)**, **Counterpoint**, **Harmony**, **Relative pitch**, **Sight-reading**, **Tonality** and so on. These present no more difficulty than the headings for any other subject, and will not be discussed here.

The distinctions between books about music, scores and recordings are not very clearly signposted within the heading itself, but some free-floating subdivisions can be used, and certain conventions are employed in the formation of headings for books and scores that indicate the difference to those in the know. Just as music libraries usually separate books about music and scores, and arrange them in different ways, so LCSH has different approaches to the headings for books and scores.

General works about music: period and place

A few years ago the headings for music in particular places and times were rationalized, so these are rather different in form from other arts subjects. Inverted headings are not used to represent the idea of nationality in music, and there are no headings of type 'Music, French' (or 'French music'). Instead, geographic subdivisions and period free-floating subdivisions are used to express music by place and time. A number of such headings are included in the published list, which you can add to as needed:

Music--15th century
Music--Austria--20th century
Music--France--20th century

As with other art forms, it isn't always necessary to use --**History** to introduce the century subdivisions, which, from the fifteenth century onwards, can be added directly to headings. In addition to these very general headings, the place and period subdivisions can also be used with headings for forms and types of musical compositions, as described below.

Composers, who can be regarded as analogous to authors in representing national musical traditions, are dealt with in a similar manner, with nationality expressed through geographic subdivisions. There is no other means of expressing, for example, English composers.

Example

```
William Byrd and his contemporaries: essays and a monograph
/ Philip Brett; edited by Joseph Kerman and Davitt Moroney.
Berkeley: University of California Press, c2007
```
Subject heading: Composers--England

Compound terms are, however, used for composers representative of cultural, ethnic and minority groups, and it is possible to find headings of the form 'Music by... composers', should you want to distinguish this from general historical or biographical studies:

Child composers
Composers with disabilities
Expatriate composers
Gay composers

Music by child composers
Music by women composers

The term 'musicians' theoretically embraces composers, but seems in practice to be used rather for performers. The same conventions apply as for music generally, and for composers, and you will not find any headings for musicians by nationality, whether in inverted or un-inverted form. However, there are headings that represent ethnicity, and other social and cultural attributes:

Deaf musicians
Lesbian musicians
Male musicians
Musicians, Black
Musicians, Romani

Genre, topics and themes

Musical form in the technical sense will be discussed below under compositions. As is sometimes the case with literature, form and genre can be difficult to separate. In music, genre may be more frequently described as 'tradition', although, again, the precise boundaries between tradition and genre are often blurred. The principal divisions into tradition are probably classical, popular and jazz, although a case might also be made for folk music, and it is hard to say where non-Western classical music should belong. Fortunately this does not really create a problem with subject headings (as it would for a classification system), although there might be a need for a local policy on the interpretation of this category of heading.

The broad traditions have a great number of subdivisions, and these various musical styles are very well represented in LCSH, as are genres defined by purpose, such as **Military music** and **Church music**. A number of these have corresponding headings for composers and musicians:

Bluegrass music
Choral music
Dance music
Glam rock music
Gospel music
Jazz
Opera
World music

Church musicians
Film composers

Overarching styles associated with chronological periods (such as Baroque music or Classical period music) are no longer provided for, but are replaced by headings of the type **Music--17th century**. Nevertheless, there are headings for artistic style in music as evidenced by **Romanticism in music, Modernism (Music), Expressionism (Music)** and so on.

Somewhat surprisingly for such an abstract discipline, there are a number of headings for specific subjects in music. It seems likely that at least some of these arise out of subjects in songs, and in dramatic forms such as operas, and a few headings indicate subject in a particular genre of music:

Anxiety in music
Crying in music
Dandyism in music
Gardens in music
Secrecy in music
Stars in music

Drinking in popular music
Mountains in opera

Free-floating subdivisions for music concepts can also be used in conjunction with main headings to express the idea of music about those subjects:

Balloons--Songs and music
Belgian poetry--Musical settings
Don Quixote (Fictitious character)--Songs and music

Summary

- Period and place in music are expressed through geographic and free-floating subdivisions.
- Periods can usually be added directly to music headings without the intervening subdivision --History.
- There are no compound terms of the kind 'French music' or 'Music, Eighteenth century'.
- Musicians and composers are similarly treated, although there are some compound headings for persons qualified by cultural, social and ethnic characteristics.
- Genre in music is well provided for, both at the level of broad tradition, and specific styles.

- There are a few headings for subject in music, and free-floating subdivisions for musical form which can qualify main headings.

Musical forces and works about them

The concept of instrumentation is crucial to the complete description of musical literature. Instruments are a necessary part of the headings for many compositions (such as sonatas, concertos and chamber pieces) and there are main headings for all kinds of instruments and categories of instruments in their own right, including the human voice. A curiosity of the headings for specific instruments is that, like parts of the body, they take the singular form:

Banjo ukulele
Bowed stringed instruments
Didjeridu
Glass harmonica
Keyboard instruments
Northumbrian small pipe
Oboe d'amore
Synthesizer (Musical instrument)
Trombone

As you can see, the list isn't restricted to the instruments of the orchestra, and very many folk instruments, mechanical instruments and instruments of non-western classical traditions are included. Musical instruments have their own pattern heading, that for **Piano**. The following is a sample of the topical subdivisions:

Piano
    --Acoustics
    --Chord diagrams
    --Construction
    --Fingering
    --Methods (Boogie woogie)
    --Pedaling
    --Studies and exercises
    --Tuning

This allows the creation of structured headings for all instruments, using these topical subdivisions, plus geographic and free-floating subdivisions as necessary:

Bassoon--Fingering--Charts, diagrams, etc.

Guitar--Chord diagrams

Organ (Musical instrument)--Performance--Belgium--History--19th century

Violin--Construction--Italy--Cremona--History--18th century

Some instruments also have their own peculiar topical subdivisions:

Violin--Bowing

Trumpet--Embouchure

Instrumental music

Almost every instrument has an accompanying heading for its music, e.g. **Flute music, Harpsichord music** (and many additionally have headings for instrument makers: **Banjo makers, Double bass makers, Organ builders**).

These broad headings for instrumental music are intended for the music itself, rather than books about it (for which the headings for individual instruments would be used). They are used for collections of music, as well as the music for specific individual pieces, and they are also the conventional form of heading used for recordings. In the examples below you can see that the heading **Oboe** is used for a general study of the instrument, whereas **Oboe music** represents both a sound recording and, in the third case, printed music.

Example

```
The eloquent oboe: a history of the hautboy 1640-1760 /
Bruce Haynes.-- Oxford; New York: Oxford University Press,
2007, c2001
```

Subject heading: Oboe

```
Masters of the oboe [sound recording].-- Hamburg: Deutsche
Grammophon, p2006
```

Subject heading: Oboe music

```
To Pauline O: for oboe solo / Louis Andriessen.-- London:
Boosey & Hawkes, c1996
```

Subject heading: Oboe music

Of course, there are very many compositions for combinations of instruments, and LCSH provides for these, some of them rather unlikely seeming:

Alphorn and harp music
Bassoon and accordion music
Tambourine and unspecified instrument music
Viola and mandolin music

Note that these headings are used for music written for both instruments, and not for, say, collections of printed music that include music for the viola and music for the mandolin (which would have two separate headings, **Mandolin music** and **Viola music**).

There are some implicit rules for the order of combination of instruments in these headings, this being: Woodwind – Brass – Bowed string – Plucked string – Percussion – Keyboard. Instruments in the same category are listed in alphabetical order, except for bowed strings which combine in pitch order (Violin, Viola, Violoncello, Double bass):

Bass clarinet and violin music
Trumpet and double bass music
Violin and celesta music

Banjo and guitar music
Harpsichord and piano music
Trumpet and tuba music

Combinations of individual instruments with ensembles take the form 'Instrument *with* ensemble' and appear to be used solely for recordings:

Flute with brass ensemble
Oboe d'amore with orchestra
Trumpet with band

Operas acts as a pattern heading for musical compositions, and further detail can be derived from the topical subdivisions there, of which the following is a sample:

Operas
  --Analysis, appreciation
  --Characters
  --Chorus scores with piano
  --Excerpts

--**Librettos**
--**Parts**
--**Scores and parts (solo)**
--**Simplified editions**
--**Vocal scores with keyboard instrument**

Further refinements of expression can be achieved by adding free-floating subdivisions:

Flute and piano music--Australia--20th century
Oboe with string orchestra--Scores and parts
Trumpet music--Studies and exercises
Violin and piano music--Simplified editions

Music for particular forms

In addition to instrumentation, another significant aspect of musical works is musical form (**Concerto, Fugue, Rondo, Sonata,** etc.). The notes in LCSH are fairly detailed, and clear about the way in which you distinguish works *about* form, from headings for compositions *in* a particular form. Generally speaking, the heading is used in the singular for theoretical works *about* the form, and in the plural for collections of compositions. Where relevant, the latter will be qualified by the instruments involved, which are placed in parentheses at the end:

Sonata--Italy--18th century
Symphony--19th century--Congresses

Chaconnes (Harp)
Concertos (Balalaika)
Concertos (Accordion with chamber orchestra)
Sonatas (Clarinet)
Sonatas (Bagpipe and continuo)
Sonatas (Piccolo and percussion)
Symphonies (Trumpet and piano)

The conventions for combinations of instruments do not follow quite the same order of combination as do those for general instrumental music. The order is as follows:

- keyboard instruments
- wind instruments

- plucked strings
- percussion instruments
- bowed strings
- unspecified instruments
- continuo.

Collections of music for particular chamber ensembles also have the instrumentation represented:

Trios (Bagpipe, hurdy-gurdy, continuo)
Quartets (Clarinet, guitars (2), violin)
Quartets (Violin, viola, violoncello, unspecified instrument)
Quintets (Basset horn, clarinet, violin, viola, violoncello)

This doesn't need to be done for standard combinations, such as piano, violin, viola and violoncello (**Piano quartets**), or combinations of three, four or five instruments from the same section (**String trios, Wind quartets, Brass quintets,** etc.).

Many of these headings will be applied to sound recordings, but in the case of printed music, free-floating subdivisions can be added for further clarification:

Concertos (Flute and oboe with string orchestra)--Scores and parts
Sonatas (Violin and continuo)--18th century--Scores

Summary

- LCSH contains very many headings for all kinds of musical instruments.
- The heading for **Piano** acts as a pattern heading for all instruments.
- These headings are used for works *about* instruments.
- Music for particular instruments is catalogued using headings of the form 'Instrument x music' e.g. **Oboe music, Drum music, Banjo music.**
- These headings are used for printed music and for recordings.
- Headings exist for music for combinations of instruments, and there is a standard order of combination.
- Musical compositions can be subdivided using **Operas** as a pattern heading.
- Headings for music by form have instrumentation in parentheses after the form e.g. **Sonatas (Clarinet), Concertos (Piano).**
- Headings for theoretical studies of a musical form use the singular version.

Vocal music
Vocal music: general works

The construction of headings for vocal music is very similar to that for instrumental music. General works on vocal music involving period and place also use the geographic and free-floating subdivisions to represent them:

Vocal music--17th century
Vocal music--Indonesia--Bali Island
Vocal music--England--16th century--History and criticism

Headings for singers of particular nationalities also require specification by geographic subdivision, although there are a very small number of headings expressing race, gender and the like:

Jewish singers
Male singers
Older singers

Genre and style are very generously provided for, and there are numerous headings for different kinds of songs, for example, and for styles of singing:

Drinking songs
Humorous songs
Sea songs
Work songs

Barbershop singing
Crooning
Scat singing

There are no headings concerned with subjects in vocal music, but, as discussed above, it seems very likely that those for music, or popular music, in general are related to lyrics of songs rather than expressionism in music.

Vocal music: scores and parts

There is no provision in LCSH for treating the voice similarly to instruments. Although there are a few topical subdivisions of **Singing**, the great majority of works on vocal technique can be catalogued only with that general heading:

Singing
      --Auditions

--Breath control
--Intonation
--Studies and exercises

As with instrumental music, musical form headings are used to catalogue printed music and recordings. There does not appear to be the same general distinction between headings in the singular and plural form to represent theory and scores respectively; the more specific forms usually don't have a singular version, although there are a few headings that can accommodate theoretical works, for example:

Ballad opera
Choral music
Oratorio
Opéra comique

Otherwise, the form heading needs to be qualified by free-floating subdivisions to indicate that the item is a work *about* the form, e.g. **Motets--History and criticism.**

Vocal form is well represented, with many kinds of secular and sacred types:

Ballads
Cantatas
Hymns
Madrigals
Masses
Operas
Psalms

A few of these vocal forms are the only remaining examples of compound and inverted headings to be found in the area of music (although not all vocal forms are structured in this way):

Ballads, Irish
Folk songs, German
Hymns, Basque

Combined voices are expressed as **Vocal duets, Vocal quartets, etc.**, up to **Vocal nonets,** with larger groups represented as **Vocal ensembles**. Accompanied voices are provided for by headings of the form:

Vocal duets with lute

Vocal trios with harpsichord
Vocal quartets with orchestra

Voices of different pitch are not represented, as might be expected, by the usual soprano, alto, tenor and base, but by **High voice, Middle voice** and **Low voice**. These are not used as main headings, but only to represent voice as a qualifier in headings for musical form. Additionally, the qualifiers **Men's voices, Women's voices, Mixed voices** and **Equal voices** are used for multiple voices. Broadly speaking, headings for vocal music are not as precise in representing the forces as those for instrumental music, and the exact combinations of voices are not included:

Cantatas (Children's voices)
Choruses (Men's voices), Unaccompanied
Songs (High voice) with lute--17th century

For mixed forces of voices and instruments, there are also some free-floating subdivisions of the form:

--Vocal scores with accordion
--Vocal scores with pianos (2)

Operas--Vocal scores with harpsichord
Revues--Vocal scores with piano

Headings for vocal music are therefore usually fairly straightforward combinations of form with the type of voice, plus any instrumental accompaniment. Free-floating subdivisions may be added to indicate the type of score.

Example

Mass in C, K. 317: the "Coronation mass" / Wolfgang Amadeus Mozart; arranged for SSA choir by Marcin Mazur. – Thousand Oaks, CA: Cantus Quercus Press, c2006

Subject heading: Masses--Chorus scores without accompaniment

Glory to God: from "The Messiah": for SATB chorus / George Frederich Handel; with keyboard accompaniment [edited and arranged by Richard Langdon]. – Ft. Lauderdale (170 N.E. 33rd St., Ft. Lauderdale 33307): Tetra/Continuo Music Group, c1992

Subject heading: Oratorios--Excerpts--Vocal scores with keyboard
                     instrument

```
Chichester Psalms: (in three movements) for mixed choir (or
male choir), boy solo and orchestra (to be sung in Hebrew)
/ Leonard Bernstein. - [S.l.]: Amberson; London; New York:
Boosey & Hawkes, [1987?], c1965
```

Subject heading: Choruses, Sacred (Mixed voices) with orchestra

Summary

- Music for voices is managed in a similar way to that for instruments.
- There are a few headings for theoretical works on musical form.
- Form headings are the general way of representing printed music for, and recordings of, vocal music.
- Headings for combinations of voices with instruments are included.
- Voices of different kinds can be incorporated into the heading, although they differ from the usual SATB.
- Some free-floating subdivisions are available for vocal scores.

Works about composers and musicians

Names of composers are formed in the usual way for persons as subject:

Britten, Benjamin, 1913-1976
Ives, Charles, 1874-1954
Mozart, Wolfgang Amadeus, 1756-1791

Names of composers normally using the Cyrillic or other non-Roman alphabets seem to pose more of a problem than do writers in the same situation, perhaps because authors are more commonly seen in writing and regular forms emerge. In any event, there is merit in using a standard for transliteration. Using Library of Congress authorities is another way of adhering to a standard, even if the results sometimes look a trifle odd:

Tchaikovsky, Peter Ilich, 1840-1893
Khachaturian, Aram Il'ich, 1903-1978

There are also headings available for well known groups of composers:

Groupe des six (Group of composers)
Second Viennese school (Group of composers)

Composers can be further qualified using the heading for Wagner as a pattern; a selection of the topical subdivisions is shown below:

Wagner, Richard, 1813-1883
--Aesthetics
--Discography
--Dramaturgy
--Harmony
--Influences
--Performances
--Performers
--Stories, plots, etc.
--Thematic catalogs

There will also be a substantial literature on performers and conductors:

Beecham, Thomas, Sir, 1879-1961
Boxcar Willie
Brendel, Alfred
Carreras, José
Coltrane, John, 1926-1967
Melba, Nellie, Dame, 1861-1931

You can also expect to find created subject headings in the Library of Congress catalogue, for all sorts of ensembles, institutions and organizations, which are, strictly speaking, corporate name headings:

Berliner Philharmoniker
King's Singers (Vocal group)
National Youth Orchestra of Wales
Royal College of Music (Great Britain)
Westminster Abbey. Choir School

Specific works of music

You might think that the simplest form of a heading for a named musical work would be a song, but in fact there are strikingly few subject headings for songs in their own right:

America (Song)
Thomas Rhymer (Ballad)
Twelve days of Christmas (English folk song)

Even songs that can be attributed to a known composer are generally catalogued using the form subdivision 'Composer. Songs', if indeed they are catalogued at all. A heading such as the one below, which conforms to the expected pattern of created works, appears to be very much the exception:

Lennon, John, 1940-1980. Yesterday (1965)

The smallest easily distinguishable unit is the album, which is generally subordinated to the performer, rather than the composer, although there is often some overlap:

Beatles. Sgt. Pepper's Lonely Hearts Club Band
Coltrane, John, 1926-1967. Love supreme

An exception would be stage musicals and shows, which are entered under composer:

Bernstein, Leonard, 1918-1990. West Side story
Rodgers, Richard, 1902-1979. Oklahoma!
Sondheim, Stephen. Sweeney Todd

Note that all the examples so far indicate works *about* the named compositions. Recordings of, or printed music for, compositions in non-classical traditions of music are normally given a genre subject heading such as **Popular music** rather than any heading relating to the name of the work or the composer.

Example

```
The dark side of the moon / Pink Floyd. - London: Pink
Floyd Music Publishers; New York: Music Sales Corp.
[distributor], c1990.
[1 score (144 p.): ill. (some col.); 31 cm.]
```

Subject heading: Rock music--1971-1980

Headings for music in the classical tradition are constructed for the individual work, in the same way as for created works in other media. The composer's name comes first, with the title of the work following a full stop (period). The title is given in the original language. Elements of a composed work can also be specified, after another intervening full stop:

Dowland, John, 1563?-1626. Lachrimae
Handel, George Frideric, 1685-1759. Coronation anthems. Zadok the priest
Mahler, Gustav, 1860-1911. Lied von der Erde
Mozart, Wolfgang Amadeus, 1756-1791. Cosi fan tutte

> **Verdi, Giuseppe, 1813-1901. Nabucco. Va, pensiero sull' ali dorate**
> **Wagner, Richard, 1813-1883. Ring des Nibelungen. Walkure**

Numbered works, such as symphonies, are given as such even where there is a popular name for the work (e.g. Mahler's Resurrection symphony or Beethoven's Eroica). Key signatures are included, although catalogue numbers, such as Koechel numbers for Mozart's works, are usually not, unless required to differentiate between two similar works:

> **Mahler, Gustav, 1860-1911. Symphonies, no. 2, C minor**
> **Beethoven, Ludwig van, 1770-1827. Symphonies, no. 3, op. 55, E♭ major**

Broader headings for groups of compositions are dealt with in a similar way:

> **Bach, Johann Sebastian, 1685-1750. Masses**
> **Beethoven, Ludwig van, 1770-1827. Overtures**
> **Faure, Gabriel, 1845-1924. Chamber music**
> **Schubert, Franz, 1797-1828. Symphonies**

Where particular instruments are involved (as in concerti and sonatas), these are listed, separated by commas:

> **Beethoven, Ludwig van, 1770-1827. Concertos, piano, orchestra, no. 5, op. 73, E♭ major**
> **Mozart, Wolfgang Amadeus, 1756-1791. Concertos, clarinet, orchestra, K. 622, A major**

All headings for specific works can be further qualified using the free-floating subdivisions:

> **Marcello, Benedetto, 1686-1739. Vocal music--Bibliography**
> **Puccini, Giacomo, 1858-1924. Madama Butterfly--Exhibitions**
> **Sullivan, Arthur, 1842-1900. Mikado--Parodies, imitations, etc.**
> **Tchaikovsky, Peter Ilich, 1840-1893. Nutcracker suite--Fiction**
> **Verdi, Giuseppe, 1813-1901. Nabucco--Criticism and interpretation**

Summary

- Subject headings for composers and musicians are formed using the rules for name headings.
- These headings form the basis of headings for specific compositions.
- The form of such headings is the composer's name and dates, followed by a full

stop (period), and the title of the work, in the original language.
- A further full stop may introduce a particular element (movement, aria, etc.).
- Numbers and key signatures are used in preference to popular names.
- Where relevant, instrumentation is indicated, separated by commas.
- These headings are used only for documents about music.

Recordings and printed music for individual works

We have already noted that recordings of songs are catalogued with the heading **Popular music**. Similarly, these detailed subject headings for classical compositions are not used for recordings, nor for printed music, where brief headings for form are the preferred method.

Example

```
Symphony no. 3 in E flat, op. 55: Eroica; Coriolan
overture: op. 62 [sound recording] / Beethoven.-- Universal
City, Calif.: MCA Classics, p1988
```

Subject heading: Orchestral music

```
Sonata no. 2, etc. [sound recording] / Chopin.-- London:
Virgin Classics, p1990
```

Subject heading: Piano music

```
Messa da requiem: editions Boosey & Hawkes [sound
recording] / Giuseppe Verdi.-- [S.l.]: Erato, p1994
```

Subject heading: Requiems

Scores and other examples of printed music use the same approach, with the addition of subdivisions for instrumentation. These are formed in the same way as the general headings for form discussed earlier.

Example

```
Requiem: for soprano, mezzo-soprano, tenor, and bass soli,
SATB, and orchestra / Verdi; edited by Michael Pilkington;
vocal score.-- London; Sevenoaks: Novello, c1993
```

Subject heading: Requiems--Vocal scores with piano

```
Konzert: d-Moll, für Oboe, Streicher und Basso continuo /
A. Marcello; nach den Quellen hrsg. von Manfred Fechner.--
Leipzig: Edition Peters [c1977]
```

Subject heading: Concertos (Oboe with string orchestra)--Scores

```
Die Zauberflöte = Il flauto magico: KV. 620: opera tedesca
in due atti / [libretto] di Emanuel Schikaneder; musica di
Wolfgang Amadeus Mozart. - [Milano]: Edizioni del Teatro
alla Scala, [1986]
```

Subject headings: Operas–Librettos

Summary

- Printed music for specific musical works, and recordings, do not make use of the name headings.
- General musical form headings (such as **Popular music**, **Symphonies**, etc.) are preferred.
- For printed music, subdivisions can indicate form of presentation (**Scores**, **Librettos**, etc.).

At the end of this rather long survey of music headings it may be useful to summarize the different categories of headings that are used for books about music, printed music and recordings.

Books (and other texts) *about* music:

- For very general works on music, headings can be constructed using geographic subdivisions and free-floating period subdivisions.
- Books about the theory and criticism of particular musical forms use headings with the musical form in the singular.
- Books about composers and musicians use their names (and where appropriate, dates) as headings.
- Books about individual musical compositions use the composer's name plus the title of the work.

Printed music (scores and parts):

- Instrumental music is catalogued using headings of the type 'Piano music'.
- Music for particular forms puts the instrument as qualifier (in brackets) after the form in the plural, e.g. Concertos (Piano).
- Vocal music follows similar conventions.
- Never use the headings for individual musical works for printed music.

Recordings:

- Recordings are dealt with in the same way as printed music, and use the same headings.
- There is nothing in the subject heading (or in the free-floating subdivisions) to indicate recording as a format.

If you should feel that this is very complicated, you would be right, but there is a great deal of help to be had from the Library of Congress subject indexes and authorities, and you will nearly always be able to find an existing heading for the item in hand. LCSH has a very large number of complicated headings and subdivisions that incorporate instrumentation already in the published list. As usual, there are always oddities and inconsistencies in the headings, so do not worry if there are occasional things that make you feel you haven't understood properly.

17 Classification Web

Classification Web is the Library of Congress's electronic version of the classification and subject headings. It is also sometimes referred to as *Classweb*.

Classification Web is only available by subscription, the price of which is related to the number of simultaneous users. This does tend to make it less accessible to small libraries, and unfortunately there is no educational rate. Nevertheless, for libraries where the budget can accommodate it, it offers a quick and easy way to use LCSH with all the advantages that a digital format affords. As the system is updated daily, it also provides the most current version.

The composition of *Classification Web*

Classification Web gives you access to both the Library of Congress Classification and the Library of Congress Subject Headings. We won't consider the classification specifically, but there are several ways in which the two are linked together that will be dealt with in this chapter.

As far as LCSH is concerned, the online tool consists of several distinct databases. The equivalent of the printed LCSH (the red books) is held in the main database, and this is what you will normally search or browse. Headings for particular forms and genres can be searched as a separate collection, although form and genre as subject are represented in the main list as well (the distinctions here are treated in more detail below). There is also a separate database of the free-floating subdivisions, which can be searched independently, or in combination using the advanced search. You can also look for name headings, which are derived from the Library of Congress name authorities. That is a useful device for establishing the correct form of personal and corporate names without having to search the name authorities as a separate exercise.

The classification data for the Library of Congress classification also forms part of the system, and various elements of LCSH link to that data, and to Library of Congress catalogue data. We will see below how this all works together.

Layout and format

Although the content of *Classification Web*'s LCSH is to all intents and purposes the same as the printed version, it looks rather different on the screen. There are also some differences in the way structured headings are presented.

Figure 17.1 shows the heading **Crocodiles**. You will notice when comparing it with the printed LCSH that the same information about geographic subdivision, LCC classmarks, the thesaurus tags and associated headings, and topical subdivisions are all included. However, the heading is combined with its topical subdivisions in the full correct form of the structured heading, so that it is not possible to confuse the subdivisions with the cross-references, as might be the case with the paper version. Note that these structured headings don't extend to combinations with the free-floating subdivisions.

Cross-references come in the form of active hypertext links, which enable you to go directly to the relevant part of the subject heading list, or to the classification schedule in the case of classmarks. The button to

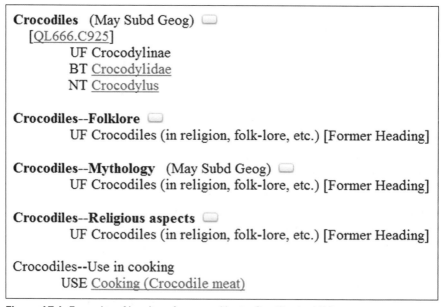

Figure 17.1 Examples of headings for crocodiles in *Classification Web*

Crocodiles (May Subd Geog)
    [QL666.C925]
        UF Crocodylinae
        BT Crocodylidae
        NT Crocodylus

| Dewey correlation |
| LC class correlation |
| MARC record |

Crocodiles--Folklore ▭
        UF Crocodiles (in religion, folk-lore, etc.) [Former Heading]

Crocodiles--Mythology (May Subd Geog) ▭
        UF Crocodiles (in religion, folk-lore, etc.) [Former Heading]

Crocodiles--Religious aspects ▭
        UF Crocodiles (in religion, folk-lore, etc.) [Former Heading]

Figure 17.2 Examples of headings for crocodiles in *Classification Web*, with cross-references in hyperlinks

the right of each heading when clicked allows you to see equivalent class-marks in DDC and LCC, and the database record for the heading in MARC format (Figure 17.2). These are considered in more detail below.

Getting started

To access *Classification Web*, go to the website at http://classificationweb.net/. The home page gives you links to information about subscriptions and legal aspects, and to the Cataloging Distribution Service home page. There is also a log on button which takes you to the main menu.

The main menu provides options to search or browse LCSH, to search genre/form headings, to search LCSH for children, and browse or search name headings, as well as access to the online Library of Congress Classification. When you have chosen one of these you will be prompted for your log in details, and having done this, your menu choice will be automatically opened up and you can start using the system.

Searching and browsing
Browsing

Whether you decide on the search or browse option, you will be confronted in the first instance by a search box. The browse facility is very simple and only asks you to type in a subject. Press the 'Enter' key on your keyboard, or click on 'Browse' to activate the system. (Don't use the 'Search' button, as it will switch you to the search mode.) This will take you straight into the alphabetical list of headings at the appropriate point. For example, a search for **Doilies** will take you straight to that heading, whereas a search for Dog leads you to the entry 'Dog USE **Dogs**', followed by **Dog adoption**, **Dog attacks**, Dog banana, and so on (Figure 17.3).

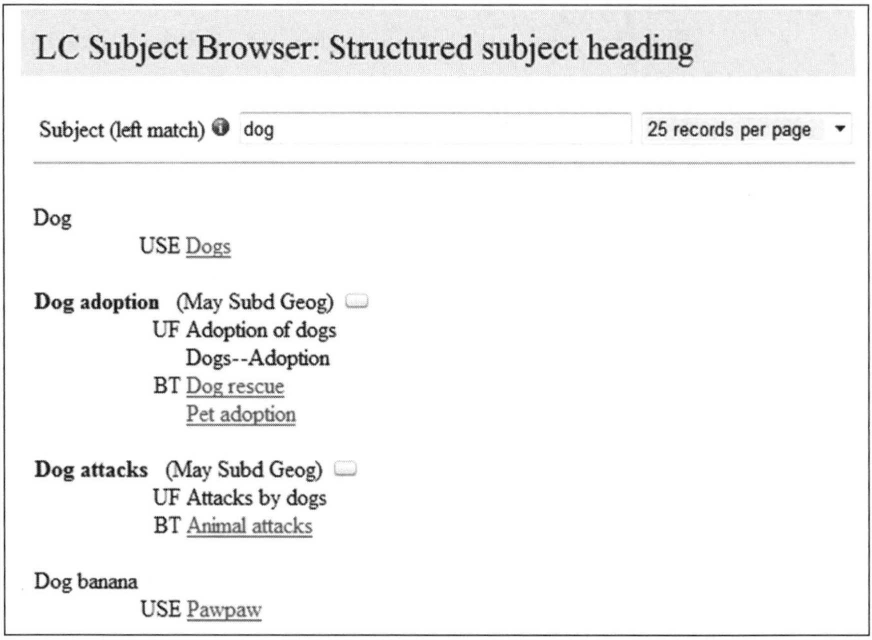

LC Subject Browser: Structured subject heading

Subject (left match) ❶ dog   25 records per page ▾

Dog
         USE <u>Dogs</u>

Dog adoption (May Subd Geog) ▢
              UF Adoption of dogs
                 Dogs--Adoption
              BT <u>Dog rescue</u>
                 <u>Pet adoption</u>

Dog attacks (May Subd Geog) ▢
              UF Attacks by dogs
              BT <u>Animal attacks</u>

Dog banana
         USE <u>Pawpaw</u>

Figure 17.3 Example of a structured subject heading in LC Subject Browser

You will see immediately that you have actually looked for a *term* rather than a *subject* and it is essentially a means of opening up the alphabetical list. In practice this is perfectly satisfactory if your subject is likely to be a heading, or the first term in a heading. If it is a common synonym for the actual heading, the USE tag will usually send you to the right place.

Otherwise the options in the Browse mode are fairly limited. You can move forwards and backwards through the list using the arrows at the top and bottom of the screen, or jump to another section via the hypertext links.

To look for another term, click on 'Browse' or 'Reset' to return to the search box. Click on 'Menu' for other options, or simply click 'Search' to take you to the search facility.

Be aware that *Classification Web* can open up another window each time you search or browse, so you may end up with several windows open, and possibly with search and browse options both active. Keep a watch on your browser bar and remember to close the windows when you've finished.

Searching

The search option (Figure 17.4) provides more flexibility and more categories of search.

```
LC Subject Search

        ⊖ Subject heading ❶  [                    ]
⊖ Free-floating subdivision ❶  [                    ]
              Keyword ❶  [                    ]
    Classification number ❶  [                    ]
        Record number ❶  [                    ]

Search tips and options
```

Figure 17.4 The search option in LC Subject Search

In addition to a variety of search types, help with searching is provided and the Boolean facility explained, via the 'Search tips and options' link. There is no option to go straight to browse from search, so to switch you will need to return to the menu.

Simple searching

A 'simple' search for a subject heading or a free-floating subdivision works in a similar fashion to the browse mode. Entering a term into the 'Subject heading' box takes you straight into the alphabetical list where that term occurs. Hence a search for 'dog' or 'doilies' achieves exactly the same result as does a subject browse. Navigation through the links or by using the forward and backward buttons is also just the same.

Unlike the browse function, the search mode keeps the search box active at the bottom of the screen, so to perform a new search you can simply put your new term in the place of the previous one. The alternative is to hit the 'Reset' button, which clears the original search.

Free-floating subdivisions can be searched for in the same way, although here you are in a separate database, so only free-floating subdivisions are returned. For example, a search for **Biography** opens up the alphabetical list at that point (Figure 17.5).

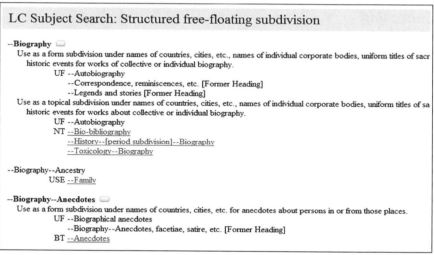

Figure 17.5 Structured free-floating subdivision in LC Subject Search

Note that the list of free-floating subdivisions has the necessary dashes preceding each entry, but you don't need to put these in when searching.

Searching for structured headings

You can search for structured headings as well as unstructured ones, but in that case you do need to put in the double dashes, for example **Jupiter (Planet)--Atmosphere** or **Barley--Diseases and pests**. Search boxes which need double dashes have a green dot on the left. Remember too that you will only find the structured headings that exist in the list – those with topical subdivisions; structured headings using geographic subdivisions and free-floating subdivisions still must be created as needed. The Library of Congress catalogue is an excellent source of those types of structured headings, since thousands and thousands have been created by the staff there, and can serve as a check on the accuracy of your own combinations. There is more information about using the online catalogue in Chapter 18.

Keyword and number searching

In this mode you can search for both subject headings and free-floating subdivisions in a similar fashion to the browse mode, but the keyword function is also available to find terms in the middle of headings, as well as at the start. Hence a search for 'library' in keyword brings up the results list:

Internet access for library users--Law and legislation
Library browsing
IUPUI University Library (Indianapolis, Ind.: Building)
Advertising--Library material preservation supplies
Kate Greenaway Medal
Homework centers in libraries
Collaborative collection development (Libraries)

This is useful, but common words may produce a very large number of results. An entry such as **Kate Greenaway Medal** is included here because 'Library' appears in the notes and cross-references. It is also the case that keyword searching retrieves many examples of narrower headings because they contain a BT reference to the original keyword. A related problem is the retrieval of the keyword as a part of a longer word. Searching for 'cat', for example, produces 3491 results, including headings such as:

Prints, Catalan
Cataloguing of hymns
Shrimp fisheries--Catch effort
Cattle herders
Insect trapping UF Insect catching
Enantioselective catalysis

There are many such headings including the word 'Catholics' or 'Catholic Church', as well as the more useful **Norwegian forest cat** or **Abyssinian cat**. Nevertheless, keyword searching is valuable for finding obscure terms in headings.

Classification number searching is only relevant if you have a classmark to hand, but it is a good way of finding appropriate headings for a book you've classified, since otherwise the subject heading-classmark correlations only work the other way round (starting from the heading). Note that this feature only applies to LCC classmarks and not Dewey.

More advanced searches

Searches can be made using combinations of different search terms, although results are usually only achieved where the terms are fairly general. For example, a combination of 'education' in the subject heading box and 'training' in the keyword box returns results where 'education' is anywhere in a heading in the complete entry (in the main heading or in a cross-referenced heading), and 'training' occurs anywhere at all (in the headings, cross-references, or other notes).

Boolean search is also available but is only effective within the keyword search. When using the basic query, Boolean AND is the default position, so in that case you need only to type the two words into the keyword search box (Figure 17.6).

⊖ Subject heading ❶	
⊖ Free-floating subdivision ❶	
Keyword ❶	education training
Classification number ❶	
Record number ❶	

Figure 17.6 The keyword search box in *Classification Web*

You can switch on the Boolean search proper by opening the Search tips and options, but when that is done you must use operators or the search won't work. For example, you may search for automobile and engines in the keyword box using the basic query, and achieve 17 hits, with the terms automobile and engines somewhere in the entries. By switching on Boolean search and typing 'automobile engines' into the keyword box this is reduced to six hits, all containing the phrase 'automobile engines'.

You can also opt for exact match searches, which will avoid the problems of truncation described in the example above of searching for cats. With 'exact match' turned on, the search for cat returns just 35 results.

General help and guidance is also available through the 'Help' link at the bottom of the menu screen.

Unless you have a very specific objective, it is probably best to stay with the default search options. The great majority of subject headings are so specific that very little is gained by the use of the extra features. If you do use the advanced options, remember to turn them off when you have finished, as the reset button only clears the search box and doesn't reinstate the default search.

Other features
Genre/form headings
You may well feel confused about the relationship between the genre/form headings, subject headings which deal with form, and form related free-floating subdivisions. You do need to think carefully about which you need, as the distinctions are often subtle.

The form/genre headings are intended for the subject cataloguing of actual resources in the particular form, rather than for the form/genre as a subject of discussion.

Bibliographic correlations
Although these are not a part of LCSH, they are a very useful tool if you are classifying books as well as assigning subject headings. They allow you to find the equivalent LC or Dewey classmarks for a given heading, and vice versa. Since the database is derived from the Library of Congress catalogue records, it includes structured headings, and as a consequence, some built classmarks.

18 LCSH in the online world

The electronic LCSH is the most significant digital tool for the cataloguer, but there are other online versions of LCSH, and ways in which Library of Congress support the work of subject cataloguing generally in a free-to-access manner. The most important of these is the catalogue itself.

The Library of Congress catalogue

Various references have been made to the catalogue of the Library of Congress throughout the text, but it seems sensible to bring them together here. The very existence of the catalogue is a major contributor to the increase in the usage of LCSH, through the easy availability of bibliographic records and their subject cataloguing data. The catalogue is a substantial resource for subject cataloguers in three major ways: the records themselves, the subject index and the authority records.

Accessing the LC catalogue: bibliographic records

A link to the catalogue is to be found on the Library's home page at www.loc.gov. (For UK users it may be worth noting that access to the catalogue is very quick and easy during the morning, but it becomes busier during the afternoon, and you may need several attempts to log in then. Weekends are not usually busy, and although there are occasional periods when the catalogue is down for routine maintenance, these don't usually happen at inconvenient times.)

The home page also provides links to other useful pages, including a number of services and resources specifically for librarians, such as information about MARC, thesauri and vocabulary, metadata standards, and the Cataloging Distribution Service, which markets LC products. Following the link to the catalogue gives you a choice between quick search, basic search, and guided search (Figure 18.1).

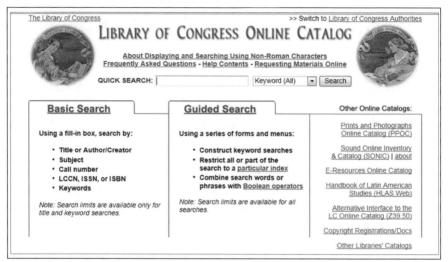

Figure 18.1 Library of Congress Online Catalog

Basic search (Figure 18.2) offers a good range of search options and, apart from the most specialized tasks, is the most useful approach for finding records. There are some tips for searching at the bottom of the screen.

Search options include keyword search in all the major aspects of the record (author, title, subject and series). You are limited to a single keyword for each of these, and searching for combinations of keywords requires the use of the Guided Search facility.

Figure 18.2 Basic search screen

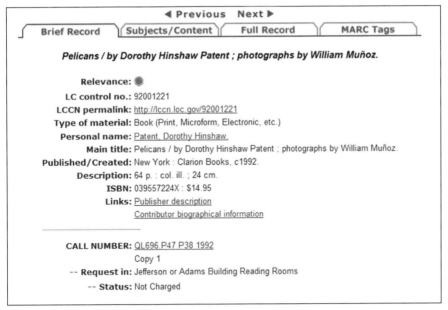

Figure 18.3 Brief bibliographic record

A basic search using a title keyword will take you to a list of titles, from which the individual records can be accessed. For example, a title keyword search for 'pelicans' returns 93 titles; clicking on any title brings up a brief form of the individual record (Figure 18.3).

The brief record doesn't contain the subject headings, but using the tabs at the top of the record will take you to the full record, in standard or MARC format, or to a summary of the subject/contents data (Figure 18.4). These

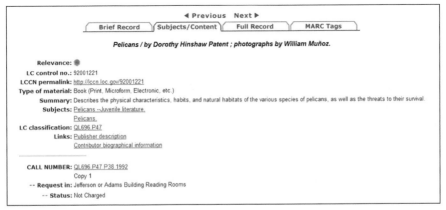

Figure 18.4 Subjects/Content record

records also contain the classification data for the work, both Library of Congress classification, and in most cases Dewey Decimal classmarks as well. This is the easiest way for you to check the headings assigned by LC to an individual work; it is helpful both in confirming the form of any structured headings, and in alerting you to additional headings you might not originally have thought of.

The full MARC record also enables you to check the correct coding for the headings in MARC format (Figure 18.5).

---

504 __ |a Includes bibliographical references (p. 60-61) and index.

520 __ |a Describes the physical characteristics, habits, and natural habitats of the various species of

650 _0 |a Pelicans |x Juvenile literature.

650 _1 |a Pelicans.

700 1_ |a Muñoz, William, |e ill.

856 42 |3 Publisher description |u http://www.loc.gov/catdir/enhancements/fy0728/92001221-d.html

---

Figure 18.5 MARC coding for subject headings

The subject indexes

Using either of the basic search the subject options (subject keyword or subject browse) will give to access to the subject index. The subject index is a database of all the subject headings used in the Library of Congress catalogue, and it is important for cataloguers (particularly beginner cataloguers) because it extends the range of possibilities for headings beyond those in the published list of LCSH.

Subject browse will take the searcher into the alphabetical index of headings where the search term is in the lead position (or as near to it as possible). Subject keyword search will increase the number of results as you will retrieve headings with the key word not in the lead position, or with the keyword in subdivisions. For example, a subject browse for 'eggs' has the following result (Figure 18.6).

You will notice that the list includes not only LCSH, but headings from some other vocabularies. The most numerous examples are from the subject headings for children, Medical Subject Headings (MeSH) and the Thesaurus for Graphic Materials, which is used for the LC collections of photographs, drawings, prints and so on. Since other libraries now contribute records under collaborative cataloguing arrangements, there are occasional references to other vocabularies, not all of them in English. If you use the subject index as a check be careful to ensure that the heading you look at is a proper LCSH heading and not one of these others.

#	Hits	Headings (Select to View Titles)	Type of Heading
[1]	1	EGGS	UNBIS thesaurus trilingual list
[MORE INFO] [2]	151	Eggs.	LC subject headings
[3]	47	Eggs.	LC subject headings for children
[4]	2	Eggs.	Medical subject headings
[5]	1	Eggs.	Thesaurus for graphic materials: TGM I, sub. terms
[6]	1	Eggs--1860-1880.	Thesaurus for graphic materials: TGM I, sub. terms
[7]	1	Eggs--1870-1880.	Thesaurus for graphic materials: TGM I, sub. terms
[8]	1	Eggs--1900.	Thesaurus for graphic materials: TGM I, sub. terms
[9]	8	Eggs--1900-1910.	Thesaurus for graphic materials: TGM I, sub. terms
[10]	1	Eggs--1910.	Thesaurus for graphic materials: TGM I, sub. terms
[11]	4	Eggs--1910-1920.	Thesaurus for graphic materials: TGM I, sub. terms
[12]	1	Eggs--1930-1940.	Thesaurus for graphic materials: TGM I, sub. terms
[13]	3	Eggs--1940-1950.	Thesaurus for graphic materials: TGM I, sub. terms
[14]	1	Eggs--1950-1960.	Thesaurus for graphic materials: TGM I, sub. terms
[15]	1	Eggs--Abstracts.	LC subject headings
[16]	1	Eggs--Alaska--1890-1940.	Thesaurus for graphic materials: TGM I, sub. terms
[17]	2	Eggs--analysis.	Medical subject headings

Figure 18.6 Results from a subject browse

The numbers immediately to the left of the headings indicate the number of records on which the heading is used. Clicking on the heading itself, or on the numbers on the far left, will take you to a list of titles which use that particular heading, and from which you can bring up the individual records.

The major advantage of the subject index is that it includes both structured headings and name headings created by the cataloguers at the Library of Congress.

Structured headings

While the subject index doesn't cover every possible combination of topical, geographic, and free-floating subdivisions, it does include a very large number of them, so it provides an excellent model for the accurate construction of headings. It also offers a quick check option for the proper form of geographic subdivisions.

Name headings

Likewise, the subject index is an excellent source for name headings of all sorts, hardly any of which appear in the published LCSH. This is another good 'quick' option for checking the form of names without resorting to the authorities, although, if variant forms have been used over the years, you may need to refer to those to establish the authorized form.

Many of the name headings will themselves have subdivisions, so further reinforce the value of the index as an authority.

··

Exercise 18.1

Note that these are just some suggestions for things to try with the catalogue to help you find your way around, so there are no specific answers.

1 Type into your browser window www.loc.gov.
2 Click on **Library catalogs** and then **Basic search**.
3 **Subject browse** allows you to search LCSH for actual catalogue records.
4 Type 'Parrots' into the box, then select **Subject browse** and **Begin search**:
   - Note that there are headings from LCSH, LCSH for children, MeSH and TGM.
   - Look at the form of the headings – in their current form they are correct for entry onto a record.
   - The results also provide a precedent for lots of structured headings.
   - MORE INFO button links you to the BTs, NTs, etc.
5 Click on the heading 'Parrots--Dictionaries' to link to the record using that heading:
   - Click on the **Full record** tab to bring up a record with headings. **Subject/content** provides just the classification and subject headings data.
   - These headings are correctly punctuated and laid out.
   - **MARC tags** provide you with a formal catalogue record, and show how the headings should be entered using MARC.

···

Library of Congress authorities

The Library of Congress authorities form the complete 'official' database of the Library of Congress headings, whether these are subject headings, name headings or title headings.

Every heading has a full record on the database, giving the correct form of the heading, any variants, a history of the heading with changes, correlation with the Library of Congress classification (if relevant) and the sources of literary warrant for the heading. The subject headings also may contain cross-references to other headings, although this isn't always the case. The records are available in MARC and labelled formats (Figure 18.7).

The historical component is particularly useful and important for geographic headings as place names may have had many changes over time, and it is an easy way to view all the different names in one place.

> **LC control no.:** sh2003012083
> **LC classification:** GT2210
> **Topical subject heading:** Umbrellas
> **Variant(s):** Bumbershoots
> Umbrellas and parasols
> **See also:** Weather protection --Equipment and supplies
> **Found in:** American Heritage dict. (umbrella; bumbershoot)
> **Invalid LCCN:** sh 85139533

Figure 18.7 Labelled authority record

Records for geographic headings also include the correct form of the heading as a main heading, and as a geographic subdivision.

Searching the authorities

Searching the authorities is usually quite straightforward, but occasionally it may take several steps to arrive at the record itself.

The initial search screen offers you the option to search for subject headings, name headings, title headings, or a combination of name and title. There is also a comprehensive keyword search.

Any search option will take you to to an alphabetical list, which may include some structured headings with subdivisions. For example, a subject heading search for 'spiders' results in the following typical list:

86	Spiders	LC subject headings
223	Spiders	LC subjects headings for children
1	Spiders	Thesaurus for graphic materials
0	Spiders & Snakes (Musical group)	LC subject headings
1	Spiders--1910-1920	Thesaurus for graphic materials
1	Spiders--1920-1930	Thesaurus for graphic materials
1	Spiders--Afghanistan	LC subject headings
3	Spiders--Alaska	LC subject headings
4	Spiders--Anatomy	LC subject headings
1	Spiders as pets	LC subject headings

Those headings with the buttons 'Authorized Heading' or 'Authorized & References' will lead to an authority record, accessed by clicking on the button.

The 'Authorized Heading' button takes you to a link to the authority record:

FIELD	Select a Link to View the Authority Record
Heading (1XX)	Spiders as pets

The 'Authorized with references' button presents you with a number of choices between the heading itself and headings for the references. Clicking on authority record brings all these options up as active links from which you can select the one you need. This is hard to describe and you are probably better to investigate this for yourself.

Exercise 18.2

Again, this exercise is just a basis for practice, and there are no particular correct answers.

1   The link between the authorities and the catalogue is at the top right of the screen. Click on it to switch to the authorities, then click **Search authorities**.

2   Type 'Umbrellas' then select **Subject authority headings** and **Begin search**:
   * The buttons in the left hand column will lead you to the Authority record for the heading.
   * Note that you may need to follow several links to get to this.
   * The record can be viewed in MARC or labelled format.

3   Search for the subject authority record for **Dog scootering** to see the origins of this heading:
   * Note the sources for literary warrant for this heading.

4   You can also search the name authorities for personal, corporate, and geographic names. You might like to try **Rhodesia, Macedonia, John Wayne** or **Elton John**:
   * Name authority searching does not support keyword searching, so names must be entered in the form 'Smith, John'.

5   Title authorities deal with series and uniform titles. Try **OED** to see how it works.

Recently the Library of Congress has been engaged in a joint project to create a large multi-national name authority file, the Virtual International Authority File. In conjunction with a number of other institutions worldwide, the object is to create a single source of data, and to link disparate versions of names together. Further details of the project can be found at http://viaf.org/ and www.oclc.org/research/activities/viaf/.

Other online versions of LCSH

In recent years the Library of Congress has made attempts to provide LCSH in different versions, and to make the basic structure of LCSH more appropriate to online use.

The complex and pre-coordinated nature of many of the headings makes them inherently difficult for machine understanding, and for interoperability, so efforts have concentrated on simplifying and to some extent deconstructing the headings. Hence we find that headings formerly of the type 'Subject in literature' have been replaced by the version 'Subject--In literature', where 'In literature' has the status of a free-floating subdivision. These only apply to certain categories of heading, so there are still plenty of the old style headings left:

Finland--In art
Plato--In literature

Birds in literature
Dance in literature
Smoking in motion pictures

This is part of a broader trend to make the structure of the headings more predictable and consistent, which is best exemplified by the Faceted Application of Subject Terminology (FAST) project.

Faceted Application of Subject Terminology

The FAST project has the aim of fulfilling a 'need for a simplified indexing schema which could be assigned and used by non-professional cataloger [sic] or indexers', suggesting that cost is a major factor in addition to any structural improvement in the headings. There is also a sense of the promotion of LCSH in situations where normally no controlled vocabulary would be used.

The FAST vocabulary is derived from LCSH with a focus on categorization of terms into what are described as facets, the original facets being topical, geographic, period, and form. Alongside this the new tool has a much simplified syntax, with the aim of operating in a more post-coordinate mode. Although there are still 'hierarchical' subdivisions of headings, there is no combination of subdivisions across facets, so, for example, a subject heading cannot be pre-coordinated with a geographic subdivision. The intention is that the cataloguer should enter these various facets independently into the catalogue record using different fields.

An example provided in the documentation shows how a structured heading from the published LCSH would be factored into constituent facets. For example:

France--History--Wars of the Huguenots, 1562-1598--Sources

becomes:

History--Wars of the Huguenots, 1562-1598 (Topical)

France (Geographic)
1562-1598 (Period)
Sources (Form)

These elements are then held separately in the database to be selected by the cataloguer in much the same way as one would use a thesaurus.

From a British viewpoint this hardly constitutes a faceted approach; conventional facet analysis of the kind promoted by Ranganathan, and developed by the Classification Research Group, starts from the premise that it is the topic (or subject) that is to be analysed, and it uses categories far removed from the above. But, if it has a misleading name, the project has achieved some impressive outputs.

The first stage of the project went on to include names, and there are now eight major categories: personal names, corporate names, geographic names, events, titles, time periods, topics and form/genre. The FAST database, freely available at http://fast.oclc.org/, has over 1,600,000 records, derived from the Library of Congress authorities, so the records look very similar.

The FAST website www.oclc.org/research/activities/fast/default.htm includes links to the database, related tools, and a variety of papers and presentations. One of the tools is a LCSH to FAST subject headings converter, and there is an ingenious search tool for geographic headings, MapFAST, which places the 'heading' on a map together with places in the same locale and their associated headings.

There is also a recently published book, *FAST: Faceted application of subject terminology: principles and application*, by Lois Chan and Edward O'Neill.

LCSH and Web 2.0

A number of studies have looked at the phenomena of folksonomy and social tagging, and how these relate to controlled vocabularies and professionally assigned subject metadata. LCSH is a popular choice as a representative of the controlled vocabulary camp, and there are a number of publications on this topic.

LCSH and the semantic web

The FAST project shows a concern at Library of Congress for tools that are more easily machine readable, and which enable interoperability. Current interest in the semantic web has prompted some research into how LCSH can be represented in web ontology languages and other exchange formats. A detailed examination of such work is outside the scope of this book, but there is plenty to read on the web itself, including a useful paper (with a good bibliography) produced by Library of Congress staff in collaboration with a W3C researcher, entitled *LCSH, SKOS and Linked Data*, at http://dcpapers.dublincore.org/ojs/pubs/article/viewFile/916/912.

19 Bibliography

General books on LCSH

Chan, L. M. (2005) *Library of Congress Subject Headings: principles and application*, 4th edn, Westport, CO: Libraries Unlimited.

Ganendran, J. (2000) *Learn Library of Congress Subject Access*, Lanham, MD: Scarecrow Press, in co-operation with DocMatrix Pty, Canberra, Australia.

Stone, A. T. (ed.) (c2000) *The LCSH Century: one hundred years with the Library of Congress subject headings system*, Binghamton, NY: Haworth.

Studwell, W. E. (c1990) *Library of Congress Subject Headings: philosophy, practice and prospects*, Binghamton, NY: Haworth.

Library of Congress publications

Cataloger's Desktop, Washington, DC: Library of Congress, Cataloging Services Division, 1994–, www.loc.gov/cds/desktop/.
(Contains AACR2, Library of Congress rule interpretations, and the Subject cataloguing manual.)

Classification Web, Washington, DC: Library of Congress, Cataloging Services Division, 2002 – http://classificationweb.net/.
(Contains Library of Congress Subject Headings, Juvenile subject headings, Library of Congress classification and correlations between LCSH, and LCC and Dewey.)

Free-floating Subdivisions: An alphabetical index (2007) 19th edn, Washington, DC: Library of Congress.

Library of Congress Subject Headings (2010) 32nd edn, 5 vols, Washington, DC: Library of Congress.

Subject Headings Manual (2008) 4 vols, Washington: Library of Congress.

Current information on LCSH

Cataloging service bulletin,
www.loc.gov/cds/PDFdownloads/csb/index.html.
Library of Congress cataloging and acquisitions homepage,
www.loc.gov/aba/cataloging/subject/weeklylists/.
Library of Congress Cataloguing Distribution Service homepage,
www.loc.gov/cds/index.html.
Library of Congress Subject Headings weekly lists,
www.loc.gov/aba/cataloging/subject/weeklylists/.
Subject Headings Manual Updates,
www.loc.gov/cds/PDFdownloads/scm/index.html.

History and principles of subject heading lists

American Library Association (1901) *List of Subject Headings for Use in Dictionary Catalogs, prepared by a committee of the American Library Association, with an appendix containing hints on subject cataloguing and schemes for subheads under countries and other subjects*, 2nd rev. edn, Boston: ALA.
Cutter, C. A. (1876) *Rules for a Printed Dictionary Catalogue*, Washington: G.P.O.
Haykin, David J. (1951) *Subject Headings: a practical guide*, Washington: G.P.O.
Library of Congress (1914) *Subject Headings used in the Dictionary Catalogs of the Library of Congress*, Washington: G.P.O.
Lopes, M. I. and Beall, J. (eds) (1999) *Principles Underlying Subject Heading Languages (SHLs); approved by the Standing Committee of the IFLA Section on Classification and Indexing*, Munchen: Saur.

Bias in LCSH

Berman, S. (1993 [1971]) *Prejudices and Antipathies: a tract on the LC subject heads concerning people*, with a foreword by Eric Moon, Jefferson, NC: McFarland.
Dickstein, R., Mills, V. A. and Waite, E. J. (eds) (1988) *Women in LC's Terms: a thesaurus of Library of Congress subject headings relating to women*, published/created by Phoenix: Oryx Press.
Johnson, M. (2010) 'Transgender Subject Access: history and current practice', *Cataloging & Classification Quarterly*, **48** (8), 661–83.
Knowlton, S. A. (2005) 'Three Decades since Prejudices and

Antipathies: a study of changes in the Library of Congress Subject Headings', *Cataloging & Classification Quarterly*, **40** (2), 123–45.

Olson, H. A. (2000) 'Difference, Culture and Change: the untapped potential of LCSH', *Cataloging and Classification Quarterly*, **29** (1/2), 53–71.

Rogers, M. N. (1993) 'Are We on Equal Terms Yet? Subject headings concerning women in LCSH, 1975-1991', *Library Resources and Technical Services*, **37** (2), 181–96.

Classification Web

Ferris, A. M. (2006) 'Notes on Operations. if you buy it, will they use it? A case study on the use of Classification Web', *Library Resources & Technical Services*, **50** (2), 129–37.

Ferris, A. M. (2009) 'They Will Use It, If You Buy It!: results of an expanded survey on the use of Classification Web', *Cataloging & Classification Quarterly*, **47** (5), 427–51.

Current developments in LCSH

Anderson, J. D. and Hofmann, M. A. (2006) A Fully Faceted Syntax for Library of Congress Subject Headings', *Cataloging & Classification Quarterly*, **43** (1).

Chan, L. and O'Neill, E. (2010) *FAST: Faceted application of subject terminology: principles and application*, Santa Barbara, CA: Libraries Unlimited.

FAST project website, www.oclc.org/research/activities/fast/default.htm.

Summers, E. et al., 'LCSH, SKOS and Linked Data', *Proceedings of the International Conference on Dublin Core and Metadata Applications, 2008*, http://dcpapers.dublincore.org/ojs/pubs/article/viewFile/916/912.

Virtual International Authority File (http://viaf.org/) and www.oclc.org/research/activities/viaf/

Yi, K. and Chan, L. M. (2009) 'Linking Folksonomy to Library of Congress Subject Headings: an exploratory study', *Journal of Documentation*, **65** (6), 872–900.

Yi, K. and Chan, L. M. (2009) 'Revisiting the Syntactical and Structural Analysis of Library of Congress Subject Headings for the Digital Environment', *Journal of the American Society for Information Science and Technology*, **61** (4), 677–87.

20 Glossary

The glossary covers a number of specialist and technical terms from the field of indexing, subject cataloguing and vocabulary construction, which occur in the main body of the text. For the most part, terms have been interpreted with subject heading conventions and practice in mind, rather than any more general classification or indexing theory. It is intended to provide helpful explanations of these terms, rather than precise technical definitions, for novices or those new to the field. I have assumed that not all readers will have a library or information service background.

about-ness: the about-ness of a document refers to its subject content – what the document is about.

abstract noun: nouns that represent ideas and abstract concepts, as opposed to physical entities, are abstract nouns, e.g. freedom, desire, socialism. Compare with **concrete nouns**.

access points: the elements of a catalogue record that can be searched for, such as author, title or subject.

alphabetical tool: a vocabulary tool where the primary arrangement is alphabetical, usually because the tool uses words for indexing rather than codes or notations; examples are subject heading lists, keyword lists and thesauri.

alphabetico-classed: a system of arrangement whereby broad classes are arranged alphabetically by name, and the items within each section ordered by classmarks. Alternatively, the broad structure is systematic, with subsequent subdivisions arranged alphabetically.

analytical cataloguing: cataloguing the component parts of a document rather than the document as a whole (which is the usual practice in libraries), for example, the cataloguing of chapters in a book.

associative relationship: the relationship between **related terms** (RTs) in a controlled vocabulary; it is generally used for non-hierarchical relationships, or relationships that are evident but cannot be precisely defined. LCSH uses the associative relationship less precisely than is the case in a thesaurus.

authority: 1) a permanent record of local decisions made about indexing, employed as a reference for future use; 2) an external (usually published) reference source of information used to inform local practice, e.g. for spelling, forms of names, etc.

authorized heading: the preferred form of heading as decided by the Library of Congress. The full records for authorized headings, giving the history, literary warrant and correct form, can be found on the Library of Congress Authorities.

automated catalogue: a catalogue in electronic form, as opposed to a physical format such as a card catalogue. See also **online catalogue**.

automated retrieval: the process of identifying relevant information in a collection by means of an electronic database or catalogue.

bias: bias is said to exist when a **controlled vocabulary** contains an unduly large number of terms reflecting the ideas, interests or position of a particular sector or field, or when terms relevant to another sector or field fail to appear. This may occur because the language of a particular group is preferred. Bias may be advantageous if the resource will be used only by the favoured group, e.g. in a scientific institution or a religious seminary. Alternatively, but less commonly, the controlled vocabulary may contain terms that imply inferiority of certain groups or views. It is very difficult to eliminate bias completely.

bibliographic information: attributes of a document (such as the author, title, publisher, date and place of publication) that are conventionally used to describe it in catalogues and bibliographies. Also referred to as bibliographic details.

bibliographic record: the formal representation of the attributes of a document as a whole; the catalogue record.

broad classification: a classification system that lacks detail, so items are located in classes not necessarily representative of their precise subjects.

broader term (BT): under a given heading, a cross-reference to another heading that is more general in scope, e.g. 'Rivers' BT 'Bodies of water'. Also known as an **upward reference**.

browsing: searching by scanning the contents of a collection or list rather than trying to retrieve specific items by some known attribute or feature. In digital collections, browsing may be supported by directory style interfaces using systematic arrangement.

BT: see **broader term**.

catchwords: words (or phrases) taken from the titles of documents and used as subject entries in a catalogue or index.

citation order: the order in which the parts of a compound subject are combined in indexing or description. The choice of citation order will affect the filing order of compounds in any sequence, and, within a particular environment, should be applied consistently.

class: a set whose members share some common feature. The word **class** is commonly used for a topic in a subject cataloguing system, e.g. the class 'chemistry' or the class 'rabbits'.

classification codes: notational codes used to represent subjects in a scheme of classification.

classification scheme: a set of classes organized in a systematic fashion to show the relationships between them; the classification consists of a **vocabulary** (the terms used to represent the classes) and **syntax** (the rules for combining classes). A classification scheme is an example of a **controlled indexing language**.

classified catalogue: a catalogue arranged in the order of classmarks applied to items. It broadly replicates the order of items on the library shelves but can include in the sequence items that are stored separately, such as non-book materials. Occasionally referred to as a classed catalogue.

collocation: the bringing together of books or documents about the same subject, usually within a classified or systematic structure. Collocation also occurs in a subject index when entries are inverted to bring together (or collocate) aspects of a subject, e.g. Chemistry, Analytic; Chemistry, Industrial; Chemistry, Inorganic.

combination order: an alternative name for **citation order**.

Compass: a subject indexing system employed by the British Library for the subject indexes of the *British National Bibliography* during the 1990s. It was a simplified form of the **PRECIS** system, which it replaced.

composite headings: see **structured headings**.

compound terms: subject terms which consist of more than one word, e.g. elastic bands, power of attorney, rock and roll.

concept: an idea or notion that is represented by a **term**. 'Concepts' are more commonly referred to in classificatory and taxonomic structures, whereas 'terms' may be preferred in word-based vocabulary tools.

concept map: a graphical representation of a subject field that shows general relationships between concepts; the concepts are usually depicted within geometric shapes, which are joined by lines to indicate any (usually non-specific) relationship between them.

concrete noun: nouns used for entities of a material or physical kind are concrete nouns, e.g. kangaroo, teapot; may be contrasted with **abstract noun**.

content analysis: the process of determining the subject of a document and identifying aspects of the subject that need representing in the subject headings.

controlled indexing language: a system used for classifying or indexing documents, which uses a more limited set of terms than are found in **natural language**. A controlled indexing language consists of a **vocabulary** (the terms used for indexing) and **syntax** (the rules for combination of terms). **Classifications, thesauri** and **subject heading lists** are all examples of controlled indexing languages.

controlled vocabulary: another name for a **controlled indexing language**.

co-operative cataloguing: a system of cataloguing where the work is divided between several institutions, and the **bibliographic records** created made available as a shared resource.

count noun: a noun representing some object that can be counted, e.g. umbrellas, turnips. Count nouns are usually pluralized in LCSH. Compare with **non-count noun**.

cross-reference: a reference from one term in a vocabulary to another that allows the user to navigate the vocabulary; in LCSH, the cross-references between headings use **thesaurus tags** to show the relationship between the two.

decimal filing: filing of numbers in which each number is treated as if preceded by a decimal point, e.g. the sequence 1, 11, 113, 2, 24, 5, 6, 67 and so on.

descriptive elements: the elements of a catalogue record that do not deal with the subject content, such as author, title and publication details.

descriptors: an alternative name for terms or keywords used in subject indexing.

dictionary catalogue: a catalogue in which authors, titles and subjects are interfiled in a single alphabetical sequence.

difference: in a compound term, the part of a term that modifies the focus or essential subject part of the term. The difference often specifies a kind or type of the focus, e.g. in the term 'Christmas pudding', 'pudding' is the focus, and 'Christmas' the difference. The difference is also known as the modifier.

direct subdivision: adding a geographic subdivision directly to a main heading without any intervening broader geographic term, e.g. 'Witch hunting--England'.

disambiguation: the use of **qualifiers** to clarify terms that are otherwise ambiguous or unclear, usually because they have more than one meaning; for example, 'Shade (shadow)' and 'Shade (colour)'. See also **homographs**.

display: the format of a thesaurus or other vocabulary tool; many such tools consist of both a **systematic display**, showing the structure of the subject, and an **alphabetical display**, listing the terms in A–Z order.

document surrogate: a somewhat dated but useful term to describe a formal representation of a document such as a citation, catalogue record or abstract. Most bibliographies, catalogues and databases consist of such surrogates, although increasingly they may be linked to full-text.

downward reference, downward link: under a given heading, a cross-reference to a heading narrower or more specific in scope, and which is lower down in the subject hierarchy. In LCSH these are indicated by the NT (**narrower term**) tag. See also **upward reference**.

effectiveness of retrieval: effectiveness (or efficiency) of retrieval is usually measured by factors such as **recall** (the extent to which all documents appropriate to the search are retrieved), and **relevance** (the proportion of useful material in the documents retrieved). Effectiveness is affected by the quality of indexing and by **vocabulary control**.

end-user: the reader in a library, or user of an information service (as opposed to the professional user of a system, such as a cataloguer or indexer).

entry term: a term that appears in the alphabetical listing in a controlled vocabulary; entry terms may or may not be used in indexing, but they all provide access for the user.

equivalence relationship: a relationship between terms in a controlled vocabulary where the terms are more or less the same in meaning, and where one only is chosen for use in indexing or cataloguing.

Equivalence relationships exist between synonyms and near synonyms. See also **preferred term** and **non-preferred term**.

Expansive Classification: a classification scheme devised by Charles Ammi Cutter in the latter part of the nineteenth century. Its major feature was its series of schedules at increasing levels of detail from which libraries could choose according to their needs. Although it was never very widely used, it greatly influenced the construction of the Library of Congress Classification.

filing order: the order in which items are arranged in any physical collection or listing.

filing value: the value of symbols used in notational codes. Letters and numbers have a natural filing value, but the filing value of other symbols (such as punctuation marks) must be specified as otherwise their value is unknown to users.

focus: the element of a compound term that is the essential subject; the focus is qualified by the **difference** or **modifier**. For example, in the term 'Fork handles', 'handles' is the focus, and 'fork' the difference or modifier.

folksonomy: a collection of the tags, or keywords, attached by individuals to web resources, which together form a kind of classificatory structure. The term is a conflation of 'taxonomy' and 'folk'.

form/genre headings: headings used where the item is in a particular format or of a particular genre, as opposed to works *about* forms or genres.

free-floating subdivision: one of a number of generally applicable LCSH subdivisions that may be appended to a wide range of headings, e.g. **--Catalogs**, **--Statistics**. They are maintained as a separate alphabetical list. Compare **topical subdivision**.

genre headings: see **form/genre headings**.

geographic subdivisions: words or phrases relating to place, which are added to main headings where appropriate, e.g. **Local foods--France**.

gerund: in English, a verbal noun that has an '-ing' ending, such as swimming, ploughing, fighting.

guard books: an early form of catalogue in which the cataloguing slips were pasted into ledgers. The space required for each section had to be estimated, with the result that alphabetical order was often only approximate.

hierarchical relationships: relationships between topics where one is a sub-class of the other. In LCSH these relationships are expressed through **broader term** (BT) and **narrower term** (NT) references, although these are not always applied very exactly.

hierarchy: a collection of terms or classes in which there are various ranked levels of subordination or containment, often expressed as a tree-like structure; in LCSH the hierarchies are implicit, detectable through the BT and NT references.

homographs: words that have different meanings and pronunciations, but the same spelling, e.g. 'bows (decoration)' and 'bows (part of a ship)'.

homonyms: words that have the same spelling and pronunciation. In an indexing vocabulary, homonyms and homographs require **qualifiers** to distinguish one meaning from another, e.g. 'plant (living organism)' and 'plant (machinery)'. See also **disambiguation**.

homophones: words that sound similar when spoken, e.g. 'aloud' and 'allowed'. Homophones create no difficulty for subject indexing.

hypertext links: active links between classes or terms in an electronic indexing language that allow the cataloguer to move directly to cross-references without the need to search or scroll through the vocabulary.

indexing: the act of determining the subject content of items and assigning appropriate subject indexing terms or notations.

indirect subdivision: using a country subdivision before adding a smaller geographic subdivision to a main heading, e.g. **Music--Austria--Vienna**.

information retrieval: strictly speaking, the process of locating information on a specific topic, usually from a managed collection or database. Information retrieval is currently used in a wider sense to refer to the whole field of information seeking, including searching, search techniques, search tools and other software, and, sometimes, the databases and resources that are searched. **Knowledge organization**, the organization of managed resources, including classification and indexing, and the theory and development of subject tools is usually distinguished from information retrieval. See also **retrieval**.

inner form: the style or form of arrangement of a work, e.g. bibliography, journal, statistical table.

insignificant words: words in a heading or title that do not tell you anything about content. They are usually conjunctions or prepositions, e.g. anxiety *in* art, church work *with* aliens. Insignificant words are often ignored by search software as they occur so frequently.

interoperability: the ability to exchange information between different institutions and systems; this is dependent on the use of common formats that are readable by a variety of IT systems.

inverted heading: inversion of the natural word order in compound terms, e.g. 'Dancing, Ballroom' rather than 'Ballroom dancing'. This was common in physical catalogues and indexes, the purpose being to bring the **focus** of the term into the lead position, and to bring together related compounds, e.g. all types of dancing. Online searching makes this practice redundant, but it persists in LCSH.

keyword list: a list of words, or descriptors, to be used for indexing documents. The keyword list is usually characterized by a lack of structure in its composition, and does not have cross-references between terms. It may be no more than an alphabetical list of terms taken from documents or previously used in indexing.

knowledge organization: the organization of resources by subject. This includes the theory and philosophy of subjects and their relationships, the application of this theory to the design and construction of **knowledge organization systems**, and the practical use of such systems to determine and describe the subject content of documents through indexing and classification.

letter-by-letter filing: filing in which compound terms or phrases are treated as continuous character strings ignoring the spaces, e.g. pump, pump action, pumpernickel, pumpkin, pump parts. Compare with **word-by-word filing**.

Library of Congress Classification (LCC): the classification scheme used by, and devised for, the Library of Congress; it is now widely used in academic libraries and in some public libraries in North America. The Classification is not structurally related to LCSH, having been constructed independently, but LCSH contains references to classmarks where correspondences exist. Generally speaking, the LCSH are more numerous and more detailed than the classes of LCC.

linear order: a one-dimensional arrangement, such as the sequence of items on library shelves, or in a physical catalogue or index.

literary warrant: the principle that there should be publications on a subject or topic before it is included in a subject cataloguing or classification system.

loan words: words (or phrases) of foreign origin that are now an accepted part of the host language, such as pizza or coup d'état.

manual catalogues: see **physical catalogues**.

MARC: literally machine readable cataloguing, MARC is a format for creating electronic records for documents, using a series of internationally agreed coded fields. The most recent version, MARC21, is the normal standard for creating bibliographic records in the English speaking world.

merged catalogue: a catalogue in which several smaller catalogues are combined, as for a group of academic institutions, or for the institutions in a particular location. Also referred to as a union catalogue. The merged catalogue allows for searches of several collections simultaneously, but the results may be compromised if the format is not consistent across all the members.

metadata: literally data about data, metadata is the term used for information attached to a document or resource that describes various features of the document such as its creator, title, date of origin, subject content and so on. Sometimes metadata can be extracted mechanically from the document, but more usually it is decided upon and assigned by human indexers, who may use a **metadata scheme** for the purpose. Metadata may be stored separately from the items it describes, as in a catalogue or bibliographic database or, in the case of digital documents, it may form part of the html code of the resources themselves.

metadata scheme: a formal statement of the various fields used to accommodate metadata. Different schemes may be used for different kinds of documents or digital objects to reflect the characteristics that users may search for, e.g. image metadata schemes may include fields for dimensions, artistic media, etc.

modifier: see **difference**.

multi-word heading: a heading that contains two or more individual words, e.g. 'Zoo animals', 'Fancy work'.

name authorities: a published source of a name used to establish its correct form. A name authority can also be created locally by recording decisions so that later occurrences of the name are dealt with consistently. Often used for personal or geographic names.

narrower term (NT): under a given heading, a cross-reference to another heading that is more specific in scope, e.g. 'Dance music' NT 'Foxtrots'. Also known as a **downward reference**.

natural language: 1) the language used in everyday speech, as opposed to the **controlled language** used in indexing; 2) specific languages such as English, Russian, Chinese, etc.

natural language indexing: indexing using terms decided on by the indexer or taken from the material indexed rather than from a standard indexing language.

natural word order: the order of words in a multi-word or compound heading that reflects the normal order in the spoken or written language, e.g. 'Bawdy songs', 'Foreign agents'. Compare with **inverted headings**.

navigation: the process of exploring the structure of a vocabulary by following cross-references to locate related concepts.

near synonyms: terms that are near enough in meaning to be treated as synonyms for practical purposes.

non-count noun: a noun representing a concept that cannot normally be counted and hence has no plural form, e.g. porridge, inter-planetary travel. Compare with **count noun**.

non-hierarchical relationships: relationships between terms that are not contained one by the other, but are related in some other way.

non-preferred headings: within a set of synonyms or synonymous phrases that are rejected for cataloguing purposes. Non-preferred headings are usually retained in the list, but with a cross-reference to the preferred form.

noun phrases: compound terms in which a noun is qualified by some other word, usually an adjective, but occasionally another noun, or, very rarely, an adverb. Examples of these include: 'artificial legs', 'stuffed animals', 'weapons industry', 'greyhound racing'.

NT references: see **narrower term**.

online catalogue: a catalogue held as an electronic database and accessed through computer terminals, often referred to as an online public access catalogue (OPAC). Note that an online catalogue need not be accessible via the web, nor indeed networked locally, although online catalogue and web catalogue are often used interchangeably.

outer form: the external format of a work, e.g. print, digital, videodisk.

pattern heading: a heading used as a pattern or model for other headings in the same category, e.g. **Piano** is used as model for musical instruments. Topical subdivisions for that category are listed only under the pattern heading, and are 'borrowed' by other headings in the category.

physical catalogues: catalogues maintained on physical media, such as cards or paper slips, or printed catalogues; sometimes referred to as manual catalogues.

plural form: headings for concrete nouns are normally in the plural, e.g. 'pencils', 'lampshades'; exceptions to this rule include parts of the body, musical instruments and species names of plants and animals.

polyhierarchy: a concept that has two containing classes (or a term with two **broader terms**) is said to exhibit polyhierarchy. For example, 'Coffee' has three broader terms, because it is a psychotropic plant and a seed crop, as well as a member of the order *rubiaceae*.

polysemous: a polysemous term has more than one meaning. Terms are usually only considered polysemous if they have some linguistic connection, e.g. 'paper' is polysemous because it can mean the substance paper, a newspaper, an article or essay, wallpaper and so on. Many terms that are **homographs** are not considered polysemous when their relationship is accidental and arbitrary, e.g. 'Reading (place)' and 'reading (activity)'.

polysemy: the state of having several different meanings.

post-coordinate indexing: strictly, a system in which the index terms (for a compound subject) are only brought together at the point of search (as in the case of descriptors or keywords in a database or an online catalogue). The index description is not used to organize the items in the collection, so there is no need to pre-coordinate the terms (arrange them in any particular order). Compare with **pre-coordinate indexing**.

pre-coordinate headings: headings for compound subjects in which the constituent elements are already combined.

pre-coordinate indexing: strictly, a system in which index terms (for a compound subject) are combined by the classifier at the time of indexing because they are used to organize the material in the collection (as in the case of a classification used for shelf order, or subject headings in a file).

pre-coordination: the combination of subject terms to make compound headings; also used to describe a situation when the terms used to describe **compound subjects** are already combined in a published classification schedule or headings list.

PRECIS: Preserved Context Indexing System. A subject indexing system devised for the British Library, and used over a number of years for the *British National Bibliography*.

preferred headings: where several synonyms or near synonyms exist for a given concept, one alone (the preferred heading) should be chosen to be used in subject cataloguing. The others (the **non-preferred**

headings) are retained in the vocabulary, but refer the cataloguer to the preferred form. Also, another name for **valid headings** or **authorized headings**.

prepositional phrases: pre-coordinated headings that contain a preposition.

qualifier: a term added to another term in order to clarify its meaning; this is usually necessary where two terms have the same spelling (**homographs**) to distinguish one from the other, e.g. 'burns (injuries)' and 'burns (streams)', or 'occupation (tenancy)' and 'occupation (profession)'. See also **disambiguation**.

quasi-synonyms: two terms that, although not exact **synonyms**, are close enough in meaning to allow one to be chosen as a **preferred term** in indexing, e.g. 'film' and 'cinema'.

reciprocal references: in a controlled vocabulary, whenever one term is cross-referenced to another, there must be an equivalent reference from the second term to the original. These pairs are known as reciprocal references.

record: in a library environment, record usually refers to a representation of an item, e.g. catalogue record, bibliographic record.

related term (RT): a cross-reference indicating another heading that is related in some general, non-specific way that is not a **hierarchical relationship**, e.g. 'Cataloguing' RT 'Books'. See also **associative relationship**.

retrieval: the process of locating indexed items by means of a search; the **effectiveness of retrieval** is closely related to the quality of the initial indexing.

Romanization: substituting the letters of the Roman alphabet for their equivalents in a non-Roman script. This is usually done to allow interfiling of Roman and non-Roman alphabets and machine manipulation of data where the software doesn't recognize the alternative characters.

RT references: see **related term**.

scope notes: notes attached to a heading that explain its meaning, or how it is to be applied.

see also references: references attached to a heading that indicate other ways in which that topic can be expressed.

semantic content: the semantic content of a document is its subject.

semantic web: the third stage in the development of the world wide web in which intelligent searching and retrieval is supported by tools that can link data and make inferences.

shelf location devices: labelling systems, such as callmarks or classmarks, that allow items to be found on the shelves.

sought terms: words that a user is likely to select when searching.

specificity: the precision with which the level of hierarchy of the subject of a document is indexed. For example, a document about zirconium indexed as 'metals' lacks specificity.

standard: 1) a published authority stating quality criteria for a product, or the way in which some process should be carried out; 2) a system or tool that is widely adopted for use by a particular community. In the first sense, there are various national and international standards for monolingual and multilingual controlled vocabularies. In the second sense, LCSH is an international standard, since it provides consistency in subject cataloguing across all those organizations that use it.

structured heading: a heading that contains more than one component, e.g. a main heading plus a geographic subdivision such as **Parks for dogs--New York**. Structured headings must be created by the cataloguer and are not routinely pre-coordinated in the subject heading list (although you will come across occasional examples).

structured vocabulary: a vocabulary for document indexing or organization purposes in which the relationships between terms or concepts are recognized.

subdivisions: extensions of headings used to express a specific aspect of the subject; for example, geographic places, form of document, or more specific topical aspects.

subject access: the process of finding information on a particular subject or topic; tools or systems that support searching by subject are often described as the 'means of subject access'.

subject authorities: detailed records of the subject headings kept at the Library of Congress that contain the history and origin of individual headings, and also the authorized form.

Subject Cataloging Manual: the Library of Congress' guide to the correct application of LCSH.

subject heading: a linguistic expression (a word or a group of words) representing the subject content of a document, and used for retrieval in a catalogue, bibliography or index.

subject heading language: see **subject heading list**.

subject heading list: a controlled indexing language used to provide alphabetical access to the subject of documents. It consists of 'ready-made' and mainly pre-coordinated headings; these are selected as needed by the cataloguer and attached to the catalogue record of each item; together they form a searchable alphabetical subject index to the collection. Unlike thesauri, subject heading lists include many pre-combined compounds of terms, such as 'English twentieth century fiction' or 'Kangaroos in art'. A formal, usually published, list of **subject headings**.

subject index: the index to, or catalogue of, a particular collection of items arranged by subject content. In an online catalogue, the subject index consists of a browsable alphabetical list of headings or other subject terms that have been applied to documents in the collection.

subject indexing: the process of deciding on the subjects of documents and assigning appropriate index terms, usually from a **controlled vocabulary**.

subject metadata: **metadata** that indicates the subject of a document or other resource.

surrogate: see **document surrogate**.

synonym control: the process of identifying synonyms in a vocabulary, and selecting one as the preferred form for indexing.

synonyms: the occurrence of two (or more) words or phrases that have the same meaning; alternatively, two or more names for the same concept, e.g. tipulidae, crane flies and daddy-long-leg. For cataloguing purposes, one synonym (the preferred form) is selected for use, and the others are cross-referenced to it.

syntax: the operating rules of an indexing system – the way in which concepts or terms are combined and the order of combination.

tagging: the adding of metadata to web resources by their creators or users; tagging uses natural language in an informal and uncontrolled fashion. See also **folksonomy**.

taxonomy: a classificatory structure showing hierarchical relationships between the constituent parts. The term taxonomy is often used to denote a fairly broad classification used in an intranet context or, more loosely, to mean any sort of subject related vocabulary.

term: a word or group of words used to label a **concept**.

thesaurus: a controlled indexing language commonly used to index documents where physical arrangement is not necessary. Thesauri consist of single terms or concepts, which are combined by the indexer to create the document description. The thesaurus relates each term to other terms in the vocabulary by indicating broader, narrower and otherwise related terms, enabling the indexer to navigate the vocabulary.

thesaurus tags: a set of codes attached to headings used to cross-refer to other headings related in various ways. The codes are **UF** (Use For), **USE, BT** (broader term), **NT** (narrower term) and **RT** (related term).

topic map: a graphical representation of a subject that shows the structure of the subject, its constituent topics, and the relationships between them.

topical subdivision: a subject subdivision of a heading, which is attached to it in the alphabetical listing, e.g. under the heading **Dogs** the topical subdivisions--**Barking** and--**Obedience trials** are found. Topical subdivisions are mostly peculiar to the heading concerned, or particularly associated with it. Compare **free-floating subdivision**.

transliteration: the practice of representing words from a language using one alphabet in a different alphabet by systematic substitution of letters, e.g. the Greek word αταραξια may be transliterated into the Roman alphabet as 'ataraxia' (which is, strictly speaking, **Romanization**). This enables the processing and interfiling of text in more than one script.

UF reference: a reference from a **preferred heading** to a **non-preferred heading**, e.g. **Hearing ear dogs** UF Dogs for the deaf.

uniform heading: a heading created on the principle that only one heading should represent a particular topic, and that headings should not exist for synonyms or variant forms; it ensures that all the material on a topic is kept under the same heading.

unique heading: a heading for a homonym that includes a qualifier; it ensures that a heading cannot represent more than one topic.

upward reference, upward link: for a given term or heading, a reference to terms or headings higher up in the subject hierarchy – more general terms. In LCSH these are indicated by the **BT** (or **broader term**) tag. See also **downward reference**.

USE reference: a reference from a **non-preferred heading** to a **preferred heading**.

valid headings: headings that can be legitimately used for subject cataloguing; preferred headings or authorized headings.

verbal noun: the noun form of a verb, e.g. 'management' for 'manage', 'education' for 'educate', 'growth' for 'grow'. Nouns are the preferred form of terms in most controlled vocabularies, and verbs should be converted to this form.

vernacular names: popular names, or names using everyday language, as opposed to scientific or technical names.

vocabulary control: the management of terms in a **controlled indexing language** in order to limit the number available for indexing; vocabulary control includes the elimination of synonyms and the choice of **preferred terms**.

Web 2.0: the second stage in the development of the world wide web, which is interactive and allows users easily to participate and contribute to content.

web-based catalogues: online catalogues accessible via the world wide web. Today most library catalogues are of this kind, and permit public access to their contents, although it should not be assumed that this is so for all automated catalogues.

word-based retrieval: the identification of relevant information using language (thesaurus terms, key words, etc.) as the basis of search. May be contrasted with searching using notational codes, or with browsing systematic structures such as taxonomies or classification schemes.

word-based tools: vocabulary tools that use words themselves for indexing, rather than codes or notations, e.g. thesauri, keyword lists and subject headings.

word-by-word filing: filing in which the spaces in compound terms or phrases precede any letter, with the effect that individual words are kept together in the alphabetical sequence, e.g. pump, pump action, pump parts, pumpernickel, pumpkin. Compare **letter-by-letter filing**.

word order: the order of words in a **compound term**. Before automation, compound terms in a catalogue or index were often inverted to bring the key element to the lead position, and hence group the subdivisions of a topic, e.g. 'cookery, Italian' or 'chemistry, organic'. Now that online systems remove the need for this, natural word order is normally preferred.

Index